The Church
A Spirit-Filled People

Second Edition

Loretta Pastva, S.N.D.
Mary Roy Romancik, S.N.D.

General Editor: Loretta Pastva, S.N.D.

Then there appeared to them tongues of fire, which parted and came to rest on each one of them.
—Acts 2:3

Benziger Publishing Company
Woodland Hills, California

Consultant
The Reverend Ronald A. Pachence, Ph.D.
Associate Professor Practical Theology
Director, Institute for Christian
Ministries, University of San Diego.

Nihil Obstat
Reverend Paul J. Sciarrotta, S.T.L.
Censor

Imprimatur
Most Reverend Anthony M. Pilla, D.D., M.A.
Bishop of Cleveland
Given at Cleveland, Ohio, 17 September 1990

The nihil obstat and imprimatur are official declarations that a book or pamphlet is free of doctrinal or moral error. No implication is contained therein that those who have granted the nihil obstat and imprimatur agree with the contents, opinions, or statements expressed.

Scripture passages are taken from *The New American Bible,* copyright © 1988 by the Confraternity of Christian Doctrine, Washington, D.C. All rights reserved.

Excerpts from *Vatican Council II, The Conciliar and Post Conciliar Documents,* Austin Flannery, O.P., ed., reprinted with permission of Costello Publishing Co., Inc., Northport, NY 11768.

Revision Editor
Celia Rabinowitz, Ph.D.

Copyright © 1992 by the Glencoe Division of Macmillan/McGraw-Hill School Publishing Company. All rights reserved. Except as permitted under the United States Copyright Act, no part of this publication may be reproduced or distributed in any form or by any means, or stored in a database or retrieval system, without prior permission of the publisher.

Printed in the United States of America.

Send all inquiries to:
Benziger Publishing Company
21600 Oxnard Street, Suite 500
Woodland Hills, CA 91367

Second Edition

ISBN 0-02-655834-3 (Student's Edition)
ISBN 0-02-655835-1 (Teacher's Annotated Edition)

4 5 6 7 8 9 10 11 12   003   04 03 02 01 00 99 98

Cover Art: *Pentecost* by El Greco, (1605 A.D.):
Rights Reserved © The Prado Museum, Madrid

Contents

Chapter

1	Finding an Image that Works for You	6
2	Biblical Images and Mystery	30
3	Contemporary Images of the Church	58
4	The Image That Others See	84
5	Experiencing the Image	114
6	Rooted in Jesus, Formed by His Spirit	144
7	Independence in the Spirit: The First Century	172
8	From Persecution to Power: A.D. 100–800	202
9	Building Christendom: A.D. 800–1500	232
10	Family Rifts: A.D. 1500–1600	266
11	From Trent to Vatican II: A.D. 1600 to the Present	298
12	Christ Gathering His People Today	328
13	Christ Calling His People to Holiness	354
14	Christ Ministering Through His People	382
	Handbook: Ecumenism—The Call to Unity	408
	Index	414

Acknowledgments

The authors wish to thank Sister Mary Joell Overman, S.N.D., Superior General, Rome; Sister Rita Mary Harwood, S.N.D., Provincial Superior of the Sisters of Notre Dame, Chardon, Ohio; and Sister Margaret Mary McGovern, S.N.D., Assistant Superintendent, Education, Diocese of Cleveland, Eastern Region, who supported and encouraged the writing of the *Light of the World* series.

Humble gratitude is also due to all who in any way helped to create the *Light of the World* series: parents, teachers, co-workers, students, and friends. The following deserve special mention for their assistance in planning, organizing, testing, or critiquing the series: Notre Dame Sisters Mary Dolores Abood, Ann Baron, Karla Bognar, Mary Brady, Mary Catherine Caine, Virginia Marie Callen, Deborah Carlin, Naomi Cervenka, Reean Coyne, Mary Dowling, Patricia Mary Ferrara, Dorothy Fuchs, Kathleen Glavich, Margaret Mary Gorman, Jacquelyn Gusdane, Margaret Harig, Joanmarie Harks, Nathan Hess, Sally Huston, Christa Jacobs, Joanne Kepler, Owen Kleinhenz, Mary Jean Korejwo, Elizabeth Marie Kreager, Leanne Laney, William David Latiano, Aimee Levy, Ann McFadden, Inez McHugh, Louismarie Nudo, Donna Marie Paluf, Helen Mary Peter, Nancy Powell, Eileen Marie Quinlan, Patricia Rickard, Mark Daniel Roscoe, Kathleen Ruddy, Kathleen Scully, Dolores Stanko, Melannie Svoboda, Mary Louise Trivison, Donna Marie Wilhelm, Laura Wingert; Dr. Jean Alvarez, Ms. Mary Anderson; Ms. Meg Bracken; Sister Mary Kay Cmolik, O.F.M.; Mr. Robert Dilonardo, Rev. Mark DiNardo, Ms. Linda Ferrando, Mr. Michael Homza, Sister Kathleen King, H.H.M., Ms. Patricia Lange, Mr. James Marmion, Mr. Peter Meler, Rev. Herman P. Moman, Rev. Guy Noonan, T.O.R., Ms. Christine Smetana, and Ms. Karen Sorace.

The following high schools piloted materials: Bishop Ireton High School, Alexandria, Virginia; Clearwater Central Catholic High School, Clearwater, Florida; Elyria Catholic High School, Elyria, Ohio; Erieview Catholic High School, Cleveland, Ohio; John F. Kennedy High School, Warren, Ohio; Notre Dame Cathedral Latin High School, Chardon, Ohio; Regina High School, South Euclid, Ohio; St. Edward High School, Cleveland, Ohio; St. Matthias High School, Huntington Park, California.

The following parishes piloted the Abridged Lessons: Corpus Christi, Cleveland, Ohio; St. Anselm, Chesterland, Ohio; St. John Nepomucene, Cleveland, Ohio; St. Thomas More, Paducah, Kentucky.

Special appreciation and thanks to Sister M. Dolores Stanko, S.N.D., for typing the final manuscripts of the series as well as for her many helpful suggestions and her insightful editorial assistance. Deep appreciation to Mrs. Anita Johnson for research; to Sisters of Notre Dame Mary Regien Kingsbury, De Xavier Perusek, and Seton Schlather; to Robert Clair Smith for special services; and to typists Sisters Catherine Rennecker, S.N.D., Josetta Marie Livignano, S.N.D., and Ms. Charlaine Yomant.

Photo Credits

Alinari/Art Research, NY, 9, 156, 167, 212, 222, 223, 331
Arnold & Brown, 17, 24, 32, 84, 146, 172, 364, 366, 369, 377, 382
Art Resource, 242

The Bettmann Archive, 247, 269, 278, 283
Bible Archeology Society, 175
Robert Bretzfelder/Photo Edit, 30

Catholic News Service, 36, 61, 63, 104, 107, 150, 218, 239, 282, 333, 343, 394, 403
Paul Conklin/Photo Edit, 250

Deborah Davis/Photo Edit, 58
Diocese of Lexington/P. Sullivan, 136

Myrleen Ferguson/Photo Edit, 100

Giraudon/Art Resource, NY, 204

Charles Hofer, 8

Lagron-Miller, Peoria, IL/Arnold & Brown, 70, 87
Erich Lessing/Photo Edit, 10, 192, 259

Steven McBrady, 118, 132, 328

NASA, 266
Michael Newman/Photo Edit, 97
North Wind Picture Archives, 53, 185, 187, 208, 217, 234, 240, 246, 248, 268, 270, 274, 288, 290, 292, 305, 313

Alan Odie/Photo Edit, 14, 63, 99, 114, 138, 148, 197, 213, 232

Peoria Notre Dame High School, Peoria, IL/Arnold & Brown, 78, 116, 334, 341, 359, 374, 386
PhotoEdit, 188, 227, 311, 349
Liz Purcell, 38, 62, 68, 79, 174, 272, 316

Reuters/The Bettmann Archive, 320, 393, 395
Jerome Riordan, 33, 178, 202

Doug Schermer, 18, 50, 155, 163, 176, 177, 195, 196, 214, 236, 251, 315, 339
SEF/Art Resource, NY, 279, 308
St. Bernard's Church, Peoria, IL/Arnold & Brown, 95, 341
St. Francis Woods, Peoria, IL/Roger B. Bean, 72
St. Mark's Church, Peoria, IL/Arnold & Brown, 42, 76, 121
St. Martin de Porres, Peoria, IL/Arnold & Brown, 78, 86, 122, 388, 400
St. Martin de Porres, Peoria, IL/Roger B. Bean, 6, 131, 298
St. Mary's Cathedral, Peoria, IL/Arnold & Brown, 144, 251, 293, 354
St. Thomas Church, Peoria, IL/Arnold & Brown, 90

UPI/The Bettmann Archive, 322

Woodruff High School, Peoria, IL/Arnold & Brown, 130

CHAPTER 1

Finding an Image that Works for You

OBJECTIVES

In this Chapter you will

- Learn about different types of images.

- Consider some definitions of Church.

- Examine some attitudes toward the Church.

- Identify your own feelings about different images of the Church.

- Experience a call to discipleship.

Recognizing that many people see Christ's light only in the lives of Christians, the council called upon the members of the Church to make this light shine more brightly by their words and deeds and so lead others to Christ.
— "National Catechetical Directory," #1

The Church: A Spirit-Filled People

SECTION 1
The Impact of Images

Images exert a powerful influence on your life. They may affect you in subtle and subconscious ways. Images are the key to the way people relate to you and how you relate to other people and the world around you.

What You See Is What You Get

What do you think is the purpose of school? How do you feel about going to school? Once you really think about and answer these questions, you should be able to predict how successful you will be in school.

Some students think school is a real community of young people whose goal is to learn what humanity has discovered to be necessary (like reading), useful (like math), and enjoyable (like music). These students are guided by dedicated adults in the community. Students with this focus often do better academically than those who have a different image of school. When these students enter the classroom, they're already on the right track. They believe that every activity, from PE to Social Studies to the Senior Prom, can be an opportunity for growth.

Other students might have a very different view. For them, school is boring. They enjoy the company of their friends. They see school as a social club. If you obey the rules, you stay in and hang out with friends. Any learning is secondary and is only part of the package, not the goal. These students will probably not do as well as the first group.

Still other students look at a school building and see a prison. They see school as a place where you're forced to go through useless activities by strict taskmasters who are

Attitude: a feeling or emotion toward a fact or experience.

Chapter 1 Finding an Image that Works for You

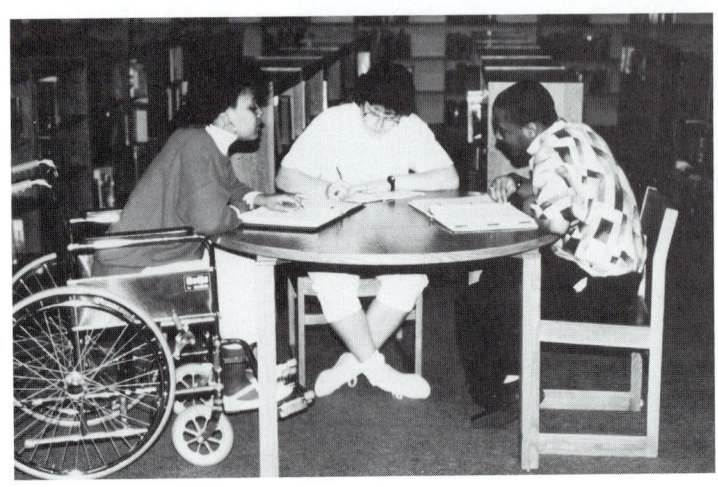

Your attitude concerning attending school will certainly affect how well you succeed in school activities.

dying for a reason to punish you. These students do poorest of all. They stay in school only because they feel forced to attend. How can students have such different images of the same school? Mostly, it has to do with their attitudes.

1. *Why do you think students have such different images of school?*

2. *Do you agree that attitude affects learning? Why or why not?*

The Power of Images

One meaning of image is a mental picture of something or someone that is held by an individual or the public. Image is all about the way you look at something, how you perceive someone, or how you understand reality.

The way you see yourself—or the way others see you—can affect who you are or how you feel. For example, a healthy computer programmer reported for work feeling fine. As a joke, several people told her that she looked terrible and unwell. She eventually left work early saying she was sick. A child who was called a "little thief" started to believe the label and began to steal. And studies

On This Rock

St. Paul, one of the greatest disciples of Jesus, used images to explain the relationship between Jesus and the Church. One of the most familiar is found in 1 Corinthians 12:12-13:

"As a body is one though it has many parts, and all the parts of the body, though many, are one body, so also Christ. For in one Spirit we were all baptized into one body, whether Jews or Greeks, slaves or free persons, and we were all given to drink of one Spirit."

The Church: A Spirit-Filled People

Iconography

In Christian art, images of the Trinity, Mary, saints, and sacred events are referred to as icons. Icon comes from the Greek word, *eikon*, which means image. As a spiritual form of art, iconography is very different from other art. Icons seek to capture the presence of the spiritual body. The role of the icon is to help us go beyond the physical body and connect us with the divine.

Icons are signs of hope. When you look at an icon, it becomes the visible image of God's presence. Icons are always expressions of the artist's faith and the faith of the Church. Icons call to mind God's act of revelation and our response in faith to this self-disclosure.

In our homes, icons are kept in prominent places for all to see. Often this is in an Icon Corner, along with a Bible and candle. To pray before an icon, we stand in silence, growing in appreciation of the holiness expressed by and in it.

Icons are used to help us go beyond the physical and connect with the divine. An icon leads us to prayer.

Chapter 1 Finding an Image that Works for You

show that when people show confidence in their spouses, they are more successful than others.

It is not clear whether positive attitudes are made or born. Do certain events or people cause someone to be the way they are? Or do people naturally tend to be with others who share the same images? We're not sure. We do know that people's images of reality have a great influence on their beliefs and actions.

---

3. *What is your image of yourself? Who and what has shaped your self-image? How has the Catholic Church contributed to that image?*

A mosaic is made up of many colored stones or pieces of glass, which when put together form a complete picture. Your life is similar to a mosaic.

The Church: A Spirit-Filled People

A Changing Mosaic

Whether you realize it or not, you have complex images stored in your mind and memory for things like government, war, picnic, mother, father, friend, priest. Like a mosaic, each image is composed of pieces, each insignificant by itself. When these pieces are fitted together, they create a meaningful whole, a complete vision of a person or thing.

How does this mosaic come into existence? A large part of it is created in your early years and through the images held by your family (especially your parents). You add other pieces through personal observation, comments of friends and enemies, education at school, the media (especially TV), and many other influences.

Because you are constantly growing, your images never remain the same. Your image of your parents probably changed the moment you realized they could make mistakes. Your personal mosaic may have been rearranged when you heard criticism of your country, or when your favorite college team was placed on probation for cheating. It is a normal part of growth for your images and understandings to change. But it is important that change is based on truth and correct information and interpretation.

4. Choose one important image in your life and describe the way it has changed over the years. What influences caused those changes?

Summary

- Different people can look at the same reality and develop different images.
- Your image of something expresses how you see reality.
- Your attitude affects your images, beliefs, and actions.
- Images are made of collected experiences.
- Images change over the years.

Mosaic: small pieces of different colored material inlaid to form a picture or decoration.

Chapter 1   Finding an Image that Works for You

SECTION 1
Checkpoint!

■ Review

1. Why are the images we hold so important?
2. What are some of the influences that images can have on our lives?
3. How can another's image of you affect you?
4. How are our images of things formed?
5. Why are our images never "finished"?
6. Words to Know: subconscious, image, attitudes, mosaic, icon.

■ In Your World

1. Write a sample magazine article for a teen magazine on the power of images over people. Use specific examples.
2. Compare a teen magazine to an adult news magazine. What are the different images used to identify the magazine? Which are used in the adult news magazine? Would the images work if they were switched? Why or why not?

■ Scripture Search

Look up the following Scripture passages: Genesis 1:1-31; Genesis 2:15-17, 3:6-7, 17-24; Genesis 6:5-8; Genesis 19:23-26; Exodus 14:23-28; Psalm 27; Song of Songs 2:8-17; Jeremiah 1:4-10; Matthew 20:1-16; Revelation 4:1-11. Identify the image of God presented in each passage. Which two differ the most? Which are the most alike? Which do you prefer? Why?

The Church: A Spirit-Filled People

SECTION 2
Examining Your Ideas of the Church

Your image of the Church has probably changed several times in the past few years. You may have come to see some Church members as hypocrites—those who act pious on Sunday, but who show no mercy or justice at work. Or maybe you are starting to recognize some of the good work done by the Church in the world and you want to be a part of it.

The Church's image of itself has developed and changed over the centuries. This growth in understanding represents the Church's openness to a changing and evolving world. The following definition illustrates part of the Church's evolution in self-image.

A Definition of Church

St. Robert Bellarmine (1542-1621) formulated a definition of the Church over four hundred years ago at the Council of Trent. The Church is the congregation of those who (a) profess the same faith, (b) partake of the same sacraments, and (c) are governed by one visible head. This definition pinpoints certain visible characteristics of the Church, but it does not cover some definitions with which you may be familiar.

5. *How many meanings of church can you identify? Make a list and include an example for each definition.*

Council of Trent (1545-1563): the Bishops of the Church gathered together to pray, discuss, and make decisions concerning the life of the Roman Catholic Church.

Chapter 1 Finding an Image that Works for You

Definitions through the Centuries

Theologians through the centuries have wrestled with the problem of defining what the Church really is. As you review the following definitions, consider which ones are closest to your own understanding of Church.

1. "They devoted themselves to the teaching of the apostles and to the communal life, to the breaking of the bread and to the prayers. Awe came upon everyone, and many wonders and signs were done through the apostles. All who believed were together and had all things in common . . . Every day they devoted themselves to meeting together in the temple area and to breaking bread in their homes" (Acts of the Apostles, 2:42-46).

2. The Church is the "universal sacrament of salvation," "a sign and instrument . . . of communion with God and of unity among all [mankind]" ("*Dogmatic Constitution on the Church,*" *#48).*

3. The Church is "a people brought into unity from the unity of the Father, the Son, and the Holy Spirit" (St. Cyprian (210-258), *On the Lord's Prayer 23).*

Some people think of a traditional altar and building when they hear the word "Church" while others see the people within the building. What do you think?

Communion of Saints

Robert Bellarmine was a scholarly Jesuit priest and Cardinal as well as an active defender of the Church against Protestantism during the Counter Reformation. Noted for the soundness of his thinking, Bellarmine was named a saint in 1928 and a Doctor of the Church in 1931. He is a patron saint of students and scholars.

The Church: A Spirit-Filled People

4. "The Church is the whole body, or congregation, of persons who are called by God the Father to acknowledge the Lordship of Jesus, the Son, in word, in sacrament, in witness, and in service, and, through the power of the Holy Spirit, to collaborate with Jesus' historic mission for the sake of the kingdom of God" (Richard P. McBrien, *Catholicism*, vol. 1, p. 714).

5. "The Church is quite simply the community of those who accept the message of Jesus and try to support and sustain each other in response to that message" (Andrew Greeley, *The New Agenda*, p. 252).

6. The Church is "a necessary but secondary structure serving as a temporal vehicle for a tradition about a certain reality" (Rosemary Ruether, quoted in *Merton: A Biography*, by Monica Furlong, p. 300).

7. "The Church may be viewed as a community of followers who support one another in this challenging task [which is] the adventure of following Jesus in new and ever changing situations" (Avery Dulles, S.J., *A Church to Believe In*, p. 10).

8. ". . . we are this church; that we are the people to whom the Father offers redemption and salvation in His Son and in the Holy Spirit . . . it is the People of God, and that as such it seeks its own unity . . . (Pope John Paul II, October 17, 1979 audience).

---

6. *How would you respond to someone who says that all churches are basically alike? Do you agree?*

7. *What are some of the distinctive features of the Church as you define it?*

Doctor of the Church: an honor given by the Church to a person because of their integrity, faithfulness and advanced learning.

Chapter 1   Finding an Image that Works for You

Experiences Contribute to Attitudes

Each person's attitude toward the Church is formed by his or her unique experience of it. As you read the following responses to a survey that asked, "What is the Church to you?" note the experiences that contributed to each person's image.

"As far as I'm concerned, the Church is another organization I belong to, except that it has better-kept buildings and grounds than most. It's just a lot of meetings and committees and programs all the time. The priest doesn't have time to talk to you." (Alanna Wack, Phoenix)

"Money, money, money. That's all you hear in our parish. Maybe they should set up shop on Wall Street. Right now I still go to church, but I'm turned off." (Greg Markovitch, Chicago)

"I don't think the Church treats us really that well. They expect a lot from us—too much. And they act like teenagers are all troublemakers." (Frank Han-Chinh, Seattle)

"You can talk forever about the love of God in Jesus, but I need something more than words. When I take part in the liturgy—we have really good ones—I know I experience God's love. That's 'it' for me. What more could I ask? The Church makes it all possible." (Fred Smith, New Orleans)

"The Church, the Catholic Church . . . you mean those pope worshippers? There's no reason for me to get excited about them . . . We've got our preacher, as poor as we are, and the Lord keeps us body and soul together. What more do we need, except jobs and money, and no church is going to help there." (Bessy Parker, Appalachia)

"You preach community, but what does our church have for us teenagers? Everything seems aimed at the adults in our parish. I'm confused about the difference between what we learn in class and what is really going on. Yet I still believe . . ." (Philip Sanders, Melbourne)

"I'm kind of searching. I never questioned the Church until I went to services with a friend of a different faith. Everyone was so warm. For one thing, we took off our coats. That made me feel more at home." (Rosaria Sanchez, Los Angeles)

If you spoke with a group of teens and asked them for their attitudes toward the Church, you would probably hear many different answers.

"When my oldest sister had a stillborn baby, my mother said something about 'God's will' and 'you'll have more.' She was almost cold-blooded. My sister was crushed. When some Protestant friends seemed a lot more sympathetic, she got interested in their faith and is now out of the Church. I guess for her the Church is the people in it." (Theresa Martin, Springfield)

"God gave us the Church. If there is something wrong with it—and I know it isn't perfect, at least not my parish—I know I'm part of the problem. You have to keep examining your conscience about what you yourself are putting in before you knock it." (Beth Spencer, Schenectady)

"I like the way the Church is getting more into politics. I can't explain it, but I feel better about being a Catholic because of it." (Barbara Leigh, Arlington)

"Our whole family goes to Church together and so the Church is like part of our family. I wouldn't know what to do if I had to break with either." (Cheryl Larson, Minneapolis)

---

8. Which of the images of the Church is closest to your own and which is the furthest away?

9. What specific experiences in your life have contributed toward your image and definition of the Church?

Chapter 1   Finding an Image that Works for You

Identifying Your Feelings Toward the Church

Directions: Let your imagination dwell on each of the images suggested below. Try to capture the feeling it creates. Then choose the one that expresses your feelings about the Church. After you have made your choice, try to find reasons or experiences that may be behind your choice.

- *a factory turning out a standardized product*
- *friends conversing comfortably in front of a cozy fireplace*
- *a stately beautiful marble building with a golden dome*
- *a black-robed judge sitting in a courtroom*
- *a responsible loving parent*
- *a plane filled with silent passengers on their way to Bermuda*
- *an elderly person hobbling on a cane*

What other images would you add?

◆

Is your image of "Church" a beautiful building, a relationship between parent and child, or is it more like friends gathered comfortably together?

The Church: A Spirit-Filled People

Unconscious Feelings

Images sometimes capture unconscious feelings that have not yet been vocalized. By expressing your image of the Church, you may also be shouting loudly what you really feel about the Church.

Understanding how you developed your present image of the Church, both the positive and the negative, will help you be honest with yourself about how you feel about the Church.

As you approach adulthood, your image of the Church will continue to undergo changes. Unless you pause to reflect on these changes, you may not be aware of what is happening to you. One secret of making your images work constructively for you is to bring them out of hiding and take a hard look at them. A guiding image is not just a beautiful idea. It includes your experiences in the Church and how you interpret them. It also includes your feelings and attitudes. The more honestly you can identify those elements, the better your chance of putting together an image that will work for you.

Summary

- There are many definitions of the Church.
- Attitudes toward the Church are formed from people's experiences of the Church.
- We can often tell our attitude toward the Church by the image we use to describe it.

SECTION 2
Checkpoint!

■ Review

1. Who was Saint Robert Bellarmine? What was Bellarmine's definition of the Church?

2. How does Acts 2:42 describe the Church?

3. What is the definition of the Church found in the *"Dogmatic Constitution on the Church,"* #48?

4. What is the difference between a definition of the Church and your experience of the Church?

5. What is the relationship between your experience of the Church and your feelings and attitudes?

6. How are people's attitudes toward the Church often formed?

7. What do our images of the Church tell us about our feelings?

8. Words to Know: Doctor of the Church, Council of Trent, sacrament.

■ In Your World

Present to the class a dialogue between a girl who states that her eight years of Catholic instruction will serve her well through life and her friend who disagrees.

■ Scripture Search

1. Read 1 Corinthians 12:12. Discuss whether Paul's imagery of the body is an appealing image for today's Church.

2. Study the Beatitudes (Matthew 5:5-12). What image of life is projected by these principles of Christian living?

SECTION 3
Need for a Guiding Image

Your image of the Church will largely determine how the Church affects you and how you will affect the Church. Without a guiding image that is personally satisfying to you, your Church participation can gradually wither and die. This image of Church should influence most of your decisions, remain firm despite doubts, and hold up when challenged by others.

Forming an Accurate Image

Since an image is a perception or view of reality, the closer an image comes to reality, the better the image. If someone with a paranoid personality sees ulterior motives in the kindness of friends, those relationships will come to an end. That's the result of an image which does not accurately reflect or correspond to reality. It is very important to form an image of the Church that is as accurate as it can be for someone of your age and experience.

A guiding image which is based on an accurate understanding needs to include some knowledge of what the Church is, how it came to be, and why it exists at all. It should take into account how others view the Church and what they think of their own churches if they are not Catholic. A guiding image should not just be a beautifully worded theory; it should really correspond with your parish and diocesan experience. If it is authentic, it will make a difference in your everyday values, priorities, and actions, and be a principle you turn to confidently in controversial or sticky issues. Finally, a valid guiding image ought to show how much you as a Church member can creatively relate to the world.

Perception: a mental awareness.

Chapter 1   Finding an Image that Works for You

10. Check the Table of Contents of this book. Which chapters do you think will help the most in shaping your image of Church?

11. What facts will you need to know to develop your image? Make a list.

The Church as They

There are probably as many perceptions of the Church as there are human beings. One of the most common describes the Church as an impersonal "they." "They're repairing the parking lot in our parish." "They shouldn't get involved in politics." Who is this mysterious "they" who is the Church?

The Church is not "out there"—in Rome, on a street corner, or in a rectory. The Church is the people of God, believers. An executive, in a discussion with her secretary, accused the Church of being rich and corrupted by power. The secretary disagreed. The executive asked, "Well, what is the Church, then?" With deep conviction the secretary replied, "You are looking at the Church right now."

Recognition that the Church is "we" rather than some depersonalized "they" usually occurs as one approaches adulthood. A psychologist of religion describes one of the characteristics of a developing adolescent spirituality as the realization that "God is no longer 'out there' and above. God is 'within,' i.e., in the natural events of the world and [in] . . . the natural feelings of the person." Mary Bourdon, R.J.M., "The Spiritual Direction of the Adolescent," *Spiritual Life,* Summer 1982, p. 97.

12. Explain what the secretary meant when she said, "You're looking at the Church right now."

13. Who do you mean when you refer to the Church as "they"? How many other "theys" can you list (example, the government)?

A Test of Knowledge

The various uses of the word "church" show how complex a notion it is. However, as you explore some of its basic features throughout this text, you will discover much about its richness.

Many students know a good deal about the Church already. Some may think they know a lot, and others are aware that their knowledge has huge gaps. The following exercise can help clarify your present level of knowledge.

What Do You Know About the Church?

1. What is the Church? Whom does it include?
2. Who are the laity? What is their role?
3. Who is the pope? What is the pope?
4. Who is the bishop of your diocese? What is a bishop? What is a diocese?
5. Who is the pastor of your parish? What is a pastor? What is a parish?
6. What do Catholics believe? Where do their beliefs come from?
7. What are the Ten Commandments? Where can they be found?
8. Who was Jesus? What is Jesus' commandment?
9. What are the laws of the Church?
10. Name the sacraments. In a word or two name the purpose of each.
11. What is the purpose of the Church?
12. How do you see your personal role in the Church?

Use this exercise again at the end of the course to gauge how much you've learned.

Your Call to Discipleship

When Jesus summoned his disciples, he called each one by name—Peter, Andrew, James, and John the fisherman; Matthew, the tax collector, Mary the Mother and model of all disciples; Mary, Martha, and Lazarus, friends and witnesses. Each one was special to him and each responded uniquely.

A People at Prayer

One of the things we look for in a Church is people gathering together in common prayer. For Catholics, this common prayer is a part of our Jewish heritage, but also comes directly from Jesus.

Jesus is shown teaching the apostles to pray. "Father, hallowed be your name, your kingdom come. Give us each day our daily bread and forgive us our sins for we ourselves forgive everyone in debt to us, and do not subject us to the final test" (Luke 11:2-4). In addition, Jesus speaks of the power of the disciples' prayer. "For everyone who asks, receives; and the one who seeks, finds; and to the one who knocks, the door will be opened" (Luke 11:10).

Just like the Apostles and disciples, you are directly called by Jesus. How you respond to this call is your decision to make in your own unique way.

The Church: A Spirit-Filled People

From the beginning, Jesus called individuals not to remain separate followers but to form a community. He said, "You are the light of the world . . . your light must shine before others, that they may see your good deeds and glorify your heavenly Father" (Matthew 5:14-16). His individual followers became a community that gave them a unique identity. Together, they brought a light to the world that had never shined before. Today, you are called to shine your light into the world—to increase the brightness of the Catholic community of believers for everyone, everywhere, to see.

14. *Have you experienced Jesus' call to discipleship? When? How was your Church community involved in this experience?*

15. *What does Jesus' call to discipleship demand of Church members today? Of you personally?*

Knowledge of the Course

However you may ultimately perceive the Church, it is important that your perception be conscious and deliberate. To come to love the Church for your own reasons, you need to know its long history. As you witness the commitment made to it by people like yourself over the course of 2000 years, you will learn what is necessary for you to arrive at your destination, a strong and active faith. Understanding how both images of the Church and the Church itself have changed and grown can help you respond to the images you see today.

Many people and institutions will compete for your heart and mind. They will challenge your beliefs and possibly question whether you have been misled. But if your image of the Church is real—something you can live with, something you love—you can stand strong in your beliefs.

If your image is genuine, if you feel good about the Church, you will cherish membership in it and will want to tell others the good news about it. You will feel a powerful need to grow in service to the Church and in love for it.

Disciple: one who follows and helps to spread his or her teacher's teachings.

Others may lose faith in the Church and seem to get along without it; but you will opt for the Church because you will be convinced that it deserves your loyalty.

Your search will lead you deeper into its mystery, make you more faithful to your commitment to it and more willing to understand and forgive its human weaknesses, which stand side by side with its divine strength.

This study will present information which will help you to form an accurate image, one that your own self-image can fit into comfortably. When the course is ended, your investigation will only have begun. Your image and love of the Church will continue to grow as long as you live.

16. How are you being influenced to continue to be a member of the Church?

Summary

- A guiding image is necessary for faith.
- The closer an image is to reality, the truer the image.
- An accurate image of the Church includes knowledge and understanding.
- The Church is not a distant "they," but is made up of people like us.
- Jesus called disciples to form a community.
- Knowledge and a positive image can help you come to love the Church.

SECTION 3
Checkpoint!

■ Review

1. What is the function of a guiding image?
2. Why is it crucial that a guiding image be accurate?
3. What does an accurate guiding image include?
4. What is a depersonalized image?
5. Why should your image of the Church be conscious and deliberate?
6. Is the call to follow Christ individual or communal? Explain.
7. To what does Jesus call his disciples?
8. Words to Know: disciple, perception, paranoid, personality, guiding image, depersonalized.

■ In Your World

1. As a class, role play the following situation: You are approached by friends to join their church. You listen to what they have to say, then explain to them why you prefer to stay in your own church or why you will go with them. What arguments do your friends offer to try to convince you? How can you answer their statements? What help do you need to make an honest decision?
2. Create a slogan to encapsulate the way you understand Jesus' call to discipleship.

■ Scripture Search

Read the call of Matthew in Matthew 9:9. What is striking about his response? Compare it with the calls of John, Andrew, Peter, Philip, and Nathanael in John 1:35-50. What similarities and differences do you notice in the responses? How would you describe Jesus' power of attraction? What different methods did Jesus use? What does all the variety tell us?

Chapter 1 Finding an Image that Works for You

CHAPTER 1 Review

■ Study

1. Why is your image of the Church so important?
2. How can the images of others affect your life?
3. Describe how our images of things are formed.
4. What influence does our growth have upon our images?
5. What is the significance of icons?
6. Write two different definitions of Church.
7. How does a definition of Church differ from your personal experience of Church?
8. How do our feelings about the Church influence our image of the Church?
9. How do guiding images shape our lives?
10. How are accurate images of the Church developed?
11. In what ways is the call to follow Christ individual and in what ways is it communal?
12. What does Jesus expect of his disciples?
13. How does our recognition of the Church change from childhood to maturity?
14. What is meant by referring to the Church as "they"?

■ Action

1. Talk to Catholic friends who attend parishes other than yours. Is their image of the Church different than yours? Make a list of the various images. Do different parishes have different images among students?

2. In some artistic and creative way, build your image of the Church. Be prepared to explain what your image represents, and why you have this image.

3. When you think of the Church, what music comes to mind? If you were music director at your parish, what music would you play? Bring examples of each kind of music to class and play it. Be prepared to explain your choice of music.

■ Prayer

In your room at home, or in the classroom, set up an Icon Corner. This is done by having a small table in the corner, along with an icon, Bible, and small candle. You may also wish to burn incense in front of your icon. Sit or stand, whatever way is most comfortable for you, in front of the icon. The way of prayer is silence.

Look intently at the sacred image represented in the icon. Think about the person seen in the icon. To what is that person calling you? As you continue to look into the icon, ask yourself what you would like to tell God. Speak these thoughts silently.

Start with five minutes a day in prayer. After a few days, increase your time of prayer to ten minutes. If you find this form of prayer valuable, you can easily work your way up to 30 minutes of prayer a day.

CHAPTER 2

Biblical Images and Mystery

OBJECTIVES

In this Chapter you will

- Learn the meaning of mystery.

- Reflect on Biblical images of the Church.

- Examine the role of a disciple.

- Study the image of the Body of Christ.

- Learn what it means to be the People of God.

The inner nature of the Church is now made known to us in various images.
— "Dogmatic Constitution on the Church," #6

The Church: A Spirit-Filled People

SECTION 1
The Wonder of a Mystery

Happiness can mean different things to different people. It might mean a giant pizza, a letter from a friend, scoring the winning touchdown, your own car, or a hug from someone special. The experience of God's love is also happiness. All of these images show a different side of that indefinable, mysterious feeling called happiness. Can you define it? Maybe not, but you have certainly felt it.

The Church: A Religious Mystery

The *"Dogmatic Constitution on the Church"* used Biblical metaphors when it tried to explain and define the Church. How could they define what the mystery of the Church really is? In an effort to form a definition, they stated, "The inner nature of the Church is now made known to us in various images" (*"Dogmatic Constitution on the Church,"* #6). Just as with the idea of happiness, images can help bridge the gap between our experiences and the true meaning and reality of the Church.

As seen by the many definitions of Church in Chapter 1, it has been hard to come up with a totally satisfactory definition of the Church in two thousand years. Will we ever be successful? Is it important? A convert from Florida put her finger on something when she said, "There's room in the Catholic Church for mystery . . . and I need that" (*Why People Join the Church,* by Edward Rauff, p. 160).

The fact is that we all need mystery. We need it because we are constantly striving to be pushed to the farthest limits of life—and beyond. Although very human, the Church is also a deep religious mystery. It touches on the sacred.

> **Sacred:** holy, set apart, entitled to reverence and respect.

Chapter 2 Biblical Images and Mystery

Catholics see the Mystery of God revealed in the bread and wine used in the Eucharist.

The Mystery of God

Religious mystery reflects the inexpressible mystery of God. It can attract us and fill us with fear because it reveals glimpses of infinity. People who have climbed high mountain peaks know mystery. People who have maneuvered a skiff in high winds have tasted mystery. Mystery is where God's presence is silent, yet so strong you can actually feel it. Thomas Merton, (1915-1968)—a Trappist monk and a famous writer—on his way to conversion, found mystery in the face of a girl praying in a church. Before embracing the faith, Saint Elizabeth Ann Seton (1774-1821) sensed it in the presence of the Blessed Sacrament when she accompanied her Italian friends to Mass. You, too, have probably sensed the mystery of the Church, perhaps in the strong voices of the congregation raised in prayer, or in the silence of a crowd kneeling in adoration.

A famous surgeon shocked the Victorian world in the nineteenth century by announcing that he didn't believe in the human soul because he had never seen one in all the surgeries he had performed. Yet we know that things like love, patriotism, and happiness are real even though we can't put them under a microscope. Divine realities are no less real! The mystery of the Church involves faith which is the acceptance of things unseen on God's word. Faith can never be fully understood or totally denied.

The Church: A Spirit-Filled People

1. *When have you experienced the feeling of mystery? How did it make you feel? How do you explain the conflicting emotions?*

2. *What do you think is the special connection between mystery and faith for the Church?*

Saint Paul and the Mystery

The roots of the Church's mystery lie in the incomprehensible design of God's wisdom and goodness. Saint Paul was the first to apply the word mystery to the Church. He called it "that mystery hidden for ages" (Romans 16:25). To discover what he meant, we can examine the meanings of the Greek word *musterion*. One of those definitions says it is a secret teaching or secret knowledge available only to a select group, something like the classified information which we connect with modern intelligence operations.

The Greeks also used this word to refer to religious rituals of initiation in which candidates sometimes acted out episodes in the lives of the gods. Through this practice, they hoped to acquire divine qualities. Saint Paul borrowed this term and applied it to the faith life of the Church in several ways.

This Greek religious artwork attempts to convey the mystery of Jesus as Lord.

Musterion: later translated by the word sacramentum, the rites of the Roman Catholic Church.

Chapter 2   Biblical Images and Mystery

On This Rock

Who were the people first drawn to the mystery of Jesus present in the Church? Early Christians lived primarily in cities. Churches were local communities identified with the city in which they were located. Greek was the main language used by the Church and the language in which the New Testament was written.

The early communities attracted many converts, especially from the socially and economically disadvantaged such as women, children, and slaves. During the first century, worship usually took place in the homes of the faithful. Only the initiated (baptized) were allowed to be present for the Eucharist. Christians were also forbidden to choose some professions such as soldier or judge.

In creating the universe, God proposed to share with humanity his own divine life. With Adam and Eve's fall, that purpose became clouded. Over the course of history, God gradually revealed his plan to restore all things to himself in his Son. Through Jesus, God's plan encompassed all people. When the Son accomplished the work his Father had given him to do on earth, the Holy Spirit was poured out to give those who believe an access to the Father through Christ. Saint Paul saw the Church as the final stage in this long process.

Paul also used the word mystery to apply to the whole sacramental life of the Church, through which God's special presence with his people was, and is, revealed. This unique presence could be known only to the initiated, those who lived within the Christian community. This "new way," which was the first name given to the early Christian life-style, was followed by spreading the Good News of the Gospel, participating in the sacraments, and serving one another in joy.

Jesus and the Mystery

The "new way" originated in the small community Jesus had gathered. Living in his presence and living as he had lived gave them an experience beyond anything they had ever known. But it was an experience that could be read two ways. For those with "eyes to see," faith, Jesus did the mighty deeds of God. To those without faith, he was at best only a preacher from Nazareth. To his followers, Jesus was the living expression of the kingdom about which he preached. To some religious leaders, he was an imposter worthy of death. Some of the crowd understood the message of the parables; others were deaf. It was the same with his crucifixion. Some saw it as a fiasco. But the community of faith saw in it supreme love and world salvation, and through it they came to possess the supreme comfort of Christ's risen presence.

It is the same with the presence of Christ in his Church today. He remains hidden in its very ordinary people—yet also very much present, in the apparently human words of an apparently ordinary book—the Bible, and in ordinary rituals and ordinary looking bread and wine—the Eucharist. The faithful see beyond the appearances and experience God's presence, always saving and always healing. The mystery of the Church is that those who live its life are given "eyes to see" that God remains in their midst. Even more importantly, those outside of the Church see God through the lives of Christian people.

3. What images are used to describe the different reactions to Jesus' life and death?

4. Is there a difference in the ways that members and non-members see the mystery? Explain your reasons.

Biblical Images of the Mystery

The heart of the mystery of the Church is God, whom only Jesus fully knew. It was the mission of Jesus to communicate this mystery. Instead of trying to explain the unexplainable, Jesus used familiar Biblical images which touch our emotions as well as instruct us.

Biblical images act like a mirror for the mystery. Through the images, the mystery is reflected in many patterns and directions. As you read and picture the images in your mind, you will find that they contain many apparent opposites like mercy and justice, judgment and forgiveness, and sin and holiness. But instead of really being contradictions, you may finally see that these images complement each other, that they reflect two sides of the same image. The power of images to reflect many sides of one thing at the same time makes these images ideal for leading us into the mystery of the Church.

5. When might you find using images easier than trying to define something?

Complement: two or more things which form a complete whole when put together.

The Sheepfold and the Good Shepherd

Many of the images used by Jesus can also be found in the Hebrew Scriptures. For example, the image of God leading the flock, Israel, to the green pastures of the Promised Land like the shepherd depicted in the Hebrew Scriptures. In the Gospel of John, the Church is compared to a sheepfold and Jesus is the one gate by which the sheep enter (John 10:1-16). These images were meaningful to a pastoral people who understood the value of grassy land and the importance of a caring shepherd.

To a sheep herder, spring lambing is a favorite event. Since newborn lambs are fragile, they can easily die from the cold without special protection. Perhaps the shepherd's care at this time makes a flock especially close to him. The shepherd learns to recognize each sheep, and older animals may even come to him for some extra attention.

Pope John Paul II, through his visits to Catholics all over the world, has been a real shepherd to the Church community.

Having grown up in sheep country, Jesus used this image to express concern for the lost sheep of the house of Israel, as well as to depict the deep relationship between himself and his followers in the Church. "I am the Good Shepherd," he said (John 10:11). As both the shepherd who laid down his life for his sheep, and the sacrificial Lamb of God who went silently to the slaughter of Calvary, Jesus formed a new covenant—binding the sheep and shepherd—in an eternal union. The images of sheep, flock, and shepherd appear nineteen times in the books of the New Testament. For sheep imagery see Matthew 8:17; Luke 22:37; Acts 8:32, 20:28; Hebrews 13:20; and 1 Peter 1:19, 2:25. For sheep imagery in the Hebrew Scriptures see Psalms 2, 23, 77, 78, 80; Jeremiah 23; Isaiah 40; Ezekiel, 34:1-31; Zechariah 11:4-17.

6. What other relationship can you think of that develops the same feelings as that of the shepherd with the flock?

7. Explain how Jesus fits the image of the shepherd and the image of the sheep.

The Vine and the Branches

Another image of the relationship between Jesus and his followers comes from John's Gospel in the parable of the vine and the branches. Like those of the sheepfold, images of the vineyard go far back in Biblical history. The community of Israel was God's choice vineyard. Jesus used the image and gave it a new and unique twist. "I am the vine, you are the branches. He who lives in me and I in him will produce abundantly" (John 15:25). The mutual abiding he describes is perhaps one of the deepest mysteries of the Church. Just as Adam ate the fruit that produced death, the new Adam—Christ living through the Church—bears the new fruit which is God's unending life. We are all branches of the vine which is the Church (see Isaiah 5:1-7; Jeremiah 2:21; Psalm 6:16; Sirach 24:17).

The image of the vine and the branches shows that we are extensions of Christ. It means that we can extend Christ's peace and love always wherever we are and

Pastoral: relating to the countryside and raising of livestock.

Chapter 2   Biblical Images and Mystery

Images in Art

Many of the images which appear in the words of the Scriptures can also be found in the artwork of the early Christian community. Artists have depicted many scenes from the Bible. Certain symbols and colors have come to have special religious meanings. The next time you visit a museum or look through a book of paintings, see if you are able to identify some of the following images and symbols.

Did you know that the dolphin is used more often than any other fish or sea mammal? It represents resurrection and salvation. The orange tree is a symbol of purity and generosity. Eyes may be an image of the the all-knowing and ever-present God. Another symbol for God is the circle, because it has no beginning and no end; it is eternal. And forty is a number which represents trial. Think of the flood which lasted forty days, or Christ's temptation in the desert.

Artists throughout history have used these familiar objects and themes to evoke emotions and responses in those who look at their work. In this way, a painting can become part of someone's spiritual experience of the mystery.

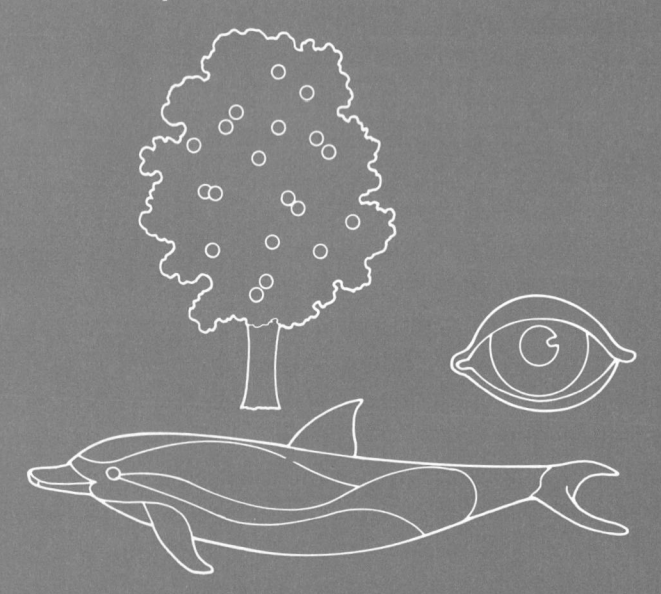

Symbolic art has been used to capture the meaning of Biblical imagery.

The Church: A Spirit-Filled People

whatever we are doing, even in the most ordinary day-to-day tasks. Every branch is in union not only with Jesus, but also with all the other branches on the vine. In that way, we share communion with Jesus and with each other.

How does one become part of the tree? The sacraments—those mysterious actions—initiate a person into the Church just as a branch can be grafted onto a vine. Through Baptism and the Eucharist, those who have experienced the mystery of salvation become part of the community of Christ.

---

8. *What other images can you think of which work as well as this one?*

9. *How does the image of a vine with many branches grafted on truly reflect the nature of the Church?*

Summary

- A mystery goes beyond our ability to fully understand and touch many of our emotions.

- Religious mystery reflects God.

- Paul used the word mystery to mean knowledge, God's plan for our salvation, and the rites which ensure our entry into the community of Christ.

- Biblical images such as the shepherd and the vine and branches were used by Jesus to describe the mystery of our relationship to God.

Chapter 2 Biblical Images and Mystery

SECTION 1
Checkpoint!

■ Review

1. Why are images used to describe mysteries?
2. What is the purpose of mystery?
3. What does religious mystery reflect?
4. What is the meaning of *musterion* in Greek?
5. How did Paul use the word mystery?
6. Why did Jesus select the images he did to describe his relationship with others?
7. Words to Know: etymology, musterion, mystery, pastoral, sacred.

■ In Your World

1. Select a new image which reflects Jesus' relationship with his Church. Make this image familiar to people today just as Jesus' images were familiar to those around him.
2. Do an etymological study of some terms you have learned such as sacrament, sacred, image, Church. Use a dictionary and other tools to trace the meanings of each word. In what language did the words originate? What did it mean then? How has the meaning changed?

■ Scripture Search

1. Read the following Scripture passages: Matthew 13:47-50; Luke 6:47-49; John 15:1-11. What images are used here? Which do you like? Which are the most effective?
2. Pick one set of images mentioned in this chapter (shepherd or vine) and look up all the Scripture references given. What sort of picture emerges when all the images are taken together? How do the passages from the Hebrew Scriptures and the New Testament complement each other?

SECTION 2
A Community of Disciples

In all four Gospels, Jesus is shown gathering a community of disciples around him. This is part of God's revelation. The image of the Church as a community of disciples became another expression of the mystery. Although Jesus called his followers to community life, he also called each one individually. His relationship with each disciple was deeply personal, and each individual joined the growing community. Every disciple experienced a conversion which involved turning away from certain things in order to follow Jesus.

Disciple and Teacher

As a Jewish son living in a patriarchical society, Jesus himself knew what it meant to be a disciple. In his father's carpentry shop he had been instructed by his father who was a master carpenter. He spent many years in observation and was gradually initiated into the art of carpentry until he was judged ready to carry on the family business.

In the Gospels, Jesus often refers to himself as a disciple in relationship to his heavenly Father. It was the same process as his woodworking apprenticeship. The "craft" he learned from his Father was the art of discipleship, which meant listening to the Father and doing God's will.

It was this vision and life that Jesus offered to the community he loved. He taught his disciples that whoever follows him is a true disciple of the Father (see Luke 10:22). After having called, instructed, and initiated his disciples, Jesus sent them off joyfully in the power of the Spirit to offer this same vision and life to others.

> **Patriarchical society:** authority is given to male members: husbands, fathers, sons.

Chapter 2   Biblical Images and Mystery

Communion of Saints

Those who convert to Catholicism from another faith often are the strongest in answering the call to discipleship. Saint Elizabeth Ann Seton, the founder of the Sisters of Charity, was the first native-born American to be canonized. She was also a convert. At twenty, she married, and eventually had five children. She converted to Catholicism in 1805 at the age of 31. Her special gift was in the education of children and she is known as the mother of the parochial school system in the United States. By the time of her death in 1821, Saint Elizabeth Seton's Sisters of Charity had branched into 20 communities. She was canonized in 1975.

The image of the Holy Family, Joseph, Mary, and Jesus, helps us to understand that Jesus grew in faith just as we do.

10. *Name some things the apostles may have given up in order to follow Jesus.*

11. *What has been the highest expression of your discipleship or that of your Church community?*

Faith Supported in Community

Following Jesus as a disciple means becoming part of his community. One benefit of belonging to any community is the interaction and mutual support of its members. In the Church, where faith in Jesus Christ is the core of discipleship, supporting the faith of all is a prime concern. Jesus said to Peter, "I have prayed that your own faith may never fail; and once you have turned back, you must strengthen your brothers" (Luke 22:32).

People don't always function at their best in a family or a business situation. They aren't always at their best in a faith community either. Community members understand that faith does not always come easily—that it often fails when tested—and that we all make mistakes and are sinners. Those people who are hurt or doubtful know that others in the community will gladly support them through the rough times.

The Church community is a source of hope and healing, not of rejection and judgment. It cares for its sick and wounded in the spirit of the Good Shepherd who went in search of the lost sheep instead of rejecting or judging them when they return.

Our Church Community

Parishes today are trying to provide new ways for Christians to experience the faith support of the Church community. Eucharistic Ministers bring the Eucharist to those unable to attend Liturgy. Others provide support to the community through prayer, Bible study groups, and continued learning experiences. Renewal activities and youth ministries are growing. The Church is also becoming more sensitive to the particular needs of people experiencing problems in married life and in the area of human sexuality. In this way, the Church provides comfort and support to the whole community. Those who are strong can help those who are going through a time of weakness. The community is composed of all types of people. The Church offers reconciliation and forgiveness to those who fall short of the ideal Christian norm of belief and behavior. In this way, the Church shows compassion toward the sinner without condoning the sin.

12. *How has your Church community helped you or someone you know through a crisis of faith?*

Chapter 2 Biblical Images and Mystery

The Call of Discipleship

The Christian community of disciples is made up of people who have accepted Christ's invitation to discipleship. They help one another to live the Christian life more fully. Each day this call to follow Christ is offered anew, and each individual has the freedom to renew his or her response. This makes discipleship an ongoing challenge. Disciples realize how important community support is in order to meet the changing challenges of faith and discipleship.

We all need to be disciples in two ways: by becoming better followers of the Lord through participation in community instruction and worship, and by reaching out to support others. We teach by our example, and often learn even while we teach others. The Church is not just a group that meets on Sunday morning. Honest discipleship requires a commitment to live the "new way" of Christ. That commitment is to the God who loves us and to all the people who are called with us.

---

13. *How can you answer the call to discipleship each day?*

14. *What could you do for someone who has lost his or her faith or who is going through a spiritual crisis?*

The Body of the Church: Paul's Image

The popularity of jogging, aerobics, and other forms of exercise shows that Americans know the value of a healthy body. Saint Paul used the human body as his favorite symbol for the Church. Paul compares the body we all share with our Biblical father, Adam, and the "new" body we acquire in the new Adam who is Christ. That new Body is the Church community, the Body of Christ. Perhaps the image of this relationship came to Paul as he was on his way to persecute the Christians and he heard Christ ask him,

"Saul, Saul, why are you persecuting me?" (Acts 9:4). Christ's question implies that there is a mysterious identity between Christians and himself.

Like the human body, the Church community is not just a collection of unrelated parts. It is a united organism. When Paul teaches that we are the Body of Christ, he focuses both on our unity with Christ and with one another, and on our diversity as unique members, each called to contribute individually to Christ's mission.

Our Union with God in Christ

As head of the body, Jesus is closely united to all its members. He is the source of the community's meaning and the center of all its activity. In his life we discover who we are to become, and he is able to bring us to our true destiny. His life is the pattern for our lives. We who die and rise with him in baptism and in our daily lives are taken up into his divine life. At the end of our time on earth, we will follow him in resurrection to share in his glory forever.

All creation is moving toward fulfillment in Christ. "For, 'In him we live and move and have our being' " (Acts 17:28). Paul also uses the image of husband and wife to suggest that the union between Jesus and the Church is as intimate as that of marriage (see Ephesians 5:25-32). Christ loves his Church just as a husband loves his wife. This union is expressed in the visible community which is a sacrament of humanity's reconciliation with God. A sacrament is a sign that carries out what it signifies—the Church community is an agent of peace and love in the world; married love produces children.

Our Union with One Another

Saint Paul's image of the body reveals the bonding role of the Holy Spirit in forming a single human society. In the same way, by grace we are united in a community transformed by the Spirit. Although this "Body of Christ" is composed of many members located around the world, it is still one body in the Spirit. Even though all members are sinners, they mysteriously share in the divinity of Christ. You are "one body and one Spirit, as you were also called to the one hope of your call; one Lord, one faith, one

Chapter 2 Biblical Images and Mystery

A Pilgrim Church

Rome, Lourdes, Fatima. Who hasn't heard of these places made famous by millions of pilgrims? Making religious journeys called pilgrimages is still popular with people all over the world. Vatican II revived the image of the entire Church as a pilgrim people. It is not a new image. The Israelites spent forty years on a pilgrimage through the desert, and Jesus' final journey to Jerusalem is depicted as a pilgrimage.

The Church, as a community of disciples, is also on a pilgrimage. The destination is union with God, as individuals, and as a group. The obstacles are sin and weakness. To reach that destination we need constant conversion and renewal. Everyone is involved in the effort to move toward a better understanding of Jesus' kingdom. We learn from our mistakes. Christ will support us just as we support one another on the journey toward the mystery which is God.

♦

baptism; one God and Father of all" (Ephesians 4:4-6). Paul stresses this unity by exhorting, "I . . . urge you to live in a manner worthy of the call you have received, with all humility and gentleness, with patience, bearing with one another through love, striving to preserve the unity of the spirit through the bond of peace" (Ephesians 4:1-3).

---

15. *How do the head and members of a body work together to function in unity (in the human body and in the Church)?*

16. *What are some ways the Church acts as an agent of peace?*

17. *What things unite all members of Christ's body and what things make them different?*

Diversity of Gifts

Paul points out the diversity of gifts in the Church by stating: "The body has many members . . . but the foot does not say, "Because I am not a hand I do not belong to the body." All the members, many though they are, are one body; God has set each member of the body in the place he wanted it to be. If all members were alike, where would the body be? There are different gifts but the same Spirit; there are different ministries but the same Lord; there are different works but the same God who accomplishes all of them in everyone" (1 Corinthians 12:12, 15, 19).

It must be obvious that Saint Paul applies the image of the Body of Christ to the Church in a nonliteral way. The members are not actual physical extensions of the historical body of Christ that died on Calvary. But in their daily living and example, they receive power from the Spirit to extend Christ's divine life into the world for all time.

18. *How does the diversity of gifts add to the beauty of the Church? How does it add to human society as a whole?*

Summary

- The Church is a community of disciples called by Christ.
- Disciples are called to follow Jesus and support others in the community.
- Parishes and communities are always trying to find ways to offer support and love.
- Paul used the image of the body to symbolize the relationship between Christ and his Church.
- We are united with Christ as head of the Church and with one another.
- The Church is composed of many individuals, all different, but united in faith.

SECTION 2
Checkpoint!

■ Review

1. How did Jesus call his disciples?
2. In what ways was Jesus himself a disciple?
3. What is the most important benefit of belonging to a community?
4. Why does the Church offer support, forgiveness, and reconciliation to its members?
5. When is discipleship offered to us?
6. Explain how the image of the body and head fit the Church community called by Christ.
7. Words to Know: disciple, patriarchical, diversity.

■ In Your World

1. Go around the class and ask each person what he or she thinks their own gift is within the Church community. Do you agree with each person's view? How would you describe the special gift of each of your classmates? How does this diversity add to the life of the group? What problems can it cause?
2. Write and act out a skit about someone who is experiencing a crisis of faith. What has caused it? How would you help and support that person?

■ Scripture Search

Read 1 Corinthians 12-13. These are perhaps the most important chapters on the Body of Christ. Think about why Paul chose this image. How is the body portrayed here, in a positive or negative way (or both)? What are the drawbacks of using this image? Why do you think that people often view the body negatively? What is the biblical attitude toward the body?

SECTION 3
People of God

Your grandparents will tell you that if you wait long enough fashions from your youth will return. Frequently it happens that over the course of time, we return to the traditions of our past. This is true for the Church as well. The Council Fathers of Vatican II restored a Church image that was used in apostolic times and then neglected for centuries—the People of God. This image has its roots even farther back in time in the Hebrew Scriptures.

The Chosen People

Identifying a people as the People of God recalls the idea of mystery. The Biblical Hebrews were God's people not by being born in a particular place, but by the action of God. They were chosen by God to witness to God's goodness. Eucharistic Prayer I mentions Abraham as "our father in faith." In the Bible, the people of Israel, and then Christians, are the People of God. Vatican II recognizes that the Jews remain God's people even though Christ brought the new Israel into being.

You may feel uneasy when you realize that, as a Catholic, you belong to the People of God. In a democratic society, we try not to claim authority or special privileges because we belong to a certain group. But there was no sense of superiority for either the Israelites or the Apostles when they used this image. The Apostles used it because it was part of their Jewish heritage and because Jewish tradition shows that being God's People was a humbling experience and a heavy responsibility. Israel became God's People by accepting God's offer of the covenant. God called the Israelites, and expected them to remain faithful. Just as people in love often take that love for granted, the Israelites sometimes rebelled or went astray. God always brought them back. God's presence among the people made them holy, capable of faith and worship (Deuteronomy 7:7, Deuteronomy 8:11-18, 1 Samuel 15:28, and Amos 6:2).

The Christian experience is the same. Christ claims everyone, without exception, as his own. Joined in his sacrifice to the Father, we are empowered, as the Hebrews never were, to worship the Father in God's own Spirit. This advantage cannot give us a false sense of superiority because it is a pure gift of God's mercy, available to all.

The first letter of Peter sums it up: "You, however, are a 'chosen race, a royal priesthood, a holy nation, a people he claims for his own to proclaim the glorious works' of the One who called you from darkness into his marvelous light. Once you were not people, but now you are God's people; once there was no mercy for you, but now you have found mercy" (1 Peter 2:9-10; see also Romans 9:25-26).

Jesus calls us from darkness into the light.

---

19. *How is the relationship of a Jewish person to God similar to a Christian person's relationship to God? How is it different?*

20. *What role do you think the Israelites played in the experience of their being chosen? Were they completely passive? What types of responses does God demand from those who were chosen?*

The Church: A Spirit-Filled People

Chosen and Choosing

In both Judaism and Christianity, scholars and religious leaders have always written commentaries on Scripture. These commentaries attempt to explore and explain Scripture. In Judaism, some of this commentary is called *midrash*. A *midrash* is a story which is used to illustrate or interpret a passage from Scripture.

There is a famous *midrash* about the events surrounding God's choosing of the Hebrews to be the People of God. It says that God originally chose another group of people, but that group would not accept the responsibilities of fidelity and morality demanded by God. After selecting several other groups, God chose the Hebrews who joyfully accepted the responsibility and honor of being God's chosen.

This *midrash* shows that it is wrong for anyone to feel superior because they are a part of the People of God. The Hebrews felt glad, and they felt humbled in the presence of God, but they did not feel better than the others. In the same way, we must always strive to be People of God. Our "membership" in this group does not mean we can be complacent. As the People of God, we are made holy by God, and must always remain deserving of the sanctity.

Imperfection among God's People

At one time when you were younger, you may have asked a priest or religious leader, "Are you God?" or "Are you married to Jesus?" As a child you probably also saw the Church through rose-colored glasses. Then, sometime during adolescence, the rose tints began to fade. You may have noticed that the pastor has a bad temper, that the choir director seems out for personal glory, or that the sister-principal can be opinionated. Someone whose opinions you value may have made a valid criticism of a Church

Chapter 2 Biblical Images and Mystery

leader, or news of a Church scandal may make the headlines. Or you may have read about the brutality of the Spanish Inquisition. As a result, you may begin to wonder whether the Church isn't just like all other organizations.

You cannot just close your eyes and deny that the members of Christ's Church have not always lived up to his expectations. There have been unworthy leaders, sinful followers, power struggles, divisions, and lack of leadership at crucial moments. These things mar the Church's image and cause some to reject it.

A People at Prayer

We think of prayer as a way of communicating with God. We pray either silently or aloud as a group. During the early Christian centuries, Christian scholars and religious leaders worked hard to develop a theology of prayer. They argued over when and how often to pray, what to pray for, and even what prayer is.

Origen, a third century Christian scholar and priest, said, "Prayer without ceasing means uniting prayer with the works that we are obliged to perform and joining fitting works to our prayer, since virtuous deeds . . . are a part of prayer . . . What we call prayer is only a small part of praying, something that we are obliged to do at least three times a day."

Origen's idea was adopted by other Church Fathers like Jerome and Basil the Great.

21. *What human characteristics do you see in the Church? When did you become aware of them and how can you respond?*

22. *What would you say to someone who rejected the Church because of the weakness of one of its leaders?*

Early Church Leaders

The situation in Jesus' time was similar to that of today. The first disciples included men who sought the first place in the kingdom, people with short tempers, and one who betrayed him. Yet they were also strong and loving people such as the teenager, John, who stayed with Christ until the end, Peter who was loving, but also afraid and especially the women who stayed with Jesus throughout his ministry even until his burial. There was also Nicodemus, an educated official who wanted to follow Jesus but who was sensitive to what others might have thought. There were others who were considered sinners including lepers, the blind, and prostitutes. It was into this soil that the Holy Spirit first planted the seeds of salvation.

It was the same in the Apostolic Church in Rome, Corinth, and Antioch during Paul's time. The vices of the general population were so awful that many people flocked to Christianity. Being part of the People of God raised the honor and dignity of the members and gave them a strict moral code. But old faults did not disappear immediately. It

The Church: A Spirit-Filled People

was necessary for Saint Paul to warn his congregations against immorality, factions, quarreling, and polarizing loyalty to particular leaders (1 Corinthians 5). Paul never hesitates to mention his own weaknesses as well. His warnings were not always effective.

Yet Paul had full confidence in the Spirit's power to bring about unity among the splinter groups, loyalty to Christ, abandonment of vice, and effective preaching in the Church. And despite selfishness, stupidity, and misguided zeal, the Spirit often prevailed in the daily witness and ministry of many ordinary people.

Paul and Peter were leaders of the early Church.

Spanish Inquisition: a Church court set up in the fifteenth century which often resorted to harsh measures to extract confessions of heresies.

Leprosy: a disease caused by a bacteria which results in the deformity of the body, paralysis, and often death.

The Work of the Holy Spirit

The Holy Spirit is still powerfully at work. God continues to work through weak and sinful people, turning all things to good. In the midst of constant setbacks, Christ still sanctifies his people, raising sinners to new life and calling new disciples every day.

When a healthy child flourishes, no one notices. But if an accident or cancer patient recovers, everyone proclaims a miracle. The history of the Church often seems like the above mentioned cancer patient who recovers. The People of God has survived ills and flourished. This is the sign of God's presence among us. That presence has been constant for two thousand years as promised, "And behold, I am with you always, until the end of the age" (Matthew 28:20).

Summary

- The Church community is identified as the People of God.
- The image of the Chosen People does not suggest superiority. It does suggest faith and responsibility.
- Being a part of God's People is a gift of mercy.
- As a human organization, the Church may display weaknesses.
- The power of the Spirit can bring about unity and strength.

SECTION 3
Checkpoint!

■ Review

1. Why do you think being chosen by God is a humbling experience?

2. What responsibilities does the Church community have in responding to God's choice?

3. How do you answer the criticism of others about the human weaknesses of the Church?

4. Why do you think Jesus chose such a diverse group to be his closest followers and disciples?

5. Words to Know: People of God, mercy, zeal, Nicodemus, Inquisition.

■ In Your World

1. Ask a diverse group of people how they understand the term "People of God." Do they have a positive or negative image? Discuss the results of your survey in class. What was your own image of this term before reading this chapter? Has it changed?

2. Make a list of the things which threaten the unity of the Church today. Include both external and internal factors just as Saint Paul did in his early warnings. What could be done to strengthen the Church against these threats?

■ Scripture Search

Read Exodus 20:1-17. This chapter and the ones following it describe the events surrounding God's choice of the Hebrews. That choice set up a covenant between God and the Hebrews. What is a covenant? What were the terms of the convenant established here? How was that covenant renewed and changed by Christ?

Chapter 2   Biblical Images and Mystery

CHAPTER 2 Review

■ Study

1. How do people try to explain something they don't understand?
2. What is meant by the term "religious mystery"?
3. What are two meanings of the word mystery used by Paul?
4. How can one come closer to experiencing the mystery of the Church?
5. In what ways do Biblical images work?
6. Explain how the image of the shepherd and the flock represents Christ and the Church.
7. Why is it important for images and symbols to come from within a culture?
8. Why can Jesus be described as both disciple and master?
9. What is the role of the Church community as a source of hope and strength?
10. Why is the call to discipleship not a one-time event?
11. How is Paul's use of the human body as a symbol successful? How is it not?
12. How does the diversity of gifts contribute to the richness of the Church community?
13. What does it mean to be a part of the People of God?
14. In what ways can the Church community disappoint or disillusion some people?

■ Action

1. Using the images discussed in the chapter as examples, create an image for the Church or for Christ's relationship with the Church as you have experienced it. Assemble pictures or draw your own.

2. Make a pilgrimage to a holy place in your city. It could be another church or a shrine. Write an account of your journey. How did you get there, what did you do, how did you feel?

■ Prayer

Set aside five or ten minutes each day to pray in your room, completely alone. Matthew 6:6 says we should pray in secret. How effective, do you think, is your prayer? At the same time, try to attend Mass every day for one week. Now you are praying in public, in the company of your faith community. Do you feel different? Are your prayers different?

Which do you prefer, individual or communal prayer? Why? What about your classmates? The early Christian Fathers did not agree on which form of prayer was the best, but they did agree that both types are equally effective. Try to balance your own personal prayer life with both types.

Chapter 2 Biblical Images and Mystery

CHAPTER

3

Contemporary Images of the Church

OBJECTIVES

In this Chapter you will

- Discover the meanings of the word *model*.

- Examine five contemporary models of the Church.

- Discuss the strengths and weaknesses of each model.

- Understand the Church as a community of disciples.

You are the light of the world. A city set on a hill cannot be hidden. Your light must shine before all so they may see goodness in your acts and give praise to your heavenly Father.
—Matthew 5:14, 16

58

The Church: A Spirit-Filled People

SECTION 1
Understanding God's Message

The documents of the Second Vatican Council demonstrate that the Church is continually growing in self-understanding. In every age, it has been invigorated by the Holy Spirit with new gifts to deal with contemporary challenges to its mission and message. Theologians constantly study God's Word in order to understand more fully its content and to express it in language each generation will understand.

Using Models to Build Images

Even though Pope John XXIII's declared purpose for the Council was the unity of humankind, one of the Council's major breakthroughs was a renewed appreciation of pluralism. In the manner of modern math, physics, and art, which reflect multiple ways of experiencing reality, the Council accepted a plurality of different ways of approaching the study of Scripture, the Church, the sacraments, and the problems of the modern world. Inspired by the Council's openness, theology has since adopted the "model" approach to its studies of the Church in order to uncover new dimensions and depths of the Church's mystery.

What Is a Model?

The word *model* has several definitions. One meaning is "an ideal": She is a model student. Another meaning is "a set of plans": This is the model of our proposed parish hall. But neither of these definitions expresses the meaning of model as the term is used in theology. For theologians—people who study religion—a model is a simplified way to describe something that cannot be observed directly or is too complex to grasp all at one time. The more complex a

> **Pluralism:** numerous groups living together within a single system.

Chapter 3 Contemporary Images of the Church

concept is, the more models we may need to investigate and understand it. For example, scientists have many models of the atom with which to work, but they still don't understand the reality. Models can be very helpful because they make it possible to think and talk about something very complex and hard to explain. The mystery of the Church becomes clearer when we use models to help us think about it.

You might be wondering if using more than one model might make things even more complicated. Actually, each model examines or represents a given thing from a different point of view, just like a prism breaks light up into the colors of the rainbow. If each color is part of the total light, then each model contributes to the total reality. Models do not compete with one another. They complement one another and help to form a complete picture of reality. The mystery of the Church cannot be confined to one model. You may recognize several models within your own parish—a miniature of the Church universal.

1. What models of your own life can you construct? For example, what different roles do you play—child, student, friend, etc.?

The Primary Model: The Trinity

The Church has come to understand itself first and foremost as intimately related to the Holy Trinity. The Church is called forth by the Father through the Son to carry forward the work of the Son in the power of the Holy Spirit. The Holy Spirit is constantly being sent to renew the face of the earth. The Holy Trinity, then, is not simply an objective truth which we must learn or understand. It is also a source of consolation and nourishment for us. Our dignity and purpose are rooted in it.

Every parish, in its own unique way, reflects the community of the Father, Son, and Holy Spirit. The union of God's people in truth (Word) and charity (Spirit) is like the unity of the divine Persons. What the Trinity does for us is the example of what we are to do in the Church.

The Father gave his Son for our salvation; the Son gave his life for us; and the Father and Son together gave us the gift of being eternally bonded in the Spirit. Each individual in the Church receives these gifts to return to God in Christ, especially in the Eucharist. Each is commissioned and empowered to share them with others. In other words, God's self-communication becomes the model for our self-communication. Our warm outreach to one another and to the world at large is the best sign and instrument of God's presence. Wherever there is love, there is God. The Divine love witnessed in the Holy Trinity is the prototype of all the other models. It is the source and ultimate goal of the Church.

2. *What other words characterize God's relationship to you?*

3. *What do you think it means to say that the Trinity is our source and our goal at the same time?*

This artwork attempts to capture the mystery of the Trinity. The large triangle shows the Oneness of God with the three persons of Father, Son, and Spirit flowing out of it.

Prototype: original form.

Chapter 3   Contemporary Images of the Church

61

Five Contemporary Models

In the 1970's, Jesuit Father Avery Dulles attempted to summarize the reflections of contemporary theologians on the nature of the Church in terms of five other models. He spoke of the Church as institution, community, sacrament, herald, and servant. In the 1980's, he drew together the models into one: the Church as a community of disciples. Each model has strengths, weaknesses, and practical applications for every Catholic.

Church as Institution

A TV director, producing a special on world religions, decided to open the segment on Catholicism with an aerial view of the massive dome of Saint Peter's Basilica in Rome. What a magnificent sight! She, like many others, probably envisions the Church as an institution housed in imposing buildings. You, too, may prefer the institutional model if your concept of your parish is the pastor, church, school, principal, parish council, and sacraments. This model stresses the Church as a structured society through which salvation comes to individual members through the preaching of God's Word and the administration of the sacraments.

This model is associated with things that can be observed—buildings, rules and regulations, offices of authority, and outward obedience. It emphasizes the hierarchy of authority from the pope, bishop, pastor, and priest down to the newest baptized infant. Along with some of Dulles' other models, this one reflects a tradition dating back to the Apostles. It holds in high esteem precise ways of worship, formulas of belief, and a clearly defined moral code.

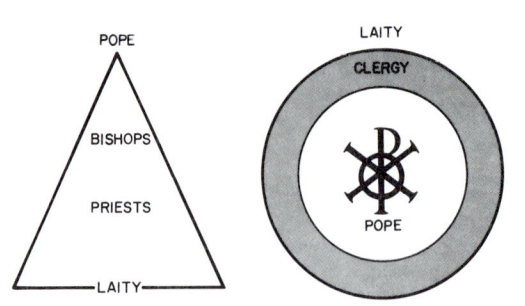

The triangle image represents a hierarchical model of the Church as Institution. The circle reflects an image of Church as every baptized person, with Christ at the center.

On This Rock

Some other models or symbols for the Church can be traced back to the very beginnings of Christianity. First century Christian writers did not have a lot to say about the Church. When they did, they used symbols to reflect on the mystery of the Church. One of those symbols is the Church as mother. As a mother, the Church brings forth children in baptism. The Church also nourishes and nurtures her members. Saint Augustine wrote: "Mother Church conceived you . . . in Christ, she was in labor with you in the blood of martyrs, she brought you forth to everlasting light, she nursed and fed you with the milk of faith . . ."

The Church: A Spirit-Filled People

The institutional model of the Church remains attractive as it provides Catholics with a clear sense of identity and a clear understanding of roles, even though the word *institution* may suggest a measure of red tape, and bureaucracy. Negative images about institutions have developed over the centuries.

In fact, institutions really aren't bad. Behind all organizations—such as hospitals, schools, or charities—there are people who are united in a belief about the value of their purpose and who share common goals. Sometimes, however, institutional structures can become impersonal, resisting change even though they were originally set up to marshal resources efficiently in the face of change. With attention and sensitivity to the Holy Spirit, they can also be lead agents for change.

Another weakness of the institutional model is that it can exaggerate structure at the expense of community. To the extent that this happens, the ordained ministry is associated with power instead of service. Even though the Second Vatican Council emphasized that each Catholic is baptized to participate in the mission of Christ, whether clergy or laity, the institutional model of the Church focuses more attention on the ordained person as minister. Such a structure does not easily respond to societal change.

Father Avery Dulles, S.J.

Institution is not a negative image. The institutional model supports those on mission caring for the sick and needy.

Hierarchy: a ranking of persons in positions of authority.

Chapter 3   Contemporary Images of the Church

63

Light of All Nations

One of the documents to emerge from the Second Vatican Council was *"Lumen Gentium"* (*"Light of the Nations"*), the *"Dogmatic Constitution on the Church."* It deals with all aspects of the Church as institution, including groups within the Church (bishops, laity), activities of the Church (liturgy, education), and with the relationships between the Church and outside groups (ecumenism, the modern world).

The document uses many Biblical images and focuses some attention on the hierarchy of the Church. This passage describes the role of the laity: "The laity are in their own way made sharers in the priestly, prophetic, and kingly functions of Christ. They carry out their own part in the mission of the whole Christian people with respect to the Church and the world" (*"Lumen Gentium"* 3.31).

This important document defines clearly the role of each member of the Church, as well as the role of the Church in the world. The work of the hierarchy is to teach, sanctify, and govern. The laity are called upon to witness to Christ through ministry and fellowship. *"Lumen Gentium"* provides the groundwork for all our models of the Church.

♦

A positive example of an institutional model would be congregations of religious men and women. The great religious orders, all of which are institutions now, evolved from inspired leaders who often aimed to correct existing institutional practices. The offices, authority, organization, laws, and policies now associated with them came into existence in order to make loving Christian service easier and to perpetuate it to future generations. Such structures create order that leads to peace and offer security when too much spontaneity would jeopardize good works. Furthermore, such structures deepen solidarity by uniting energies toward a common goal.

4. *When you see a picture of St. Peter's in Rome surrounded by people, which do you immediately identify with the word "church," the building or the people surrounding it? Discuss your choice.*

5. *What other institutions can you name? How are they structured? What are their advantages and disadvantages?*

6. *What are the advantages of this model for the Church? What characteristics does it contribute? What are your feelings about the Church as an institution?*

Summary

- The Second Vatican Council shows the Church's evolution in self-understanding.

- Theology has adopted a "model" approach to its study of the Church.

- A model helps to clarify a complex reality.

- Many models may be needed to understand a reality.

- Understanding the Trinitarian model is fundamental to understanding all other models.

- The institutional model of the Church focuses on its organization and structure.

- Although institutions can grow static, they can still provide for the needs of those they serve.

SECTION 1
Checkpoint!

■ Review

1. Why do you think it is important for the Church to grow in its self-understanding?

2. What are the strengths and weaknesses of a pluralistic society?

3. What is the purpose of a model?

4. Why are several models often necessary to understand complex concepts or realities?

5. Explain the statement: God's self-communication is the model of our self-communication.

6. What is the hierarchy of the Church?

7. Words to Know: pluralism, model, hierarchy, institution.

■ In Your World

1. Create a montage which illustrates the Church as an institution. Explain why you chose the pictures you did and what each represents.

2. Conduct a poll. Ask people what their definition of an institution is, and how they view the Church. Present your results to the class. Do people have a positive or negative view of institutions in general? Do they see the Church as an institution?

■ Scripture Search

1. Read Timothy 3:1-13. What can you tell about the structure of the early Church from this passage? What concerns does Paul voice in this letter about deacons and bishops?

2. How is the model of Trinitarian love exemplified in Ephesians 3:17-21? Name some practical ways that you and the Church can convey this love to the world.

The Church: A Spirit-Filled People

SECTION 2
Examining Other Models

The next three models which Father Dulles proposed center on the Church community, its nature, and its function. These models focus on the relationships between all the members of a community, and between the Church community and the larger society in which it is located.

Church as Community

If you feel accepted in your Church and your fellow parishioners are caring friends, your parish fits into the community model. A community is just what the word suggests: A unity of people working together in a common purpose. Because community requires structure to function, it is, at times, in tension with the institutional model. Perhaps because of rapid advances in technology or the breakdown of family life, people today seem eager to feel part of a community. Even though our period of history seems to value individuality more than any prior period, we still seek out the community of others every day.

Community as Relationship

The main task of a community is to cultivate personal growth through interpersonal relationships leading to mission. This model views the Church as a family joined in love and sharing in the inner bonds of faith and union with Christ. "It was in one Spirit that all of us were baptized into one body" (1 Corinthians 12:13). The community is a kind of bridge that provides us with the solidarity of a family within the structure of an institution.

Chapter 3   Contemporary Images of the Church

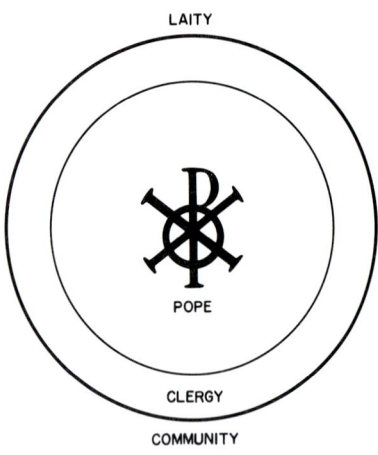

This design captures the idea of the People of God clearly. Every baptized person, pope, bishop, priest, layman or woman is an equal member of the community of faith.

The visible aspects of the institution remain, but only as an external expression of the internal reality. In this model, the Church is not viewed as a dispenser of sacraments, but as a society that assumes responsibility for the total growth of its members. It expresses the reality that God is given to us in Christ and in one another. This model is often referred to as "The People of God."

The People of God

Parishioners and priests are the People of God—servants of the people. The community's concern for its members, modeled after the love of Christ for us, is the supreme sign of his presence in the world. This model reflects an image of the Church from the New Testament which healed and helped sufferers of every kind. The revised code of canon law (the law governing the institutional Church) defines a parish in terms of community—the people—rather than, as in the past, the office of the pastor.

Recent efforts to foster the Church community have focused on human needs: supporting family life, strengthening neighborhoods, and reinforcing community associations within which people can find support and direction for their lives. Smaller communal groups are growing within the parish where, in a circle of trust, people can reflect together on the faith, the Scriptures, their family and work lives, and shared socioeconomic concerns.

There are also signs of inter-parish activity, sometimes called an experiment in "area Church," or parish clusters. Sharing of programs, policies of sacramental administrations resources, and cosponsoring of organizations result when parishes cluster around a bishop or other leader to relate Church life to larger social, political, and economic issues.

The Church as a Unique Community

The Church should not be seen as a community like all others. Christ's unique Body is different from other communities and groups—health care agencies, for example—which might be just as caring and supportive as a parish. Parishes, dioceses, or nations might become focused on their own exclusive community to the neglect of the intended Church family.

It is important to remember that the Church, unlike other communities, originates not in the desire of people to unite in some endeavor, but springs from God's call. The Eucharist, a shared action which brings Christ into our midst, is both the source and sign of the Christian community. The Eucharist is also the supreme sign of the central belief of the community: Jesus is Lord (God).

---

7. Why do you think people want to be part of communities? How can individuality and community work together?

8. How does your parish express its concern and support for all the members of your Church community?

9. What ideas and programs does your parish share with other parishes? What different kinds of inter-parish activities would you suggest?

10. How do you think the Christian community differs from your neighborhood and other forms of community? How is it the same?

Church as Sacrament

If Sunday worship within your community is a source of energy, excitement, and inspiration during the hectic pace of your week, you are experiencing the sacramental model. Vatican II stressed that the Lord is present in many ways: in word, in the community at prayer, in the sacraments, in the minister, and in the mission of all to serve one another. The Church is not the only place he said he'd ever be, but it's the place he said he'd *always* be. It is when we draw apart from the public places that we discover God's special presence. When the community gathers for Eucharist, the rich symbolism and ritual of the sacred drama nourishes life at its deepest roots; and God's People, united with Christ's life, death, and resurrection, are healed ("Constitution on the Sacred Liturgy," #7).

Chapter 3   Contemporary Images of the Church

The Sacramental Church

The sacramental character of the Church is not confined to its system of sacraments. God was with the blind man before the man approached Jesus. Jesus took him aside from the crowd and healed him. That was sacrament (see Mark 9:22-26). There are the liturgical feasts during the year, along with daily prayer—the Liturgy of the Hours—through which time itself is sanctified (see Matthew 18:20). Christ's love is also specially present in the ecclesial community. He promised to be there where two or three are gathered in his name. In their good works, Christians are sacraments of Christ to the world (see Matthew 10:42). The Scriptures, too, are sacramental. They put us in touch with Christ and his saving grace. The visible "institution of the Church, of which the Holy Father is the unifying symbol, is a sacrament of this special [sacramental] presence in the world" (*"Constitution on the Church in the Modern World,"* #41).

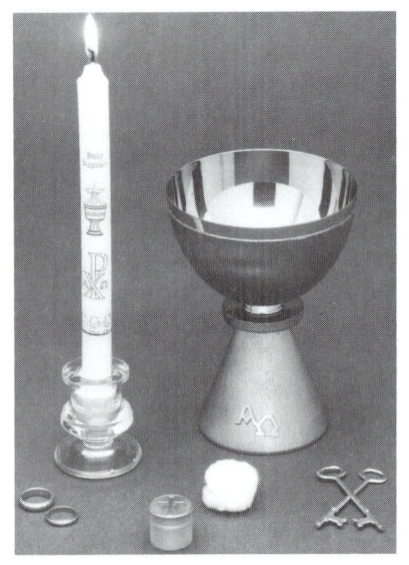

Using and Abusing the Model

One weakness of this model, as is true for the community model as well, is to concentrate on the sacraments (or community) and ignore the needs of the world. In both the community and sacrament models the focus must remain on the Church's mission of proclaiming the Good News, bringing Christ to the World. It is possible in this model for worship to become too mechanical, e.g., "going to Church" to fulfill an obligation. A third pitfall is to think that salvation is attached exclusively to religious symbols, actions and places rather than in recognizing that the Church and sacraments are reminders that God's saving presence is universal.

Getting the most from the sacramental model means that we must work to make the sacramental symbols more visible and believable. It also requires us to cultivate a deep faith which will enable us to find God throughout the world.

These objects represent the sacramental Church. How many objects can you identify, and with which sacraments do they go?

11. *What does your physical presence in Church say about your faith or inner convictions?*

12. *In what ways can you and your parish keep the words of Scripture alive as a sacrament?*

The Church: A Spirit-Filled People

Understanding Scripture

Understanding and interpreting Scripture is an important part of Christian belief and action. Because it was written long ago, using many different styles and formats, Scripture has been misread and misunderstood throughout history. One form of study is geared to help us better understand the Scriptures. This study is called *exegesis*.

The word *exegesis* means explanation or interpretation of a written text. We use *exegesis* every day when we read the newspaper or a magazine article or when we write about the meaning of a poem. When we do these things, we are interpreting what we read. *Exegesis* is concerned with understanding and interpreting written materials. *Exegesis* of Scripture is a special job which involves education and training.

You often hear *exegesis* when you listen to a homily, or sermon, where the meaning of a Scripture verse is explained. The purpose of interpreting Scripture is not only to understand the Word of God, but to apply it. This makes *exegesis* a very exciting activity. Scripture study is at the heart of many models of the Church because of its central role in the daily life of the institution, the community, and each individual Christian.

◆

Church as Herald

"Details at eleven!" the newscasters promise. They are heralds of the news. In old England, town criers were heralds. They proclaimed the news aloud so that all would know the message of the King. If your parish concentrates on religious education, it fits the herald model. In this model, the Church is regarded primarily as a people who eagerly receive the Good News and go out to share it by word and deed. Churches fitting this model are responding to Jesus' command to make disciples of all nations

Communion of Saints

Saint Francis Xavier was born in 1506 in the Spanish city of Navarre. He was a companion of Ignatius of Loyola, and was appointed by him to be a missionary, or herald, of the Church. He traveled far from Europe to spread the Good News. In 1542 he reached Goa in the Portuguese East Indies.

At first he did little to learn the language and customs of the people he baptized. Later, when he reached Japan in 1549, he realized the importance of understanding the beliefs, customs, and language of all peoples. He, and the other heralds with him, learned the language, history, and traditions of the Japanese people.

Saint Francis Xavier died in 1552 on his way to China. The mission of the Church as herald was permanently changed by his travels. He is the patron of all missions of the Catholic Church.

(Matthew 28:19). Through preaching, teaching, and Christian example, people are evangelized, baptized, and continually renewed in their Christian commitment. In a religious education system, perhaps unparalleled anywhere, catechists, teachers, and missionaries, in union with their bishops, explain the faith and prepare people for authentic Christian living. Educators of all kinds, including theologians and charismatic speakers, prayerfully study, interpret, and proclaim the fruit of their reflections, sowing God's Word everywhere.

The Church as Herald model is built around the mission every baptized person has to proclaim the Good News.

The Word in the Church

A weakness of this model is that, if it is exaggerated, it can result in a religion which is too centered on the book, and not enough on bringing the Word to life. It can de-emphasize the communal for the sake of private scripture devotion. Without guidance from the whole Church, Gospel interpretations can become too rigid (fundamentalism) or too free (radical liberalism). It can also lead to a divorce from the institutional Church that originally gave us the Scriptures. Jesus spoke, but he also lived among us. He is the Light of the World, but he is also within the community gathered by his Word. The purpose of the announcement of the Word is not just understanding or personal enrichment and consolation. The Word is announced, as the first letter of John states, "so that you too may have fellowship with us" (1 John 1:3). A strength of the herald model is that through it, the Church becomes a community which brings the Gospel alive in love.

Integrating Models

Often, to get a clear picture of the Church, it is necessary to bring several models together. This is true in the case of ecumenism. Catholics who formerly saw the Church primarily from the sacramental model, and Protestants who recognized the herald model, are seeing that each tradition offers something of value. The sacramental model understands Christ to be active and alive in signs and symbols. The herald model sees Christ most present in the proclamation of Scripture. Through integrating their models, Catholic and Protestant have both been enriched in their understanding of the Church.

13. *Explain how you think education and action are related. How do you and your parish act as heralds of the Gospel?*

Summary

- The task of community is to encourage personal growth through interpersonal relationships.
- The Church community supports its members and reaches out to other parishes.
- The Church is a unique community called by God.
- As sacrament, the Church reveals the presence of God in worship.
- Sacrament and service must be joined together.
- The Church heralds the Gospel by educating and preaching.
- Education should be guided by the Church through its living community.

Charismatic: a special way of responding to the gifts of the Holy Spirit; a type of worship.

Fundamentalism: a form of biblical interpretation which emphasizes the literal meaning of the text.

Ecumenism: the expression of unity and cooperation between Christians.

SECTION 2
Checkpoint!

■ Review

1. How can a person grow through his or her relationships with others?

2. What kinds of smaller communities exist within the larger Church community of your parish?

3. In what ways can you be a sacrament of Christ to the world?

4. Why do you think the idea of Church as sacrament looks at so many different aspects of the Church, not just on the system of sacraments?

5. Discuss the following statement: Education should be for its own sake. What are the dangers in thinking this way?

6. How does religious education go beyond the walls of your classroom?

7. Words to Know: community, sacrament, herald, fundamentalism, ecumenism.

■ In Your World

1. Design an activity which could unite two parish communities in action. What would be its focus? How could the two communities share resources and talent?

2. Become a herald of the Gospel by participating in the education process of your parish. Try teaching a group of younger students for one lesson, conduct a Scripture study for your class, or become involved in an ecumenical program. What challenges face you? What goals do you have? Did you meet all of them?

■ Scripture Search

1. Read Luke 2:41-52; 1 Kings 3:3-14. In what ways are the young Solomon and the young Jesus described as wise? Read Matthew 28:18-20 and Mark 16:14-18. Which model do these passages reflect? How are the disciples told to spread the Word?

2. The connection between faith and sacrament is made especially clear in the miracles of Jesus. Read Matthew 9:18-29 and Luke 5:12-13. How are faith and Jesus' action related in these passages? How do these examples help show that the Scriptures are sacramental?

The Church: A Spirit-Filled People

SECTION 3
Being of Service

Does your parish run clothing drives for the poor, organize mail and telephone campaigns, or run a soup kitchen? The watchwords of a servant Church are action and service. The word "servant" does not have a very positive meaning in today's society. Yet even in our times those who are generous enough to give of themselves for the welfare of others are held in esteem. Every year the President honors those who risk their lives to save the lives of other people. And all the people who work in government service on behalf of our whole society are called civil servants.

Church as Servant

The servant model views the Church as a healer of human affliction—poverty, homelessness, violence, oppression, and discrimination. Its job is to gather Church resources to bring about God's reign as it unfolds on earth. This model sees Church members as imitators of Jesus who came to serve and not to be served (Matthew 20:27), and who went about doing good—healing the sick (Luke 9:11), restoring outcasts to the community (Luke 17:12), and forgiving sins (John 8:11).

As an integral part of the human family, the Church regards human liberation as part of its mission—from the fulfillment of basic human needs to liberation from sin. It uses the achievements of culture, such as education, medicine, technology, government, industry, and even the arts, to help the underpriviledged and oppressed of every community. Servant Christians imitate Jesus—the man for others—not only in individual works of mercy for members

A People at Prayer

The Sermon on the Mount presents a picture of the hopeful future of those who act as servants of God, and those who are in need of the service of others. Jesus tells his listeners that their worldly condition will be rectified in the kingdom of God: "Blessed are the poor in spirit, for theirs is the kingdom of heaven. Blessed are they who mourn, for they will be comforted. Blessed are the meek, for they will inherit the land. Blessed are those who hunger and thirst for righteousness, for they will be satisfied. Blessed are the merciful, for they will be shown mercy. Blessed are the clean of heart, for they will see God. Blessed are the peacemakers, for they will be called children of God. Blessed are those who are persecuted for the sake of righteousness, for theirs is the kingdom of heaven" (Matthew 5:3-10).

Being of service to others in need is one way that you can bring your faith to life.

of their own community, but also in collective efforts to transform all unjust social structures that victimize their members through proclaiming the Gospel and putting the Gospel into action.

14. What do you think of when you hear the word servant?

15. Who are the sick and the outcasts of today's society whom Jesus would serve?

16. Where in your community and the world do you see oppression, violence, and injustice which could be healed by the efforts of you and your Church community?

The Serving Church

The Church today teaches that one cannot be Christian without actively entering into society to transform it. But Christians may not fall into the trap of identifying or replacing the kingdom of heaven with a worldly paradise. In the Hebrew Scriptures (Isaiah 9:1-6), the kingdom of God is identified with a reign of earthly peace and justice among humankind. But in the New Testament, a more personal

The Church: A Spirit-Filled People

and interior concept of God's rule emerges. A serving Church works for universal justice while realizing that "you always have the poor with you" (John 12:8). Christians persevere, but they understand that when their plans and projects fail, the Lord is still there.

In a Church composed of human beings, it is to be expected that the ideal of humble service is not always lived out. We acknowledge that even as we individually fail in service, the Church too is a wounded healer. This understanding leads to forgiveness when members forget their servant role; we ourselves should always remember to act with justice when we preach to the world.

---

17. What have you and your parish done to make your community and the world better places?

18. How do you think the idea of service can be corrupted by people who value power or wealth?

Pulling the Models Together

Each of the models described in this chapter expresses some essential features of the Church, but none of them represents all aspects of the Church. Even all the models together do not adequately describe the Church. Just as in the total spectrum of light, there are intermediate colors and colors that we cannot see, so in the Church their are aspects that we do not yet clearly understand.

People, parishes, dioceses, and nations each play different roles in the Body of Christ. Your parish may see itself clearly in one or another of the models, depending on the history of your community, the interests of the parishioners, or the special opportunities that present themselves. The challenge is to recognize how it could meet the greater needs of the community if it sees itself from the image of a new model.

Chapter 3 Contemporary Images of the Church

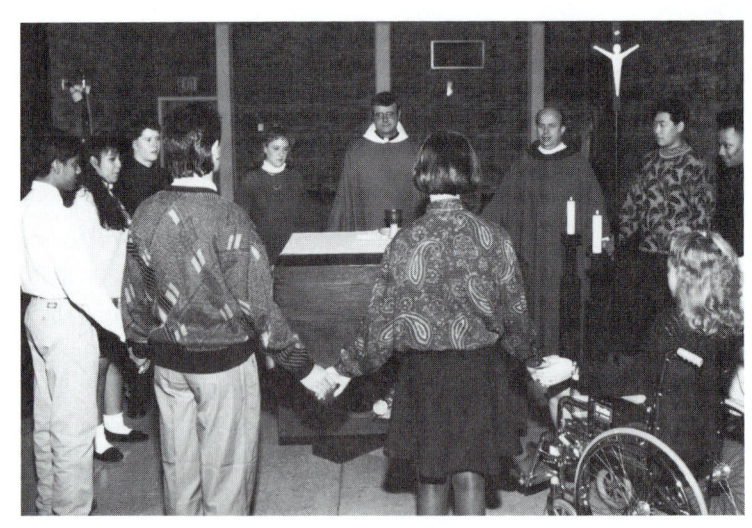

Take advantage of the special moments you have now to celebrate with classmates. Give thanks for all the gifts which you share together.

Your Special Gifts

Just as we recognize models in the parish, we can recognize them in our own life. Your own life certainly shows some aspect of all the models, but your natural gifts may draw you to specialize in one or more of them. If you enjoy sharing your faith, you may feel called to be a catechist after the herald model. A love for people may give you a special inclination for making your parish a warmer community. At the same time, you should always be aware of your deficiencies and try to work on those areas of yourself. If you don't enjoy being part of organizations, find a way to help a Church committee so you can have a new experience.

You have a lot to offer to your parish community. Get involved and make a difference.

Follow the Star

Of the five models you have just investigated, two serve as models of what the Church is: *institution*, which sets up structures for smooth group relationships, and *community*, which fulfills the primary need we have for personal relationships.

The other three models describe what the Church *does*: it sanctifies and cultivates faith, it educates and converts, and it serves the community and the world.

According to Thomas Downs, in the book *Parish as a Learning Community*, these five models can be shown as the arms of a five-pointed star.

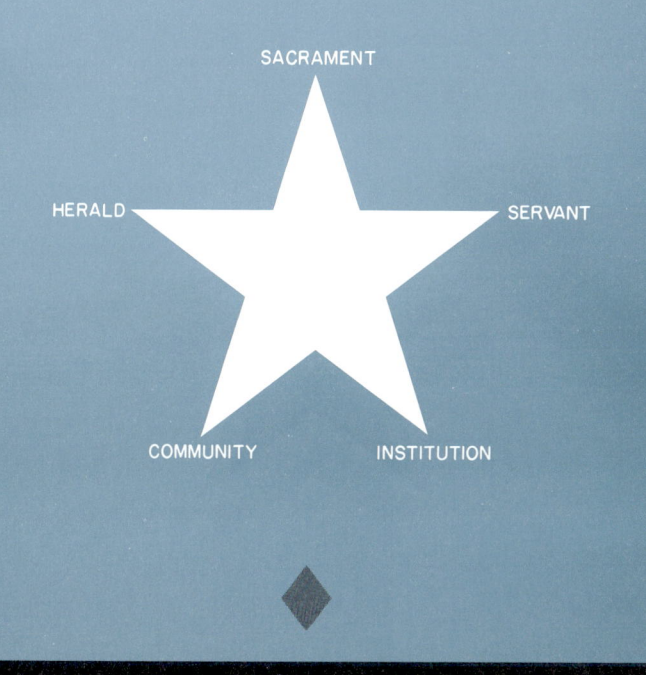

A Community of Disciples

All models of the Church may be drawn together into the model of the Church as a community of disciples—people who follow Jesus on the journey to the Father. Disciples are prayerful and open to continual conversion. They acknowledge their constant need for penitence and they implement the teachings of their leader in the world.

As disciples of Jesus, we must always be ready to move ahead, to brave the dangers of the way, and to change our course if necessary. We need to see the Church revealed in its rich beauty, and yet realize that we travel in hope behind a crucified Lord. We humbly acknowledge that we have a way to go before God is present fully in our lives and in the Church we love.

19. Which of the models does you parish most strongly represent?

20. What are your own strengths and weaknesses? Which models appeal to you the most? Why?

Summary

- A servant Church does good for the community and the world.

- The task of the servant Church is serving the needs of people.

- Efforts to transform may not always occur without roadblocks.

- All the models together contribute to a better understanding of the Church.

- The Church is a community of disciples.

SECTION 3
Checkpoint!

■ Review

1. What is the function of someone who is truly a servant?

2. What can the Church do to help individuals inside the Church community? Outside it?

3. How is the idea of selflessness related to the idea of service?

4. What are additional models of the Church not described in this chapter?

5. Words to Know: servant, transformation, disciple.

■ In Your World

1. Choose one way your class can serve your Church community and devise a program of service. How will you transform and serve?

2. Create a slide or photograph presentation which documents the various ways your Church community acts as servant. Try to capture as many different aspects of its service as possible, such as soup kitchen, clothing drive, letter writing, visiting the elderly, and others.

■ Scripture Search

Examine the following passages: Luke 1:36-38; Acts 4:23-30; Romans 1:1; Matthew 14:1-3; and Mark 1:20. What are the different ways the word servant is used in these passages? Create your own dictionary definition of the word using these passages as a guide.

Chapter 3   Contemporary Images of the Church

CHAPTER 3 Review

■ Study

1. What are the three meanings of the word "model" given in this chapter?
2. Why are multiple models needed to understand certain concepts?
3. How is the Church related to the Holy Trinity?
4. In what ways do we act as instruments of God?
5. Name three components of the institution model.
6. What does the model of Church as institution contribute to the Church?
7. What are the characteristics of an institution?
8. How does the Church flourish as a community?
9. Describe how Scripture and liturgy are part of the model of Church as Sacrament.
10. What is the unique function of heralds in the Church?
11. Why does the model of Church as servant have roots in the actions of Jesus?

■ Action

1. Devise a system of images to characterize the models discussed in this chapter. Be creative. Be prepared to explain your choices.

2. Conduct a survey on people's preferred model of the Church. Ask for at least two reasons for each person's choice. Keep track of the age and gender of everyone you ask. Tally up your results and try to determine if there are any patterns based on age, sex, etc.

3. As a class, choose one model and plan a course of action to live that model within your own Church. Discuss how you will make your collective contribution and be sure everyone gets involved.

■ Prayer

Prayer is both a collective and an individual activity. The prayers we say in private are the way we communicate with God our innermost thoughts, wishes, and fears. The prayers we say out loud with our community demonstrate our faith and our hopes as a group.

Try to compose a prayer which you can share with your class or Church community. Think about the prayers you say during communal worship. Talk to your classmates, parents, and priest about what prayer means to them. And reflect on what it means to you.

Share your prayer with your class or family. Perhaps you can begin class with a different prayer every day. What is the purpose of praying as a community? How has your class been transformed by this activity?

CHAPTER 4

The Image That Others See

OBJECTIVES

In this Chapter you will

- Observe what is distinctive about the Church.

- Identify the four visible marks of the Church.

- Learn what is characteristic of each mark.

- Think about what makes you remain a Catholic.

Christ established and ever sustains here on earth his holy church, the community of faith, hope, and charity, as a visible organization through which he communicates truth and grace to all people . . . This is the sole Church of Christ, which in the Creed we profess to be one, holy, catholic and apostolic.
— *"Dogmatic Constitution on the Church,"* #8

The Church: A Spirit-Filled People

SECTION 1
The Visible Image

When you are too close to something, it's hard to get the total picture. Artists step back from their paintings in order to gain perspective. Writers submit their manuscripts to editors for an objective evaluation. You may have received insight into a family problem from comments made by a friend.

Looking at the Church

What do people see when they look at the Church? Probably the most striking thing to outsiders is its solidarity. "Looking at it from the outside, I've often wondered what holds the Roman Catholic Church together, why hasn't it splintered into myriad denominations as we Protestants have?" (Howard E. Royer, quoted in *U.S. Catholic,* May 1979, p. 20).

The Roman Catholic Church in the United States numbers close to sixty million people, more than any other religious body in the country. Worldwide, one out of every six people is a Catholic. Three-fourths of a billion people from Baltimore to Bangladesh profess Jesus as their Lord and God, 22 percent of the world's population. They worship him in the same sacraments, believe the same teachings, live in accordance with his laws, and experience fellowship wherever they meet.

How Others See It

The stability of the Church has made an impression on many people. Evelyn Waugh, a British novelist and convert, depicted the pervasiveness of the faith in the lives of Catholics in his novel *Brideshead Revisited.* Another convert, whose business was selling candles to churches, was

On This Rock

The Council of Nicaea was the first ecumenical (worldwide) council in Church history. Vatican II was the twenty-first ecumenical council. Nicaea gathered 318 bishops, but only 220 of their names are known. It began on May 20, 325 and ended on July 25, 325.

It is the one line: "We believe in one, holy, catholic, and apostolic Church," which has given us a way to establish our identity. Vatican II lasted from October 11, 1962 until December 8, 1965. Its conclusions are contained in the many documents published after the Council ended. These councils, and the nineteen held in-between, are a witness to the continuing unfolding of the revelation of God through Christ.

Receiving the Eucharist is a very "Catholic" thing to do.

sitting in the back of a cathedral in a big city and noticed that those who approached the altar for Communion were quite diverse. He was impressed because there was no distinction of race, color, or social class.

Martin Marty, a well-known Protestant theologian, summed up his view of what is distinctive about Catholicism when he wrote that it isn't being born to the faith, and it isn't just being part of a distinct group or believing in an idea that makes Catholics different. The difference, he says, is in being churchly. A Catholic is "one who knows what it means to be active in the body of Christ, responsive at Eucharist, publicly professing what your Baptism committed you to." It is not to be "all ground up and refined," Marty said, "but to be 'lumpy,' so that everyone can recognize a Presence in the world; that is the only kind of Catholic that makes a difference. To hold and loudly assert the Truth (which is Jesus, risen and alive) in a special way, and not just mumble it" (*U.S. Catholic,* May 1979, p. 23). Lumpy here means real and perceptible.

The Church: A Spirit-Filled People

What Is Distinctive?

Some people who notice the Church's many fine buildings might say that wealth is the Church's outstanding quality. Others see as distinctive the great power in our worldwide hierarchy centralized in Rome. Still others might consider the sacramental rituals as most characteristic. The high visibility of the Church reflects that it is indeed "lumpy." It is diverse and varied in its outward expression. This visibility is a sign of the intensity of its faith life. It cannot remain invisible, but instead is almost too visible—constantly in the newspaper headlines. This paradox is part of the Church's mystery. Even though the Catholic faith touches people's inner spirit, it is at the same time a most visible Church.

---

1. *How would you define the word "lumpy" in Marty's statement? How do you think the Church is lumpy?*

2. *What do you think are the distinctive characteristics of the Church?*

3. *Why do you think it is necessary for our inner faith and spirit to be shown outwardly?*

When you see these four objects together like this, what is the first image that comes to your mind?

Paradox: something which seems contradictory, but true.

Chapter 4 The Image That Others See

Incarnation of the Incarnation

Human nature is such that we need to see and touch things in order to know them. In the divine providence, God works with our nature, making things signs of invisible grace (see Exodus 33:20). To give us clear knowledge of the invisible God, the Father incarnated the eternal Son, sending Jesus as a person we can all relate to. The Church, too, is consistent with our nature. It is "an incarnation of the Incarnation" (William J. Bausch, *The Christian Parish*, p. 13). The Church is a sign that God is at work among us. All its visible forms express the interior mystery of God's presence and unfolding plan for the world's salvation.

Some of the more obvious visible features of the Church include

- *the worldwide Church community united by a visible head, the pope,*
- *seven distinct sacraments celebrated in all Catholic churches,*
- *a unified body of teaching and morality,*
- *a celibate priesthood, and*
- *the Catholic veneration of saints, especially the Virgin Mary.*

4. *What other features do you think make the Church visible today?*
5. *In what ways does your Church act as an "incarnation of the Incarnation"?*

The "Marks" of the Church

You can identify any member of your family in a flash. Each has particular features, a characteristic way of walking, and certain unique gestures that you would know anywhere. In the early Church, four signs or marks identified the Church of Christ. As listed in the Nicene Creed, these signs mark the true Church as one, holy, catholic, and

The Church—A Visible House of God

In both Judaism and Christianity, the place where people meet for prayer is called a House of God. Of course, no one thinks that God lives only inside the physical building, but that holy place is marked as a place where God dwells, especially when people are gathered there for prayer, study, and fellowship.

These special places have their own visible "marks" which make them distinct from other buildings in a community. A building with a cross on top can usually be identified as a Christian church of some type. Catholic churches have their own characteristic marks, both inside and out, which have been adapted throughout history from the architecture of various cultures.

The earliest churches were based on the model of a Roman basilica (hall of justice). It has a hall large enough to fit a crowd of spectators, aisles on the sides, a row of columns, an entrance at the west end (called a narthex) where the unbaptized sat, and a semicircular space at the east end (called an apse) for clergy. You can see that it was an elaborate design. Later on, space was added to make the building into the shape of a cross. As the Church grew and developed, so did the building for the Church. Space for a choir was added. Architectural developments in France, Italy, and England provided new ideas, such as towering ceilings, stained glass windows and flying buttress construction to support loftier designs.

Your own Church was probably built on the same basic model as the earliest churches. In this way there is a line of continuity, not only in belief and teaching, but even in the places where we meet for worship. The visible architectural marks of your Church are good examples of the way the Church has been able to absorb and transform elements from the cultures around it.

Incarnate: of the flesh; to have a body.

Nicene Creed: formulated at the Council of Nicaea in A.D. 325, to express publicly what the Church believes.

Architecture: the method or style in which a building is constructed.

apostolic. *Mark* expresses theologically a gift God has given the Church. It is different from a quality, like your hair color, which you can change without affecting your identity. Marks cannot be changed, and express what is essential to the Church.

Although the marks of the Church express an inner reality, they are outwardly visible to anyone who takes the time to look. Roman Catholics everywhere are faced with the task of reexamining who they are and what makes them unique. The answer lies in the fact that other Churches may share some or all of Catholicism's four marks, but no other Church displays the four marks of the ancient Church in the same form or degree as does the Catholic Church.

Even so, this distinction should go hand in hand with sensitivity to the beliefs of others. "The decree on Ecumenism [of Vatican II] has stressed a sensitivity to others' beliefs. No longer does the Church proclaim itself the 'one, true Church.' Rather, today the Church says, gently, that within the Catholic Church is the fullness of the Christian message. However, the Catholic Church does not deny that those embracing another faith may rightfully believe that they too are participating in the fullness of Christ" ("Whatever Happened to Convert-Making?" by Sister Mary Ann Walsh, R.S.M., *U.S. Catholic,* October 1979, p. 27). The

The mark of the Church, Catholic, means that the message of Jesus is to be proclaimed to everyone, everywhere.

The Church: A Spirit-Filled People

"Decree on Ecumenism" says, "all those justified by faith through baptism are incorporated into Christ. They therefore have a right to be honored by the title of Christian, and are properly regarded as brothers in the Lord by the sons of the Catholic Church" (#9). Because of its pilgrim status, the Church will not reach its full identity until the end of time. Therefore, each of the marks also serves as a goal yet to be achieved. Like physical fitness, each mark needs to be developed as each member or group of Catholics strives to become a people of one mind and heart in God.

6. How do you think members of other faiths might be participating in the fullness of Christ?
7. What do you already know about each of the four marks of the Church?

Summary

- Outsiders often note the stability and solidarity of the Church.
- The Catholic Church is "lumpy" because it establishes a recognizable Presence in the world.
- Many characteristics make the Church visible to the outside world.
- The Church is a visible sign of the work of God in the world.
- There are four marks of the Church identified by the earliest Christians—the Church is one, holy, catholic, and apostolic.

SECTION 1
Checkpoint!

■ Review

1. What is the value of looking at something by stepping back?

2. What do the Catholics of the world share?

3. Explain what Martin Marty means by describing the Church as "lumpy" and not "ground up and refined."

4. Why is the faith life and visibility of the Church a paradox?

5. How has God been made known to us?

6. What is the meaning of the word "mark"?

7. Words to Know: perspective, paradox, to incarnate, mark of the Church.

■ In Your World

1. Talk to some of your non-Catholic Christian friends. Ask them what they think is distinctive of Catholicism. Ask the same questions of some of your non-Catholic non-Christian friends. How are the answers the same and how do they differ?

2. Create a montage of some of the visible signs of the Church. Use real items where possible and supplement them with photographs, drawings, or other pictures. Explain the role each item plays in the visible Church.

■ Scripture Search

Read the following Scripture passages: Genesis 1:3-5; Genesis 6:5-8; Exodus 19:16-20; Exodus 33:17-23; John 1:14. What images of God are given here? What is their purpose, and how do they fit in with our knowledge of the true nature of God?

SECTION 2
The Church Is One and Holy

You know how hard it is to keep peace even in a small family, or to have a committee come to a unanimous decision. But unity is one of the strongest and clearest characteristics of the Catholic Church. It is one in teaching and faith, worship, liturgy, and government. Hundreds of millions of members from many nations and backgrounds enjoy worldwide solidarity because the Church is one in all essentials.

Unity of Teaching and Faith

With the first doctrinal confession, "Jesus is Lord," the early Christians declared their faith in the fundamental dogma of Christ's divinity. Many Christians today are divided on doctrinal issues, including this one. Catholics, however, profess Jesus' Lordship and they accept all that Jesus taught as sacred. As a result, all Catholics hold the same faith throughout the world and have throughout history.

Describing a Catholic sermon he heard before becoming a Catholic, Thomas Merton said, "behind those words you felt the full force not only of Scripture but of centuries of a unified and continuous and consistent tradition . . . What was more, I sensed that the people were familiar with it all, and that it was also . . . part of their life . . . just as much integrated into their spiritual organism as the air they breathed" (*The Seven Storey Mountain*, pp. 208-209).

This unity is proclaimed in the creeds universally accepted by Church members. It is exercised in the Church's teaching office by the lawful pastors of the Church who

Dogma: an authoritative principle or teaching.

Chapter 4   The Image That Others See

93

Church Teaching—How Much Do You Know?

Because of your Catholic education—in school, in Church, and at home—you may feel that you have already "learned it all." Test yourself, your classmates, or work in teams and see how many of the names, places, and dates listed below you can identify without using any outside materials. Try this quiz on members of other classes, your parents, or even your teacher! Take the quiz again at the end of the year and compare your results.

Council of Jerusalem
Council of Nicaea
barbarian
Edict of Milan
A.D. 451
Saint Augustine
Saint Benedict
A.D. 1545–1564
Joan of Arc
Teresa of Ávila
Vatican II

---

teach the same truths everywhere. It is visible in the readiness of Catholics to accept all that the Church teaches and in the censure of those who refuse to do so.

Sometimes this unity of belief is broken in such a way that an official censure is required. Censure and even excommunication are rare today, but they do occur. Archbishop Marcel Lefebvre, who rejects Vatican II, was suspended for ordaining priests in 1976 and ultimately excommunicated along with his followers in 1988.

---

8. *Describe ways in which you have witnessed the unity of the Catholic Church.*

The Church: A Spirit-Filled People

Unity of Worship and Liturgy

Wherever the Catholic community gathers to worship, whether in a grand cathedral or in a basement church, around a dining-room table or from the back of a military van, Christ forms the center of unity. Where two or three are gathered in Jesus' name (Matthew 18:20), an encounter of a new kind takes place. As members of Christ's prayer community, we are bonded to him and to one another in our worship of the Father.

This mystical unity is the visibly expressed celebration of the same sacrificial meal, the same sacraments, and the same outward signs of the sacraments. This is especially clear in the two principal sacraments of Baptism and the Eucharist.

9. *If you were to attend Mass in a Catholic church in a foreign country, how would the unity of worship and liturgy be apparent to you?*

The Laity is active in Catholic worship today as musicians, lectors, and Eucharistic ministers. How can you be involved?

Chapter 4   The Image That Others See

Unity of Government and Obedience

Catholics are united in Church government, acknowledging their leaders as the successors of the Apostles. The bishop of Rome holds primacy over the whole visible Church. The pope approves all newly consecrated bishops in the name of all other bishops. Pastors exercise leadership authority under their diocesan bishops.

Unity of government is visible in the laws and precepts of the Church and in the obedience of the faithful to them. The main body of Church law is called the Code of Canon Law. Regulations are often called precepts. Disobedience of individuals or groups may cause scandal, but it does not destroy the overall unity of government.

Unity, Not Uniformity

The Oneness of the Church is not based on uniformity in its teaching, worship, or government. Like a variety of band instruments played in the performance of one song, unity allows individuals to remain unique while they are incorporated into a unified group. Uniformity means that individuals in a group are all "identical."

The interpretation of Scripture, for example, can take one of several positions, provided that basic revelation is not denied. Conservative approaches adhere strongly to traditional interpretations. Liberal views are less literal and more open to change. A pluralism of opinions does not threaten the Church's heritage. It enriches it.

The unity of the Church does not forbid diversity in liturgical ceremonies, language, or styles. In East Africa, the people give their morning sign of Eucharistic peace by passing a tuft of grass from hut to hut. If some family refuses to accept the grass from another family because of hard feelings, the Eucharist is postponed until all are at peace. In India, the offertory procession is a ritual dance almost always involving the lotus, the beautiful national flower. No matter how local liturgical customs differ, Catholic unity means worshiping with and in Christ.

In government, too, there is room for differences. Dioceses apply disciplinary laws according to local custom.

For instance, Eastern Catholics (Catholics who do not observe the Roman, or Western, rite) have different laws for fasting, and their penances are much more demanding than those of Roman Catholics. Canadian and Mexican Catholics observe different holy days of obligation than Catholics in the U.S.

The reason this priest dresses differently than other priests you know is that he is a priest of an Eastern Catholic Rite.

Efforts Toward Greater Unity

Recognizing that the human race is still far from unified, the Church engages in sincere efforts to form greater unity within its body. Synods, councils, and conferences are formed in order to encourage dialogue on every level.

As Catholics, we strive for unity, first in our families, parishes, neighborhoods, and places of work, and then among our Churches, both East and West. There is a clear call for collaboration with separated Christians. Recent pastoral/theological developments reflect a shift from interfaith dialogue (concerned with how we differ) to ecumenical dialogue and agreement (concerned with how we are similar). In this way, differences may be worked out. The Church has the further duty of working with Jews, Muslims,

Primacy: being first in rank.

Synod: a meeting or assembly that has governing power.

Chapter 4   The Image That Others See

Communion of Saints

Saint Maximilian Kolbe was born in Poland in 1894. He became a Franciscan priest and studied theology and philosophy in Rome. He was strongly drawn to the devotion of Mary, and he founded a devotional association, monthly publication, and a religious center all dedicated to the Virgin. He even helped begin devotional institutions to Mary in Japan and India. Saint Maximilian returned to Poland in the 1930's and was arrested in 1939 for his anti-Nazi activities. He was released, but arrested again in 1941, this time for helping Jews and the Polish underground. He was imprisoned in Auschwitz. There, he volunteered his life in the place of a condemned fellow inmate. He was starved, injected with a drug, and cremated. In 1982, Saint Maximilian was canonized by Pope John Paul II and declared a martyr.

and people of other religions—as well as with people of no religion—to spread God's love throughout the world. Jesus prayed for this unity saying, "so that they may be one, as you, Father, are in me, and I in you, that they may also be one in us" (John 17:21). In recent years, Pope John Paul II has met with leaders of the Protestant, Orthodox, and Jewish communities as well as with representatives of other religious groups in order to promote peace and understanding.

---

10. Why do you think uniformity is discouraged in the Church?
11. What unique contribution does your parish make to the Oneness of the Church?
12. What can you do to promote unity first at home and in school, as well as in your Church community and in the world?

The Church Is Holy

When you put your face up very close to your mirror, every bump, blemish, and wrinkle seems to jump out at you. Likewise, living very close to the people in the Church can cause you to see only imperfections where others see the beauty of God's holiness shining through. The Church is holy because, as Saint Paul wrote, "Christ loved the Church and handed himself over for her . . . that he might present to himself the church in splendor, without spot or wrinkle or any such thing, that she might be holy and without blemish" (Ephesians 5:25, 27). It is holy in its founder, purpose, ministries, and members.

God alone is holy by nature. Because we are made in God's image and filled with his presence, we are good. In Christ, God's presence and the person Jesus are one, making him an equal sharer in God's holiness. Having loved his Father and us infinitely, Christ became the center and source of our holiness, sanctifying us in his Spirit. Having him as founder makes the Church holy.

The Church: A Spirit-Filled People

The Church's Holiness

The Church is holy in its purpose. It was brought into being to share Christ's mission of saving all peoples. The supremely holy action of the Eucharist sums up the Church's purpose: to be Christ worshiping the Father in its members, and through them gradually transforming the world. At worship, Christ is present, the Gospel is proclaimed, and the Eucharist is shared in love, as part of the community. Christians are made more like Christ in order to serve him through others, and to hasten the process of reconciling all things to God in Christ.

The Church is holy in the means it uses to achieve this holy purpose: its ministries of Word, sacrament, service to the needy, and its organization, offices, and programs. As the Mystical Body of Christ, the Church makes the Good News human, offers fitting worship to God, and undertakes works of charity and social justice.

Finally, the Church is holy in many of its members, who in every generation and age, and from every walk of life, are able to attain holiness, sometimes to a heroic degree. From the times of the Apostles and martyrs, the Church has publicly recommended men and women of outstanding holiness—called saints—as examples to the faithful. The religious and clergy also witness to the holiness of the Church.

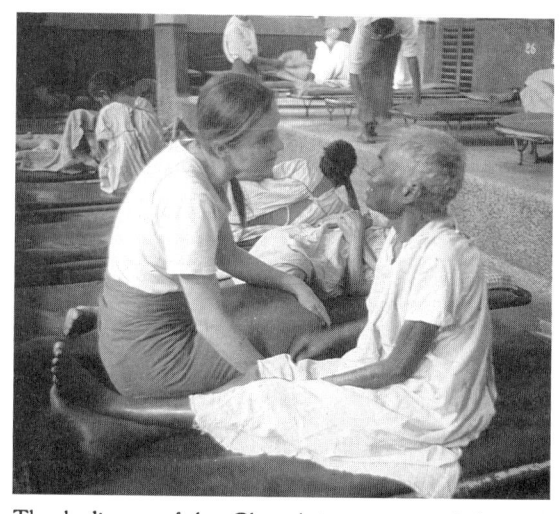

The holiness of the Church is recognized through the action of its members.

Holiness: being filled with the presence of God.

Chapter 4   The Image That Others See

While all Christians are called to holiness, each person chooses as an individual to follow the path of holiness or not.

The Holiness of Christians

In the past, it was thought that the age of miracles, healing, and martyrdom that characterized the early Church and influenced so many to believe had passed. But the Spirit is as active today as ever. The charismatic movement, for example, has witnessed to an outpouring of prayer, preaching, and healing. And it is estimated that in the present generation alone the Church has had more martyrs than in all previous ages put together.

This does not mean that all Christians are holy. The history of the Church reveals that popes, bishops, priests, religious, and laity have not always lived up to the message of Jesus. Their unholy lives demonstrate both the freedom Christ allows in his call to discipleship and his power to sustain the Church in spite of human resistance and weakness.

But even if everyone in the Church were to fail in his or her efforts, the Church would still be holy because of the supreme holiness of its founder, Jesus; of its purpose which is to sanctify the world; and of the means it offers to be joined to and converted in him. But the holiness of the Church cannot be triumphant and self-righteous. Since we are a pilgrim Church, weak and sometimes sinful as individuals and as community, we must keep ourselves open to conversion.

13. Where do you see holiness in the people you know?

14. What kinds of things make it hard to be holy and to reflect God in your life?

Summary

- Unity is one of the strongest characteristics of the Catholic Church.

- The Church is one in teaching and faith. Its creeds are accepted by all and they express faith in Jesus as Lord and God.

- There is unity of worship and liturgy among Catholics everywhere.

- Catholics are united in their leaders and laws.

- Unity allows for a range of options and diversity in customs and language so long as the basic revelation is not denied.

- The Church is holy because it is filled with God's presence in its founder, purpose, ministries, and members.

Charismatic movement: ecumenical gathering including Catholics, who gather for prayer and thanksgiving, filled with the gifts of the Holy Spirit.

Chapter 4   The Image That Others See

SECTION 2
Checkpoint!

■ Review

1. What are the three ways that the Church displays unity?
2. How is unity in faith expressed by Catholics?
3. How is the unity of worship made visible?
4. Which leader has primacy over the Church?
5. Explain the difference between unity and uniformity. Give an example.
6. What responsibilities does the Church have in its relationship with other Christian and non-Christian groups?
7. How is God's holiness different from ours?
8. What is the purpose of the Church?
9. Words to Know: unity, primacy, uniformity, synod, holiness, charism.

■ In Your World

1. Become an armchair anthropologist (someone who studies the nature of human societies). Read about Catholic worship in a different culture. Where is the unity of worship evident? Where is there diversity according to the customs or traditions of a people? Present a report to your class describing one type of worship as if you had observed it yourself.
2. Prepare a presentation that demonstrates the ways your parish reflects the four aspects of holiness: in its founder, purpose, ministries, and members. You can use photographs, slides, drawings, and music. How does your Church community reveal God's image?

■ Scripture Search

1. Paul speaks of the unity of the Church in Ephesians 4:4-6 and 11-16. Read Deuteronomy 6:4. How do you think the unity of God and the unity of the Church are related?
2. Read the following passages: Matthew 5:43-48; Luke 6:35-36. Does Jesus mean that we can be as perfect and merciful as the Father? How do we participate in God's perfection and mercy?

The Church: A Spirit-Filled People

SECTION 3
The Church Is Catholic and Apostolic

In the creed we profess belief in a Catholic and Apostolic Church. The word Catholic—first applied to the Church in the writings of Saint Ignatius, bishop of Antioch, a Christian martyr in the year A.D. 110—comes from the Greek word meaning universal. It refers to the Church's extension over the whole world. Apostolic refers to the Apostles whom Jesus commissioned to teach all nations everything he commanded. Jesus also promised to remain with his Church until the end of time (see Matthew 28:18-20). Thus the Church of Christ also has the mission and duty as well as the gifts to proclaim all that Jesus revealed for all generations to come.

The Mark of Catholicity

The word *catholic* has a deep and rich significance. The mark of catholicity means that the Church is open to all, regardless of race, nation, or social class. The Church is eager to receive all, and its message is preached throughout the world. Of course, the Church does not literally reach every village on earth nor speak every language. Its geographic and cultural universality means that it might be known to all and may not exclude anyone.

The Church's catholicity is seen in its ability to recognize, draw out, cleanse, and use what is noble and beautiful in all cultures. Christ's humanness affirms "an element of the divine" in all peoples. Throughout history, the Church has absorbed and transformed aspects of many cultures.

Pentecost foreshadowed "the union of all people in the catholicity of the faith by means of the Church . . . which

For Example

Some cultural elements the Church has absorbed are the thoughts of the Greek philosophers Plato and Aristotle, and the art, literature, language, and architecture of Rome.

Chapter 4   The Image That Others See

By ordaining men from all cultures as priests, the Church prepares to serve people of every land with respect.

speaks every language and embraces all tongues in charity and this overcomes the dispersion of Babel" (*"Decree on Missionary Activity,"* #4).

It was revealed to Peter and Paul that the Gentiles were called to faith, and so the infant Church, though reaching out to only a few areas of the Roman Empire, was already universal. The Second Vatican Council declared that today "the Church, the salt of the earth and the light of the world, is even more urgently called upon to save and renew every creature, so that all things might be restored in Christ and so that in him people might form one family and one people of God" (*"Decree on Missionary Activity,"* #11).

Finding Christ in the World

One of the Church's biggest challenges lies in finding and bringing to full development Christ's presence in our world. "The Church is faithful to its traditions and is at the same time conscious of its universal mission; it can, then, enter into communion with different forms of culture, thereby enriching both itself and the cultures themselves" (*"Constitution on the Church in the Modern World,"* #58). Thus the Catholic Church is not, strictly speaking, the Church of Rome (a title used in honor of the primacy of Peter), or a church for one particular race, or a church for the middle class. It is a world Church.

Sometimes being a world Church is not easy. Humans—out of fear, ignorance, or distorted values—tend to reject what they find as different. Although the church welcomes all, occasionally some local churches have been less than hospitable. Wars have been fought in the name of religion. The Church has not always spoken quickly on issues of justice, like slavery or the Holocaust. In other areas of social concern, as society opens its arms to the disadvantaged, the physically challenged, and other groups, the Church should be in the forefront witnessing to Christ's universal love, especially to his preference for the oppressed and weak. The Church is now publicly acknowledging these mistakes and bishops are lending their authority to public moral and religious issues.

For instance, Bishop Joseph Francis of Newark, N.J., one of the first African-American bishops, wrote in *America:* "Today, black Catholics have come of age . . . Black Catholics are saying to the Catholic Church that the church has been and will continue to be poor in the United States without accepting the richness of their contributions of faithfulness and loyalty . . . They have come this far by faith and it is that faith-experience they wish to contribute to the Catholic Church. Simply, they wish to share the truth, which has become the symbol and substance of their quest for freedom promised to the children of God" (March 29, 1980, pp. 256-257).

Universality Means Openness

Universality also implies an openness to differences in point of view and spirituality. Within the Catholic Church there are many examples of each, with people traveling at their own pace. There are those who believe that the Church will be preserved only by their own efforts. In order to protect it from outside harm, they sometimes end up going in circles. Then there are those who are incapable of even the slightest change. They travel in a straight line from one thing to the next. Others plunge ahead, trying to anticipate the future, and usually leaving everyone else dizzy as they race by. Some Christians move steadily forward gently and peacefully. Catholic liturgies, services, activities, and courses should accommodate as many travelers as possible. The sea of the Church is big enough to embrace all.

Babel: see Genesis 11:1-9.

Holocaust: the slaughter of 13 million Jews and other people by the Nazis during the Second World War.

15. How does your own Church community reflect the catholicity of the Church?

16. What evidence do you see of the cultural, linguistic, and artistic elements absorbed by the Church from all over the world?

17. Have you ever rejected something or someone because it was different? How has your opinion changed as you learned more?

The Church Is Apostolic

The first Church members were called followers of "the Way" (Acts 18:25). As followers of the disciples, it is only in communion with one another that churches can manifest the unique "way of salvation" given to us by Christ through the Apostles (one sent on a mission). The apostolic concern for church communion is shown in several ways. The early Church worked together to solve problems. Both the outlying churches and the central Jerusalem Church sent delegates to one another in order to come to agreement on matters of doctrine and practice (Acts 15:1-35). Letters were sent to the local churches to keep them mutually informed. Consensus was never easy, as can be seen from the Council of Jerusalem, where there was "much discussion" and it took the authority of Peter, apostle to the Jews, to settle the issue (Acts 15:7). Galatians 2 also reports on the Council of Jerusalem and recognizes Paul as the Apostle to the Gentiles. Throughout the Church's history, bishops who could not agree with the community consensus were excommunicated, and churches that were ignorant of some teachings were instructed. The deliberations entered into by all the churches in the first Council have served as a model of how a united church discerns God's will.

Apostolicity Is Continuity and Communion

Apostolicity is the quality of continuity in Church authority. The Church has had an unbroken line of popes and bishops from Peter and the Apostles. Novelist-convert

Katherine Burton wrote, "To me, succession [means] a long lifeline of hands touching hands, . . . a church which went back . . . to Christ Himself" ("The Outstretched Arms," in *Where I Found Christ,* p. 14, edited by John A. O'Brien, Doubleday, 1951). Apostolicity also means the Church has maintained communion with the Apostles' teaching and practices, handed down first orally and a little later in the writings of the New Testament.

Although the apostolic source of divine revelation was complete with the death of the last Apostle—traditionally John—the Church has reflected on, clarified, and defined the truths of that original revelation. It will continue to explain the Faith in terms that each generation will understand. Many learned, wise, and holy scholars have unfolded and continue to unfold the meaning of revelation, as has been seen in the latest Church Council (Vatican II, 1962-1965). But the mystery of Christ will never be exhausted.

Though the truths of faith do not change and nothing new can be added to what was revealed in Christ, the Church grows in its understanding of revelation. Like a diamond, which sparkles in the light, new aspects of revelation appear as doctrines are probed, only to reflect back what was held from the start. Mary's Immaculate Conception and Assumption, defined in 1854 and 1950 respectively, are examples of truths contained in original revelation, even though these doctrines are not directly stated in Scripture. The Church, by defining doctrine, assures us that it comes from the original revelation; for the Church teaches as the Apostles taught—that is, under the guidance of the Holy Spirit.

Bishop Joseph Francis.

Efforts at Apostolicity

With the recent revival of interest in tracing family roots, people are awakening to a greater reverence for the past. Respect for the revelation given to and through the Apostles can open our hearts to the teachings of the Holy Father and our bishops. Doctrinal declarations of the Church are to be received with respect, and infallible pronouncements adhered to with obedience of faith and understanding.

If we have questions or reservations about the Church's teachings from time to time, it is important to bear four things in mind. We should always: 1) remain sincerely disposed to continuing our inquiry; 2) adhere to Christ and the Church; 3) respect the teaching authority of the pope; and above all, 4) try not to harm the common good. Questions should always be raised with genuine love and sympathy as we seek unity in essentials, diversity in nonessentials, and charity in all things.

18. How do you think reading the Scriptures can help you understand the mark of Apostolicity?

A People at Prayer

The Catholic Church welcomes all who sincerely desire to join the community of the People of God. At Vatican II, the rites for initiating people into the Church were revised. Here is a prayer from the rite:

"All-powerful God, help our brothers and sisters as they deepen their knowledge of the Gospel of Christ. May they come to know and love you and always do your will with generous hearts and willing spirits. Initiate them into a life of holiness, and count them among your Church so that they may share your holy mysteries here on earth and in the everlasting joy of heaven. We ask this through Christ our Lord. Amen."

The Call to Be Catholic

The four distinguishing characteristics of the early Church—oneness (unity), holiness, catholicity, and apostolicity—identify the Church as being of Christ. These are gifts the Catholic Church has guarded as the precious legacy of Jesus. Although never perfectly witnessed in the Church, not one has been lost, and nowhere else can they be found exactly as they are present in the Roman Catholic Church.

Many people outside the Church admire its stability, tradition, and truth. Though nearly two thousand years old, the Church remains vibrant. But not everyone becomes a Catholic. If the marks of the Church do indeed identify the Church as Christ's own, why do so many sincere people choose *not* to belong?

For one thing, the imperfections in the Church may hide its true splendor from some people. For another, most people find peace and blessing in the faith of their ancestors. Vatican II teaches that all peoples, even the non-Biblical and the unevangelized, possess saving gifts that come from the Father through Christ in the Spirit. By responding to these gifts with generosity and love, true seekers can become holy.

But there are many who feel driven to search beyond the faith of their family and friends for a deeper involvement with God. Those who choose Christianity center their faith

"Born" Catholics Speak Out

When asked why they are Catholic, some "born" Catholics gave among their reasons:

". . . the Catholic Church helps me discover Christ in the most unlikely places." John Deedy, author, past managing editor of *Commonweal*.

"The Church remains for me a sign of the transcendent . . . above all, it is the Church of the Eucharist . . . the link with Jesus the founder and head." Abigail McCarthy, author, lecturer, educator, mother.

". . . we have to say that we do not know the answer to that question [Why am I a Catholic?], for the answer lies in the realm of God's grace and his providence." James Hitchcock, author, historian, scholar.

"(1) I treasure my Catholic heritage . . . (2) I like the company I keep . . . (3) I believe in institutions . . . (4) I am helped by the Church's moral code . . . (5) I am provided with a perspective . . . (6) For me, Christ is central." Sister Candida Lund, O.P., college professor and past president, author.

"Catholicism . . . has given me nothing but questions. But they are much better questions than I've had for a while. One good question is worth ten thousand answers." Arlo Guthrie, in "Singing a New Song" by Pam Robbins, *Sign*, May 1977, p. 15.

"At those times when I think of the Catholic Laity, I don't always think of myself as being part of that huge and diverse group . . . Simply put, I find I meet God in others—in their love and concern and attention. I believe, because there is always one small moment, some small miracle which occurs to give me reason to hope." Kathy Petersen Cecala, "Meeting God In Others," *Commonweal*, July 14, 1989, pp. 400-402.

Chapter 4   The Image That Others See

in Christ as the fullest revelation of God. Some embrace Catholicism because they recognize in it a unique historical continuity with, and fidelity to, Jesus and the apostolic Church in the essentials of Church life: teaching, worship, and community. Others give different reasons for their choices.

However, logical reasons really do not fully explain why anyone is a Catholic. You may know people who express a desire to join the Church, but who do not persevere. There may be others who agonize over certain questions about doctrine or morality, but who finally feel free enough to join the Church.

Jesus told us, "It was not you who chose me, it was I who chose you." (John 15:16). Although faith requires a free personal response, faith is a gift of God, bestowed as gifts of grace as God chooses. The main task of every human being is to respond sincerely and wholeheartedly to his or her personal call. God will do the rest.

19. Do you know any converts to the Catholic Church? How do they explain their choice?

20. Why do you remain Catholic? How have you responded to God's call?

Summary

- The word catholic means universal or worldwide.
- The Church has been able to affirm and use positive elements from many different cultures.
- Universality means witnessing to Christ's love for the weak and being open to different points of view.
- The apostolicity of the Church reflects our continuity with the earliest followers of Jesus.
- Through constant reflection and study, we continue to clarify the revelation of God as did the Apostles.
- Not all people respond in the same way to God's call, but God offers all people the gift of grace and salvation.

SECTION 3
Checkpoint!

■ Review

1. What is the meaning of the word Catholic?

2. How is the Church's catholicity seen in its history?

3. How is the Church becoming more involved in the world through its witness?

4. Describe the different approaches to change in the Church mentioned in the section.

5. How did the Apostles maintain Church communion at the Council of Jerusalem?

6. Why is the mystery of Christ still being clarified and explained?

7. What are the four steps for dealing with questions of Church teaching?

8. What is involved in the act of faith? How do God and the person of faith interact?

9. Words to Know: catholic, universal, Babel, Holocaust, apostolic.

■ Scripture Search

1. Read the following passages: Romans 10:12-13; Galatians 3:25-29. How do these passages reflect the catholicity of the Church? What other pairs of seeming opposites could you add?

2. Read Acts 9:1-31. How did Paul respond to God's call? How did Paul maintain the apostolic continuity of the Church?

■ In Your World

1. Reenact the Council of Jerusalem. Read the account of the Council in Acts 15, as well as Paul's version in Galatians 2. Choose class members to represent the two sides in the debate. Present your arguments, clarify the conclusion as it is presented in the Scriptures, and describe what happened at the conclusion of the Council.

2. Look around your Church and your parish community. Identify elements which you think might have been absorbed from other cultures. Using encyclopedias of history and art, describe the origin of these elements and how they are used in the Church. For example, both Latin and Greek are important languages in the Church.

CHAPTER 4 Review

■ Study

1. What characteristics do outsiders often use to describe the Church?
2. Why is a "lumpy" Church better than a "refined" one?
3. Explain the statement: "The Church is an incarnation of the Incarnation."
4. Define the term mark and identify the four marks of the Church.
5. Why are the marks of the Church still developing?
6. In what ways does the Church demonstrate unity?
7. What is the role of diversity in the oneness of the Church?
8. What is the role of the Church in both interfaith and ecumenical dialogue?
9. What are the four facets of holiness in the Church?
10. How does the Church remain holy even when some of its members are not?
11. What efforts is the Church making to remain conscious of its universal mission?
12. Why is the apostolicity of the Church so fundamental to its continuity?
13. How has the meaning of revelation been continually unfolding?
14. What is the teaching of Vatican II about the holiness of those outside the Church?

■ Action

1. Design a logo for the Church which illustrates each of its four distinguishing marks. Be prepared to explain the meaning of each design.

2. Attend a class for catechumens being held in your Church or a neighboring one. What kinds of questions do the students ask? Ask some of them what led them to seek conversion. Bring your impressions back to class and discuss them.

■ Prayer

The holiness of the Church is often most evident in its members, those we call saints. These men and women contribute to the holiness of the Church, and Catholic Christians often turn to the saints to intercede for them through Christ to the Father.

Catholic Christians believe that those who have died "in the peace of Christ" continue to be active in the world. Saints have been recognized by the Church for their achievements while on earth. Individuals sometimes feel close to a particular saint and choose to honor and pray to him or her.

Choose a particular saint whose life speaks to you. Learn about his or her life. Find an icon of the saint (a picture or statue). Kneel or sit in front of it. Focus on the image. Be conscious who it represents. Know that your saint is interested in you and joins with you in love of God.

Think about and discuss with your classmates how this prayer activity differs from other forms of prayer.

CHAPTER

5

Experiencing the Image

OBJECTIVES

In this Chapter you will

- Learn about the role of all members of a parish.

- Study the mission of a parish.

- Read about parish organization and vitality.

- Observe how parishes design activities for all members.

- Learn how parishes began and how a diocese is organized.

A diocese is a section of the People of God entrusted to a bishop to be guided by him with the assistance of his clergy so that, loyal to its pastor and formed by him into one community in the Holy Spirit through the Gospel and the Eucharist, it constitutes one particular church in which the one, holy, catholic and apostolic Church of Christ is truly present and active.
— "Decree On Bishops In The Church," #11

The Church: A Spirit-Filled People

SECTION 1
The Image in Action

For most Catholics, the single most important part of the Church is the parish. In your parish the Biblical and contemporary images of Church take on flesh and blood, and you experience "the image in action."

Every Catholic, no matter how old, starts off with baptism in a parish. The parish witnesses and blesses the drama of birth, growth, marriage, friendship, and death played out in every life. It is a primary shaper of our view of life, positively accenting the divine dimension of everything that occurs on earth. Through it you enter into the Lord's own community of followers.

A Living Community

Through liturgy, catechesis, service, and social life, and by the influence of family, priests, religious, youth ministers, athletic coaches, and fellow parishioners, the parish tells you what the Church is. Ideally, it is in the living community of your parish that you experience the love of others as an image of the love of God. Here you receive comfort in sorrow and the support you need to live your faith in a world where Christian influence is decreasing. Interaction with others who share your faith and commitment can act as a positive and encouraging reinforcement to deeper faith.

What Is a Parish?

Someone once observed that, for some Catholics, the Church is only a place to be hatched, matched, patched, and dispatched. Some Catholics center their lives on their parish. Others hardly ever see the interior of their church except for baptisms, weddings, and funerals. Why is the parish different things to different people?

Being a member of a parish means getting involved in the activities of a parish.

The parish is not meant to be a "filling station" where the clergy "dispense salvation" which the parishioners accept passively. Neither is the ideal parish a place where people simply follow the rules and pay their dues to insure that they make the guest list for the Heavenly Banquet. Nor is a parish just the buildings where the Church gathers. Even when a parish church has been destroyed by fire, we have witnessed parish life continuing, often strengthened by the ordeal.

Your parish may seem simple—a group of people gathering to express, in public, their communion with God and one another—yet in describing it, you will see a parish community different in some ways from all others. Whether it is a huge, thriving body of believers living in the congested suburbs, or a tight-knit rural community set in remote hills, or an inner city parish struggling to survive, the variety of parishes and parishioners mirrors the universal Church. The parish is, in fact, the Church in miniature.

Ways Parishes Differ

Think about all the ways parishes may differ from one another. They are as varied as our population. Many parishes reflect the patterns of residence in American society, and so may seem segregated. Others have managed to be very inclusive, recognizing neither nationality, status, age, or gender (1 Corinthians 12:13). But we must always recognize, and remember, that our parishes will always reflect the diversity of society.

The Church: A Spirit-Filled People

Think about how the people of two parishes might be different in some of the following aspects:

- *locality from which they come;*
- *race and nationality;*
- *age range and gender composition;*
- *level of education;*
- *values and experiences;*
- *ways in which they seek God.*

All this variation and diversity makes the Church a truly universal body.

1. How would you describe your role in your parish?
2. Does your parish reflect the diversity of your community? In what ways?

Master Plan for a Parish

At the Second Vatican Council there was a renewed emphasis on the parish. As a result, the U.S. Bishops' Committee on the Parish proposed a blueprint for the Catholic parish in a short document called *"The Parish: A People, a Mission, and a Structure."* The parish, they said, "seeks to become ever more fully a people [community] of God through sharing Christ's mission and developing the structure necessary for supporting its community life and carrying out its mission" (*"The Parish,"* #8). Rather than a description, the document sketches an ideal toward which pastors, parishioners, bishops, and diocesan committees should continue to strive. It is a vision meant to "direct our energies for renewal, guide programs of formation for parish ministry, and identify priorities for diocesan service" (*"The Parish,"* #8).

Chapter 5   Experiencing the Image

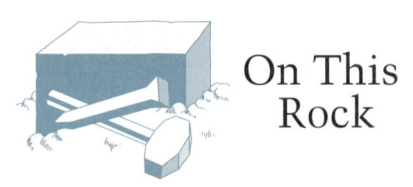

On This Rock

The relationship between the priests and parishioners is important. Neither group alone can make up the Church. The *"Dogmatic Constitution on the Church"* tries to make clear the responsibilities of each group to the other and to the Church.

"The baptized . . . are consecrated into a spiritual house and a holy priesthood. Though they differ from one another in essence . . . the common priesthood of the faithful and the . . . hierarchical priesthood are nonetheless related. Each of them in its own special way is a participation in the one priesthood of Christ" (#10). Through the ages, followers of Christ have recognized that all the baptized are called to share in the holiness of Christ. This document from Vatican II shows that the Church is the people worshiping and working together.

A People

"The parish is first a people," an ecclesial community: it is a people "called together by God and empowered by the Spirit" to share and develop a faith in Christ and to build up and express it ever more visibly (*"The Parish,"* #9). From the unity generated by the Eucharist, members of the community are led to care for one another and to extend the Church through various forms of Christian witness.

The ecclesial community is not just a group of people doing good together, but rather a priestly people called in Baptism to witness Christ's enduring presence and thereby to transform the world into a more graced fellowship of true brothers and sisters in the Lord (*"The Parish,"* #10). Christian laity and religious all participate in the witness to Christ. The laity, "by their very vocation, seek the kingdom of God by engaging in temporal affairs and by ordering them according to the plan of God" (*"Dogmatic Constitution on the Church,"* #31).

Most important to every parish is the quality of its sacramental life because it is through the prayer life of the parish that God acts in a unique way. The individual sacraments are "graced events of God's action and our response. In all its celebrations of the sacraments the parish makes every effort to attend to the mystery of God's action, to open itself to the power of the sacramental symbols and to show care for the people engaging in these rites" (*"The Parish,"* #18).

One way to judge the quality of a parish is to observe how people celebrate the sacraments.

The Church: A Spirit-Filled People

Clergy and Laity

Within the community, the leadership role of pastoral ministers is very important. These ministers enable the community to form an ever closer union with Christ through the Gospel and the Eucharist. In collaboration with the bishop they "encourage a sense of community within the parish" and make it "their special concern to know their parishioners" (*"Constitution on the Sacred Liturgy,"* #42). Every group in the parish is to be the personal concern of the pastor. Pastors are charged with seeing that "either personally or through others . . . each member of the faithful shall be led by the Holy Spirit to that full development of his/her own vocation in accordance with Gospel teaching" (*"Decree on the Ministry and Life of Priests,"* #6).

No parish can mature today without the development of lay ministry with both women and men assuming leadership roles. And the Church cannot flourish unless vocations to all forms of church ministry are encouraged, especially in the family.

Priest and Parishioner

Close cooperation and mutual respect between the pastoral team and parishioners is vital if parishes are to reach their ideal development. Instructed by the Council to "recognize and promote the dignity and responsibility of the laity in the Church," pastors are further counseled to encourage their initiative to "willingly use their prudent advice and confidently assign duties to them in the service of the Church, leaving them freedom and scope for acting" (*"Dogmatic Constitution on the Church,"* #37). On the other hand, parishioners are urged to develop the habit of working in close union with their priests and they "share their priests' anxieties and help them as much as possible by prayer and active work so that they may be better able to overcome difficulties and carry out their duties with greater success" (*"Decree on the Ministry and Life of Priests,"* #9).

The bishops' document sets the parish in a wider context: "The parish community does not exist in isolation, of course. It is present in larger and wider communities. Under the bishop it is part of the local church and recognizes the

Ecclesial: from the Greek word *ekklesia*, which means "called forth," a name for the community of Christians.

Laity: defined by Vatican II as all the faithful except those in holy orders and those in religious life.

Chapter 5   Experiencing the Image

A People within a People

Christians have always been a community existing within the larger communities around them. Jesus' command to spread the Good News throughout the world meant that his followers could always be found everywhere. From the beginning, Christian leaders realized that maintaining unity and communication in the Church would be difficult. Christians also had to learn to live and work among non-Christians.

Sometime around the year 124, a non-Christian called Diognetus (which was not his real name) wrote a short essay on the life of Christians at that time. It contains important information about the place of Christian communities within the larger society. The author says, "The difference between Christians and the rest of mankind is not a matter of nationality . . . Christians do not live apart in separate cities of their own. They . . . conform to ordinary local usage in their clothing, diet, and other habits. Nevertheless, the organization of their community does exhibit some features that are remarkable . . ."

Diognetus observes that Christians love those who hate them, and support the poor even if they are poor themselves. This short essay shows that from the earliest times, there were strong and supportive communities of Christians that were making an impression even on those who had not yet received the Good News.

♦

need to share in the mission of the whole diocese. Under the pope, it is part of the universal church, whose tradition and teaching guide it. It also exists in the broader human communities: local, national, and international. As the parish forms itself into a community, it also acknowledges its place in these other communities" (*"The Parish,"* #14).

In these ways, the parish attempts to become more and more a community of faith.

3. What are some of the groups within your parish? How does the pastor show concern for the different groups?

4. In what activities are lay people in your parish involved? How have you been active as a lay person in your parish?

5. Name as many local and global communities as you can to which you and your parish belong.

A parish community reaches out to serve the needs of all its members.

A Mission

The parish doesn't exist for itself, but rather to carry out Christ's mission. It is a mystery of God's working among us. Catholic parish life aims at the "glory of God the Father in Christ" (*"Dogmatic Constitution on the Church,"* #3). We glorify God first by accepting the salvation he has given us, second by participating in Christ's life, death, and resurrection, and finally by living as Jesus taught us by his word and example. All ministry—of clergy, lay persons, parishes, and dioceses—aims at that goal for each Catholic. God's "glory consists in people's conscious, free, and grateful acceptance of God's plan in Christ and their manifestation of it in their whole lives" (*"Decree on the Ministry and Life of Priests,"* #2).

Called to minister to one another and to those with whom they live and work, "the staff and members of the parish must be willing to take the time individually and together to heal, console, listen to, and help people in need" (*"The Parish,"* #21), especially by supplying the needs and championing the rights of the poor and alienated.

Behind all parish activity lies the call and commitment to grow in and to share the faith at all stages of life and personal development (*"Dogmatic Constitution on the Church,"* #12). The parish encourages its active members to more mature faith, invites alienated or inactive Catholics to return to the Church's beliefs and worship, and brings the Gospel alive for all by the vibrant witness and warm hospitality of its members. In an effort to nourish the Christian life, the parish provides formation and support for family life, which is so important to its own life. It also shows concern for the needs of single parents and others of all ages who lack family support. Its primary duties are the instruction and formation of its members, especially through sacramental programs; opportunities for small group reflection; and ongoing catechesis throughout the life of every member.

When we gather for prayer as a parish, we form a community of faith. Jesus is truly in our midst.

The parish also reaches out to "build a society where there is justice, freedom, and peace for all," to support home and foreign missions, and to do everything in its power to promote unity with those of other Christian churches as well as with other religious groups (*"The Parish,"* #25; *"Decree on the Apostolate of Lay People,"* #10).

6. *How does your parish serve poor and alienated people?*

7. *What education programs does your parish provide for its members?*

8. *How does your parish try to live as Jesus taught us, and how do you personally contribute to that life?*

Summary

- The parish is the Church in action.

- Parishes reflect the larger reality of the universal Church.

- A parish is a community of people called to witness to Christ's presence in the world.

- Cooperation between priests and parishioners is essential.

- The mission of the parish is ministry to those people both inside and outside the community through education and outreach.

SECTION 1
Checkpoint!

■ Review

1. How does the daily and weekly life of the parish illustrate the reality of the Church?
2. What is the purpose of a parish?
3. In what ways might two parishes be different?
4. Explain the role of pastors and the role of parishioners within the community.
5. What can parish members do specifically to offer support to other members and concern for society as a whole?
6. Words to Know: parish, ecclesial, diocese, laity, pastoral ministers.

■ In Your World

1. Using your own parish as a guide, describe the following activities as they are carried on: Eucharistic celebration; educational services (schools, adult education); service to the community; justice programs. Now compare this to a parish which you will invent. Develop a parish located either in the business district of a large city (with mostly transient members) or a campus ministry parish at a college or university. What programs do they have and how do they differ from yours?
2. How would you talk to a member of your parish who feels alienated from it? Set up a scene between two people. What complaints are voiced? How do you try to understand and offer support?

■ Scripture Search

1. The Church is a community of all people. Read 1 Timothy 2:1-7; James 1:22-25, 2:1-7. What instructions about the structure and responsibilities of the Church did the Apostles leave the early Christians?
2. God's covenant with Moses and the Israelites established a community of the faithful. Read the following passages: Exodus 19:1-6, 28:1-6; Leviticus 10:8-10. How was the community formed? What is the function of the priests?

The Church: A Spirit-Filled People

SECTION 2
Evolving Parish Structures and Programs

Today, the Church is being forced to rethink its organizational structure by the increased mobility of its population and the decline of the neighborhood community. As a result, the diocese is being restored to its more ancient position as the basic element in Church structure and the bishop to his role as the chief sign of unity and solidarity among the People of God. At the same time, new programs to serve the local Church community are always being developed.

New Parish Structures

The Constitution on the Sacred Liturgy avoided a strictly administrative and legalistic concept of the parish. Instead, the document described it in theological terms focusing on its purpose, center, and mission.

In the past, people were assigned to a parish based on their location. These were called territorial parishes. Today, experiments with new parish structures are being conducted. The faithful may choose a parish where their liturgical and spiritual needs are satisfied. Such experiments are called non-territorial parishes. Another development is the involvement of a greater number of people in a wider variety of ministries within the traditional territorial parish. Some parishes may be led by a team. Each team member —such as co-pastor, director of religious education, liturgical coordinator, or any other parish leader—is responsible for his or her area of ministry.

Chapter 5   Experiencing the Image

Communion of Saints

Throughout history, there have been Church leaders whose attempts to live the Gospel have been controversial. Such a person was Saint John Chrysostom (347-407). He became a priest in 386 in Antioch (an ancient city in modern-day Syria). In 398 John was consecrated archbishop of Constantinople. His sermons were often directed against the economic excesses and corruption of the wealthy. Chrysostom lived simply, donating much of his money to local hospitals and orphanages.

Chrysostom's harsh sermons were not well-liked and he was expelled from the city. He died in 407. Saint John Chrysostom, meaning "Golden Mouth," is remembered for his preaching, which was always directed toward improving the life of Christians and the Church.

Leadership

Leadership is essential to parish development. Leaders must be personally faithful to God's call. They must work to make the mission of the parish clearer. Most of all, good leaders call forth the leadership of others and coordinate the many gifts provided by the Spirit within the parish community. Parish leadership must be creative but remain subject "to both the Gospel and the total experience of the Church, which is tradition" (*"The Parish,"* #29-30, see also the *"Decree on the Ministry and Life of Priests,"* #9).

Developing structures which allow for shared decision-making encourages the fullest possible collaboration of all members of a parish. This decision-making covers various ministries including worship, formation, education, evangelization, ecumenism, and social service (*"Dogmatic Constitution on the Church,"* #37).

Although structures may differ from parish to parish, all structures within the parish are geared to foster community and to facilitate its mission. The Bishops' Committee names the parish council as "the most promising way" to ensure optimum participation. They recommend that the members be properly trained for their responsibilities, and include representatives of those actually carrying out the ministry of the parish. The council's purpose is "to develop the correct understanding of the parish's mission, and to formulate policies" for properly carrying out its ministries (*"The Parish,"* #31).

The Pastor

The pastor (or pastoral team) is the primary leader of the parish (*"Decree on the Ministry and Life of Priests,"* #6). He unifies parish worship activity, coordinates the spiritual and organizational life of the parish, and connects the parish to the larger Church of the diocese. He not only serves the people of the parish, but also makes it possible for the parishioners to minister, one to another, and constantly to deepen their commitment to Christ.

Under the pastor's guidance, small groups develop within the parish, giving parishioners greater freedom to profess, study, and better understand their own faith. As a team,

The Church: A Spirit-Filled People

people are able to initiate projects of outreach that might be impossible if single individuals tried to accomplish the same task.

In the past, the list of people directly involved in the day to day life of the parish was small. The modern parish may include many individuals and groups starting with the ordained pastor and his associate pastor (or parish team of co-pastors). The pastor is sometimes assisted by:

- *a permanent deacon or a deacon to be ordained to the priesthood;*
- *members of the parish council, parish committee representatives, and consultants, such as leaders of parish associations or groups;*
- *the director of religious education (DRE), the principal of the parish day school and its faculty, the principal of the parish school of religion (PSR) and catechists;*
- *religious sisters in various parish ministries;*
- *ministers of the Eucharist, of the Word, of music, of youth, and of pastoral needs, acolytes, ministers of hospitality, and sacristans.*

---

9. Can you name the people who fill the the leadership positions outlined above in your parish?

10. How is your own parish structured? Is it territorial? Are there members from other locations?

Parish Committees and Programs

Parish structures work to deepen the Christian life of the community in two directions: they provide opportunities for personal spiritual growth, and they offer opportunities for outreach to parishioners and other people. Traditionally, parishes have sponsored missions and devotional services as well as programs to support the needy through special collections, benefit affairs, and donations of food, clothing,

Chapter 5 Experiencing the Image

Baptizing Adults—New Life for the Church

The Rite of Christian Initiation of Adults (RCIA) was adopted at Vatican II. The RCIA, recapturing an ancient practice of the Church, was to improve the way adults were incorporated into the People of God. The early Church, with many more adult baptisms than children, understood the concept of adult initiation. Returning to this ancient rite strengthens the Church with a treasure from its past.

For unbaptized adults who wish to become a part of the Church community, there are three stages in the RCIA process. First, they enter a period of inquiry and study; then they actually become catechumens—a technical term applied to those who are part of the Church family, but not yet baptized—sponsored by a godparent; finally, they are prepared to receive the sacraments. The entire parish community is a part of the spiritual development of the catechumens. Pastors and teachers are responsible for their formation and others in the community support them through personal witness and prayer.

The acceptance of a new adult member into the parish becomes an event for everyone to experience, and the entire community shares in the new life. The RCIA offers the parish an opportunity to renew itself and its mission as it welcomes new members into the Body of Christ.

and household items. Today, new ministries are available in such structures and programs as Liturgy Committees, Religious Formation and Education Committees, Finance Committees, the Rite of Christian Initiation for Adults (RCIA), Evangelization Committees, and Peace and Justice Committees. Sometimes programs are sponsored jointly with neighboring churches, whether Catholic or not, to broaden the parish's outreach. Cooperation with others in facing community problems, running projects for the elderly or people with handicaps, peace and justice programs, and ecumenical services fall into this category.

11. What committees does your parish have as expressions of its own ministries?

12. What local and world issues could a Peace and Justice Committee in your parish be concerned about?

Parish Vitality Today

Wherever priests and laity have responded to the call to revitalize their parishes, signs of new life are evident. Whether through small communal units, such as Cursillo or a renewal program, Marriage Encounter, or the charismatic movement, or through parish-wide programs like the RCIA, the parish is enjoying a renewal of spiritual life that is nurturing more caring communities and spilling over into Christian service. Greater lay participation in a variety of new ministries is one consequence of this widespread renewal. This is especially true in the area of Youth Ministry.

Many youth have felt that there is no place for them in the parish. In many cases, the parish didn't know how to incorporate youth into its structure. The parish needs the gifts brought by youth—faith, vision, enthusiasm—and the youth need the parish's history, tradition, and experience of faith. Youth are the future of the Church, but only in so far as they become vital members now. That is why most parishes have begun well-developed programs for Youth Ministry, often hiring a Youth Minister to work full-time with parish teens.

13. How do you think your involvement now in the life of your parish will contribute to its vitality in the future?

Chapter 5   Experiencing the Image

Many parishes today are paying close attention to the needs of their adolescent members through youth groups and youth ministry.

Portrait of a Parish

Father William Bausch is pastor of Saint Mary's Parish in Colt's Neck, New Jersey and author of *The Christian Parish*. He feels the following ideas are key to the forming of a good parish.

- *Shared decision-people feel more at home and also more important when parish decisions are as much theirs as the pastor's.*

- *The feelings of a parish as an extension of the home, giving the sense of openness and welcome. Kids can stop in to use the bathroom, and they feel like it's their place.*

- *Listen to the needs of the parish and find out people's real hunger. Know what concerns parents have about their kids. Why call it a spiritual center? What do you do there?*

- *Develop a special place designed so that people just don't come to the parish for Mass. This can be a place where families and individuals go for retreats, prayer days, days of recollection, Scripture studies, overnights for kids, parish spirituality, and cultural and community things, like theater or arts and crafts shows.*

The Church: A Spirit-Filled People

- *Instead of begging for money, ask the people to give one hour of their time each week to God. Every Tuesday, for example, from three to four is God's hour—specifically and consciously. Whatever you make in that hour ought to go to God.*

- *Don't make every activity a money-making affair. Run events that may lose money but build community spirit. Have trips every year. That's as much a part of parish spirituality as anything else.*

- *Don't let the parish be known as an "active" parish. That's not a compliment. It would be better if people would say, "They have a great spirit there," or "I sense the presence of Christ (adapted from an interview with Fr. Baush, U.S. Catholic, February 1981).*

Reprinted with permission from U.S. Catholic, published by Claretian Publications, 205 W. Monroe Street, Chicago, IL 60606.

According to Father Bausch, the parish should be a place where people feel comfortable gathering, not just for religious activities, but social and action activities as well.

Chapter 5 Experiencing the Image

131

Some Parish Activities

St. Mary's Church in Colt's Neck, New Jersey is an alive and active parish. In trying to address the real needs of parishioners, the following groups and activities have been established (adapted from *The Christian Parish: Whispers of the Risen Christ*, by William J. Bausch, XXIII Publications, 1981).

- ***Instructional**—Parish booklet (describing organizations, services, and parish calendar) which is given to all parishioners. A newsletter is sent to college students from the parish to keep them in touch. Advent/Lent Packets (with ideas for family activities) are developed to address parish needs. Bible vacation school, Preschool (3 to 5-year-olds), and leadership training workshops round out traditional instruction programs for children and youth.*

- ***Spiritual Life/Liturgical**—Overnight retreats are held for fifth, sixth, seventh, and eighth graders. Special worship activities include Lenten stations (conducted by parish families), the Moppet Mass (children's liturgy monthly), All Saints and Epiphany costumed celebrations by children, Passiontide crosses (life-size, made by parishioners for Good Friday procession), and an exciting music ministry.*

- ***Service**—Families keep the parish grounds neat, do the Christmas decorating, and serve in the Lazarus Confraternity (helping with wakes and funerals). Parish youths minister to the aged, staff food collections, and join the "Samaritans" (serving the sick, doing works of mercy). Another group is the One-on-One ministry to people with special problems like job loss or divorce.*

The priest is not the same as the parish. But the quality of parish life often takes its direction from the priest. What kind of parish do you envision from this photo?

The Church: A Spirit-Filled People

- **Social**—The parish offers many opportunities for parishioners to gather together: Mini breakfast after Mass (monthly), Welcome Wagon (for newcomers), parish trips, Singles Group, Sunday afternoon movies (for kids), Easter egg hunt, Saturday night dinner in the rectory, staff day away.
- **Evangelization**—The parish makes a special effort to reach out to those Catholics who feel alienated from the parish, as well as the RCIA.

---

14. How can parish leaders make even the financial needs of its members a community activity?

15. Compare the activities in your parish with those at St. Mary's. Are there any activities in your parish that are not included in the list above? Are there some listed that your parish doesn't have?

Summary

- Parish structures are evolving in order to meet the needs of the faithful.
- Parish organization allows for shared leadership and decision-making.
- Various committees and programs touch the lives of all parish members.
- There are many signs of vitality in parishes today as seen in the example of St. Mary's Parish.

SECTION 2
Checkpoint!

■ Review

1. What is a non-territorial parish?
2. What is the function of parish leadership?
3. How do the pastor and parish council enhance the life of the parish?
4. Name some of the committees that might be found in a parish today.
5. How does the pastor of St. Mary's Parish encourage participation in the life of the Church?
6. What are a few specific activities of St. Mary's aimed at reaching out to all?
7. Words to Know: territorial parish, non-territorial parish, co-pastor, parish council, RCIA.

■ In Your World

1. In your parish find out about one activity from each of the categories mentioned in the section on parish activities. Choose one every week. At the end of the month, either write a short essay reflecting on what you've learned or report back to your class. What new side of the Church did your participation in this activity show you?
2. Prepare an overall composite picture of your parish either on paper or in photographs. What is the age, gender and racial makeup of the parish? What types of jobs do people have? About how many children are in the average family? Is your parish territorial? Are there transient (temporary) visitors?

■ Scripture Search

Read 1 Corinthians 1:1-17, 5:6-6:8, 12:4-11. What are some of the causes of disunity in Church? What are the quarrels about? And how does Paul try to resolve the struggles? Explain how the diversity of the Church contributes equally to both its unity and disunity.

SECTION 3
The Parish: How It Developed

Today, we take parishes for granted. Parish rectories and churches are part of Catholic culture. But it wasn't until the fourth century that priests began to live outside the bishop's house, and not until the mid-sixteenth century that pastors were permanently assigned to parishes. That happened at the Council of Trent (1545-1563) when the entire parish system was reorganized. But the organization of Christian communities began with the Apostles and their followers.

The Early Centuries

In the early Church, bishops headed every portion of the Christian community. They were assisted by priests who were called presbyters. The word parish came into use after 150, when it was used to designate individual, geographic communities cared for by the bishop. In the Hebrew Scriptures, "parish" meant the earthly dwelling of Israel considered as a sojourn in a foreign country. In the New Testament Church, it was adopted to represent the earthly lifestyle of the Christian community, whose true home is God's kingdom, and then to an individual Church community. After the destruction of the local churches by the barbarian invasions, feudal landowners rebuilt them, reducing the clergy to servant status. Later bishops regained possession of their churches, but lost them once more when, under secular governments, parishes became privately owned.

When the Council of Trent (mid-16th century) separated the duties of pastors and bishops within the parish and set up parish boundaries, the authority of the bishop over local parishes narrowed while that of the papacy grew.

Presbyter: elder, refers to the priests in the early Church.

Feudalism: a system of political organization in which landowners demanded loyalty from tenants.

Papacy: a term used to describe the office of the pope.

Chapter 5 Experiencing the Image

16. *As the Church grew and spread over a wide geographical and cultural area, why do you think it became necessary to reorganize the system of parishes and to redefine the duties of bishops and pastors?*

The Coat of Arms for Bishop J. Kendrick Williams, first bishop of the Diocese of Lexington, KY. The left side of the shield represents the diocese and the right side is symbolic of Bishop Williams' personal history.

A People at Prayer

Confirmation is a sacrament normally celebrated by the bishop of a diocese. Here is a prayer spoken by the bishop to those about to be anointed: "All-powerful God, Father of our Lord Jesus Christ, by water and the Holy Spirit you freed your sons and daughters from sin and gave them new life. Send your Holy Spirit upon them to be their Helper and Guide. Give them the spirit of wisdom and understanding, the spirit of right judgment and courage, the spirit of knowledge and reverence. Fill them with the spirit of wonder and awe in your presence. We ask this through Christ our Lord. Amen" (Rite of Confirmation).

The Local Church

When you first hear the term "local church," you might think "parish"; and when you hear the phrase, "head of the local church," your first thought might be "pastor." However, the parish is not an autonomous unit because the pastor depends on the bishop for his pastoral appointment. He cannot preach or administer any sacraments besides Baptism unless he has received faculties (permission) from the local bishop. Faculties serve to promote unity within the Church. Therefore, the basic complete local church unit is the diocese, known especially since Vatican II as the "local church." The Bishop is called the "local ordinary" of the local Church. A diocese—a geographical area—is a section of the People of God entrusted to a bishop, and constitutes one particular church in which the one, holy, catholic, and apostolic Church of Christ is truly present and active (*"Decree on the Pastoral Office of Bishops in the Church,"* #11).

Apostolic Leadership

The earliest Church communities were called churches, or assemblies. Individual churches were identified by the places where they were located, like the Church of Corinth or the Church of the Thessalonians. Except for James and John, who governed in Jerusalem and Ephesus—respectively—the Apostles did not head individual churches. Instead, they formed a collegial grouping (college) under Peter's leadership. After the death of the Apostles, each of the local churches was headed by a bishop who also governed surrounding rural assemblies. Not until the thirteenth century was the term diocese adopted to represent a territorial grouping of assemblies (parishes).

As a successor of the Apostles, the bishop governs the diocese or local church as chief shepherd and teacher, answering only to the Pope, who appoints all bishops. Bishops in communion with the pope form the supreme governing body of the Church, especially when gathered in council. Their working together is known as collegiality. A bishop, together with his priests, who exercise their authority as delegates of the bishop, form a brotherhood.

Diocesan priests are ordained for a diocese. Religious order priests, on the other hand, work in dioceses, but are not attached to one. They are moved in and out of dioceses at the need of their leader, usually called a Provincial. While in a diocese, a religious order priest is under the authority of that particular diocesan bishop.

The pope is the Chief Bishop of the Church and is called the Bishop of Rome. As the direct successor of Peter, he possesses the highest (primacy of) jurisdiction over the entire Church.

The Bishop

The word bishop is from the Greek *episkopus* which means "overseer." The Second Vatican Council described the bishop's pastoral duties as follows: "In exercising his office of father and pastor, the bishop should be with his people as one who serves, as a good shepherd who knows his sheep and whose sheep know him, as a true father who excels in his love and solicitude for all" (*"Decree on the Pastoral Office of Bishops in the Church,"* #16). If a local

---

Autonomous: able to function independently.

College: an organized body of persons having common interests or duties.

Diocese: from a Greek word which means "to keep house" or "to govern."

church is extensive, a bishop may be assisted by one or more bishops who are auxiliary or coadjutor bishops. They share in the authority of the bishop. Auxiliary bishops are bishops in their own right, but are under the authority of a local diocesan bishop. Co-adjutory bishops are in line to succeed when a bishop dies or resigns.

---

17. Can you name the bishop of your diocese? How many parishes and people make up your local church?

Diocesan Organization

As the number of Catholics increases worldwide, new organizational patterns have evolved in order to serve individuals and parishes more effectively. Every diocese is composed of individual parishes. Groups of parishes, usually geographically close to one another, form a deanery. Even though it is common knowledge that a pastor heads a parish, it is often not known that a priest called a

This bishop is seen wearing his **miter** (hat) and **crosier** (staff), two symbols of the office of bishop.

Leadership

The ministry of the Church can be traced back all the way to the commissioning of the disciples and the Twelve Apostles by Jesus. It is believed that a threefold ministry—composed of bishops, presbyters, and deacons—developed early, along with the roles of teachers and evangelists.

By the third century, there were bishops, presbyters, deacons, sub-deacons, acolytes, exorcists, readers, and doorkeepers—each position was known as an order. The Council of Trent defines the gift of Holy Orders (priesthood) as a sacrament. As a sacrament, it gives its recipient an indelible character, just like Baptism.

The earliest known written rite of Ordination—from A.D. 215—comes from Hippolytus. We can see that the need for strong leadership has been evident since earliest Christian times. The guidance of the Holy Spirit has provided structures and systems for the continued direction and care of the Christian community.

♦

dean heads the deanery. Some parishes today are run by a team of priests. Dioceses are grouped into provinces headed by an archbishop or metropolitan.

Different organizational patterns exist in other rites of the Church. The archbishop is also called a patriarch, especially in the non-Latin rites like the Byzantine rite. A rite is a particular way of worshiping and governing. Most Catholics belong to the Latin (Roman) rite.

Chapter 5   Experiencing the Image

Diocesan Curia

Within an individual diocese, the bishop enjoys the services of many different people, experts who assist him in the administration of the diocese. What follows is a partial list.

- ***Vicar General**—exercises episcopal jurisdiction in the bishop's name, often in different diocesan regions.*
- ***Officialis/Diocesan Tribunal**—handles marriage cases and other legal proceedings, such as dispensation from religious vows and various matters requiring communication with Rome.*
- ***Chancellor**—prepares all written documents used in the administration of the diocese.*
- ***Offices**—Secretary of Education, for Parish Life and Development, for Evangelization, for Social Service.*
- ***Consulting Groups**—Diocesan Pastoral Council, Priests' Senate, Sisters' Senate.*

Organization in the Church assures Catholics that Christ's Church will always be visible, that bishops will be able to carry out their functions, and that people's spiritual welfare will be attended. In other words, the structure of the diocese must include everything necessary to continue Christ's mission.

Summary

- The word "parish" was first used to mean the earthly life of Christian communities.
- Pastors were not permanently assigned to parishes until the Council of Trent.
- "Local church" refers to the diocese.
- The bishop is the chief pastor and teacher of the diocese.
- The pope is the Bishop of Rome.
- Within a diocese, there are many professional offices which assist the bishop in his duties.

SECTION 3
Checkpoint!

■ Review

1. What were the duties of bishops and priests in the early Church?
2. How did the roles of bishop and priest change between 150 and 1535?
3. To what does the term "local church" refer?
4. What is collegiality?
5. What are the responsibilities of the bishop?
6. Explain the purpose of three professional diocesan offices.
7. Words to Know: presbyter, parochial, local church, territorial parish, diocese, collegiality, episcopus, coadjutor bishop, dean, *episkopus*.

■ In Your World

1. Prepare a detailed map of your diocese. Start by drawing its boundaries. Plot the location of each individual parish. Does your diocese contain any Catholic colleges? How many Catholics make up the diocese? Draw a chart starting with the bishop, and name some of the groups and individuals who assist the bishop. How old is your diocese? Where would you go for this information?

2. A friend of yours who is not Catholic observes that, from the outside, the Church seems like a huge organization, almost like a business or a corporation. It seems very impersonal and removed from the daily life of its members. How do you respond to this? What do you say about who really makes up the Church and what is the purpose of the structure?

■ Scripture Search

As we have seen, the bishop is entrusted with the spiritual well-being of his community. He is described as a shepherd. The parable of the Good Shepherd in Luke 15:4-7 presents the image of a good bishop. How? Read the parable well and think about the way it illustrates the qualities of a good minister. Present your findings to the class.

Chapter 5   Experiencing the Image

CHAPTER 5 Review

■ Study

1. Which services and activities of your parish define it for you?
2. How is the parish meant to be a "two-way street"?
3. How does the parish community function as a body of individuals?
4. What are some of the important roles of pastors and other priests?
5. What forms of lay ministry add to the diversity of a parish?
6. How can a parish contribute to the society and the world?
7. What are some ways a parish can minister to its members?
8. Why is shared leadership important?
9. Explain how committees and joint programs can affect the spiritual life of parishioners.
10. How does St. Mary's Parish demonstrate vitality in its activities?
11. What is the relationship between pastor and bishop? Between bishop and pope?
12. How have the functions of these Church leaders changed and evolved over the centuries?
13. What is the work of the Vicar General and the Chancellor in a diocese?

■ Action

1. Prepare a report on your parish. Make an appointment to spend time with your pastor. First find out about the history of your parish. Then chart out the relationship between all the committees and programs carried on in your parish. Try to speak to some of the leaders and organizers about their duties. Ask the pastor or another leader to attend your class and to discuss the workings of the parish.

2. Do a study on one other parish in your diocese. Try to choose one which seems different from your own. Visit the parish. How is it different and how is it the same? Invite some students from that parish to visit yours. Discuss those things (membership, programs, etc.) which characterize each parish and compare. What can you say about the universality of the Church as a result of your study?

■ Prayer

So many committees, activities, and programs from which to choose! How do you know which is really the one for you? What are your special gifts to give to the Church? What is God's will for you? Prayer can help you to know the will of God. We cannot be passive receivers of the will of God. Instead we must be active participants, using our talents and our brains.

Develop a prayer service using the following passages from Scripture: Psalm 40:1-11, Hebrews 10:1-7. The prayer should be designed to call each student to a greater awareness of the ministry around them. The class can share this service together.

Prayer for self-understanding and discernment of God's will can lead you to recognize and use your talents for the good of your parish community.

CHAPTER 6

Rooted in Jesus, Formed by His Spirit

OBJECTIVES

In this Chapter you will

- Think about the importance of roots and history.

- Ask yourself, "Did Jesus really found the Catholic Church?"

- Trace the beginning of the Church from Jesus through Pentecost.

- Learn about the earliest characteristics of the Church.

- Recognize the role of the Church as a guardian of revelation.

The Holy Spirit was sent on the day of Pentecost in order that he might continually sanctify the Church, and that those who believe might have access through Christ in one Spirit to the Father.
— "Dogmatic Constitution on the Church," #4

The Church: A Spirit-Filled People

SECTION 1
Looking to Your Roots

In recent years, there has been a renewed interest in searching for family roots and tracing family trees (genealogy). When you visit a Catholic Church you can touch both your present and your past. You experience the pain and the pride of your common bond with Catholics of all times and all places. Your visit brings you in contact with some of the distant influences on yourself, people and events which helped to form the person you are—a family member of the Catholic Church.

Your parish Church might put you in touch with your own personal past, like the lives of your great-grandparents. If they worshiped in the same Church, you may pray at their graves in the parish cemetery. This same Church can also focus your attention on the many people who have found the peace of Christ in the Church. Like any family or nation, they form generations of people whose experiences stretch through time and into eternity.

The Perils of Rootlessness

Imagine what it might be like suddenly to lose your memory and wake up in a world of strangers. With help you might survive, but it wouldn't be easy. If you didn't remember anything from your past, it would be almost impossible for you to function. You'd have to start all over. You could never be sure people were telling you the truth.

Like individuals and families, nations and states have a need to remember their past. An American philosopher, George Santayana (1863-1952), said that to ignore the past is to repeat its mistakes.

On the other hand, to explore the past is to benefit from both its wisdom and its mistakes. Catholics who try to understand and live their faith without a grasp of their

On This Rock

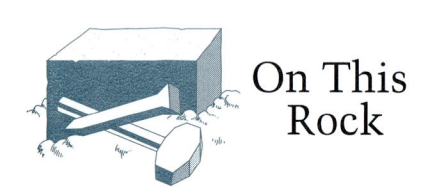

The quick spread of Christianity throughout the Roman Empire was an assurance to early followers of Christ of the truth of his life and message. When Christians were criticized or persecuted, the faithful followers of Christ often spoke eloquently of the truth of their mission. For example, Tertullian (160-240), a native of Carthage in North Africa, defended Christianity from its critics by noting the stamina of the Church even in its very beginnings: "We are but of yesterday, and we have filled everything you have—cities, islands, forts, towns, . . . camps, palace, . . . forum."

To its members, the spread of Christianity was a visible, living proof of its truth. It reflected the continuing presence of Christ.

Knowing the story of your ancestors can help you face the challenges of your own life.

religious heritage travel like people without a compass. Without any past, people lose perspective. Without a vision of the whole, faith floats unconnected to its origins and unsure of its direction.

1. *How are your personal family history and the history of the nation similar?*
2. *What difference would it make in your life if you knew nothing about your past and the past of your family?*

Christ's Family Tree

Unlike psychological amnesia (the loss of memory), which cannot always be cured, cultural amnesia can be remedied by investigation. As you assume the responsibility from your ancestors of continuing to build the Body of Christ, you will want to acquaint yourself with God's salvific history. That includes the foundation, the work and the development of many people over the past twenty centuries, along with what is recorded in the Hebrew Scriptures. Only then will your addition to the design be in harmony with the whole and create an impact satisfying to you, your contemporaries, and those who will follow after you.

The Church has inherited a vast store of spiritual wealth, wisdom, and weakness; yet, for the most part, it is in you that the Church is best seen by others. For some, accepting that responsibility is a frightening prospect. But with help from the Spirit, the Church has survived human weakness, persecution, heresy, and division. From a tiny seed, it has grown and flourished to become a worldwide and enduring religious faith. As one Catholic put it, "We must be doing something right to have lasted that long." Jesus promised to be with his Church until the end of time (Matthew 28:20), and he is with you as you join other members of your generation in continuing the family tree.

---

3. *How do you think learning about the history of the Church will add to your contribution? If history is so valuable, why do you think so many people say they dislike it?*

4. *Describe how you have benefitted from your knowledge of the past.*

It is through you that the Church is best seen by others.

Chapter 6   Rooted in Jesus, Formed by His Spirit

The Modern Questions

Tracing the Church's roots through time ought to bring you back to Jesus, who is recognized by Catholics as the founder of the Catholic Church. However, even Catholics ask, "Did Jesus really found the Catholic Church?" or "Did Jesus found a particular church at all?" If these questions represent sincere faith searching for a better understanding, there is every reason to try to find a satisfactory answer. Faith and the Spirit will act as our guides.

The image of the dove is a symbol for the Holy Spirit. What other images symbolize the Spirit?

Is Church Membership Necessary?

Though all Christians believe in eternal life on Jesus' word, not all agree that it is necessary to belong to the visible Church to be saved. Many people of other faiths struggle to answer this question as well. Some avoid the institutional Church because of an unfortunate encounter with an insensitive priest or minister or because of the demands of some moral regulation. Others ask sincerely, "Do I really need the Church to get to God, or can I find salvation directly in Jesus by contact with him in prayer or in Scripture?"

Liberal and Conservative—Who Are They?

As we have seen, attitudes about the necessity of the Church vary widely.

Catholics and Mainline Protestants—Standing in the center of the spectrum, these Christian communities accept the authority of tradition and Scripture, and allow a wide range of diversity among their members. Catholics will emphasize tradition more, while Protestants will place a stronger emphasis on Scripture. Many are devoted to the transformation of the world through social justice. Some mainline Protestant churches are called evangelical from the Greek word *euangelion*, Good News.

New Evangelicals—Somewhat to the right on the spectrum, these groups stress the primacy of Scripture over tradition and the authority of the Church. Their members characteristically support the prevailing culture and government, and generally follow gifted preachers upon whose interpretations of Scripture they rely heavily.

Fundamentalists—Those people described as fundamentalists accept the primacy of God's word. They usually insist on a literal understanding of Scripture (the belief that every word of Scripture is literally true), and interpret Scripture very narrowly. Another distinguishing feature about fundamentalists is the importance of a "born again" experience for their religious faith.

Your study of the founding and development of the Church based on the word and teaching of Christ will help you recognize people of different beliefs. Understanding the history of your own faith community will equip you to evaluate the views of others, especially if you are challenged about your faith by someone from a different religious tradition.

The Church Is Unnecessary?

As you meet people from different social circles and segments of society, you may find those who feel that they don't need the Church. They believe that if they accept Christ in their personal lives, they will be saved. Some Protestants, for instance, believe that Jesus never intended to create a Church because he spoke of the immediate coming of the kingdom. In fact, they say, he gathered followers precisely to liberate them from oppressive ecclesiastical institutions such as the temple system. His doctrine was simply love of God and neighbor. In their view, it was the Apostles who "created" the Church when it became evident that the Second Coming was still some way off. If the Church is merely the creation of human beings, they say, it can't be essential to salvation. It can be changed at will or dispensed with.

The majestic scope of this church architecture expresses the faith of the people who built it—God is magnificent.

The Church: A Spirit-Filled People

The Church Is Unchangeable?

Other people you may meet, who are often called fundamentalists, teach that the Gospels contain a verbatim account of Jesus' words—as if Jesus' words had been recorded and then transcribed. According to their belief, Jesus left us a blueprint for the Church, with all the forms of the sacraments exactly as we have them today, with the Apostles organized as bishops over well-defined dioceses, and with a shaped body of laws. From this viewpoint, nothing in the Church can ever change, and there can never be new ways of living out the Faith. No one is saved except those who follow every biblical prescription to the letter.

---

5. How important is the Church to you in your spiritual life?

6. Do you know any people who hold any of the views described above? How do they explain their position?

7. How will a study of the history of the Church help us reach the answer to our questions?

Summary

- The history of the Church puts you in touch with God's salvation history.
- Many Christians ask if the Church is necessary in order to attain salvation.
- Some people say that only God's love, not an institution, is necessary for salvation.
- Some people claim that the Church must remain literally true to Scripture, allowing little room for adaptation or change.

Verbatim: word for word.

SECTION 1
Checkpoint!

■ Review

1. What are the benefits of knowing about the history of your family, your country, and your Church?

2. How would you interpret George Santayana's statement about history repeating itself?

3. What perspective does knowledge of Church history give?

4. Why might someone ask if Jesus really founded the Catholic Church?

5. Describe the two negative answers to the modern question of faith.

6. Words to Know: genealogy, fundamentalist, verbatim.

■ In Your World

1. Establish a place for your parish within the long history of the Catholic Church. Check with your pastor or director of education to see if there are any old photographs and written materials about your parish. Prepare a small presentation which tells about your parish and its place in the universal Church. Are there any families who have been members since the beginning? Has the Church always used the same building?

2. Conduct a survey on the meaning and importance of the Church. Select fifteen people: five Catholics, five Protestant Christians, and five non-Christians. Ask them how important the Church (or their place of worship) is to them and why. Discuss your results in class.

■ Scripture Search

Read the following passages: Genesis 1:1-2:3; Genesis 12:1-3; Genesis 20:10-17; Exodus 20:1-20; Matthew 1:18-25; Matthew 3:13-17; Mark 5:25-34; and Mark 16:1-8. What do all these events reveal about God's salvation history? How are they all parts of the search for our Christian roots?

SECTION 2
Jesus, Founder of the Church

"To found" means to originate something, like a college or a hospital. The founder proposes the basic vision and usually establishes the way the project is to be carried out. The founder of a college does not always directly organize all of the departments that may be added during the course of time, but he or she is indirectly responsible for them. In the same way, Jesus did not directly organize the Church as we know it today, but the way it evolved flowed from what he said and did and was.

What He Said, Did, and Was

He preached that the kingdom of God was breaking into history: "This is the time of fulfillment. The kingdom of God is at hand" (Mark 1:15). He also demonstrated that the kingdom had indeed arrived in his Person by performing miracles. "But if it is by the finger of God that [I] drive out demons, then the kingdom of God has come upon you" (Luke 11:20). Yet Jesus taught that the kingdom will not be completed until the end of time. Therefore, he had a vision of time in which the kingdom was to be brought to fulfillment. This is understood to be an example of salvation history—the record of God's saving power in the world.

But it was principally by who he was and by his great act of redemption that Jesus founded the Church. As Son of God and Son of Man, Jesus' death and resurrection accomplished his mission of saving the world. Then he turned the work over to the community he had prepared so that it might be extended until the end of time.

Chapter 6 Rooted in Jesus, Formed by His Spirit

8. What do you think it means for a thing to be already present, but not yet completed? Can you give an example?

Communion of Saints

One of the people who was instrumental in establishing the People of God throughout the world was Saint Patrick (390-460). He was born in Britain where Christianity had already been established. Raised a Christian, Patrick was captured by the Irish pagans when he was sixteen. During his captivity, he prayed to God, and eventually he escaped. Upon returning home, he dedicated his life to Christ. He was sent to Ireland as a bishop and spent the rest of his life there evangelizing, ordaining clergy, and educating the people. For this reason, he is known as the "Apostle of the Irish."

The courage and conviction of Christians like Saint Patrick resulted in the spread of the Faith all over the world. For it to continue in the future, new saints must arise willing to pay the price necessary to proclaim the Good News.

The Role of the Apostles

Jesus did not bring the kingdom to completion by himself. After praying for guidance, he chose disciples and Apostles, instructed them, and then sent them out to baptize, preach, and heal in his name. Jesus singled out Peter from the other Apostles to be their head. The Apostles, as seen in the Gospels, don't seem to have been the best choices to build God's kingdom. They fled the scenes of Jesus' last hours. Crushed in spirit and humiliated before the populace of Jerusalem by the crucifixion, they took refuge in an upper room.

Despite their cowardice and weakness, the risen Lord appeared to them and took them into his confidence by "opening their minds to the understanding of the Scriptures" (Luke 24:45), especially to his fulfillment of thousands of years of prophecy. "When they saw him, they worshiped," (Matthew 28:17). He authorized them to baptize, to teach in his name, and sent them to "make disciples of all nations" (Matthew 28:19). Then, before his final departure, Jesus reassured them, "And behold, I am with you always, until the end of the age" (Matthew 28:19-20). Jesus ascended and instructed them to "stay in the city until you are clothed with power from on high" (Luke 24:49). Not knowing what to expect, they returned to the upper room with Mary his mother to pray and wait (see Acts 1:13-15).

After the Ascension

Only after the Ascension did the great work of organizing the Church begin. Jesus didn't leave his followers to fend for themselves. He sent his Spirit to guide the operation. Through the Spirit, Peter came to understand what Jesus had intended when he said: "You are Peter, and upon this rock I will build my Church" (Matthew 16:18). He, together

The Church: A Spirit-Filled People

with the other Apostles, and then others in their place, were to bring to the world the salvation that Jesus had won. Jesus founded the Church, but he left the organization and growth of it to his followers, who acted under the special guidance of the Spirit in all their undertakings. Other actions, such as anointing and laying on of hands, were soon understood to be sacraments of Christ's redeeming love. We call the early days of the Church "normative" because the Spirit's special presence during this time made what the Apostles did and said a standard or norm for all time.

There are only two gospel references to the Church, but more than seventy in Paul's letters, Acts, and Revelation, which deal with the post-resurrection Church (see Matthew 16:18 and 18:17).

---

9. *How do you feel about the reaction of Jesus' followers at the time of his death?*

10. *What other experiences or questions might result in a test of faith?*

11. *What do Jesus' words to the Apostles tell you about the mission and organization of the Church?*

Churches come in many shapes and sizes.

Peter: the name Jesus gave Simon; means "rock" in Greek.

Chapter 6 Rooted in Jesus, Formed by His Spirit

The Revelation of Pentecost

It may well be that the assembled community felt a sense of destiny as Peter, the acknowledged leader, rose to direct the choice of a replacement for Judas to restore the number of Apostles to twelve, a number symbolic of the twelve tribes of Israel. Matthias was chosen. Like the other eleven, he was baptized by John and experienced Jesus' life and teaching. He shared the Apostles' mistaken expectation that the "power from on high" would be Jesus himself, returning majestically in a Second Coming, to launch the messianic kingdom. Somehow, everyone present knew that Israel's sacred history was coming to fulfillment.

The Day of Pentecost

On the day of Pentecost, "there came from the sky a noise like a strong driving wind, and it filled the entire house in which they were. Then there appeared to them tongues as of fire, which parted and came to rest on each one of them. And they were all filled with the holy Spirit and began to speak in different tongues, as the Spirit enabled them to proclaim" (Acts 2:2-4). So this was the power Jesus promised to send: power to praise God and to teach all nations; power to act in his Name; power to establish the community of the Church and make it grow! Transformed by the Spirit, they understood the promise of Jesus, "The Advocate, the Holy Spirit that the Father will send in my name—he will teach you everything, and remind you of all

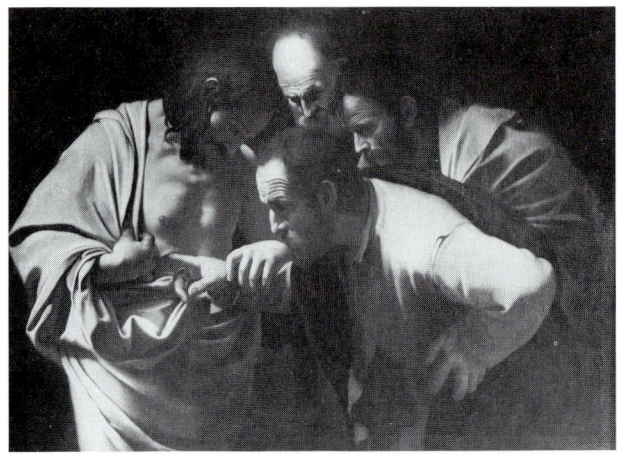

Caravaggio—"The Unbelief of St. Thomas"
The doubts of the Apostles disappeared completely after Pentecost.

The Church: A Spirit-Filled People

that [I] told you" (John 14:25-26). Empowered by the Spirit, the previously fearful Apostles rushed outdoors to preach about Jesus. Their ability to speak so that all understood symbolized the restoration of unity that was destroyed at the Tower of Babel (see Genesis 11).

Luke's account of Pentecost uses imagery and symbols from the Hebrew Scriptures, as well as what he used to announce Jesus' birth and the start of his exodus journey. The wind and fire of Pentecost recall the Mosaic covenant and reception of the Law in thunder, smoke, and flame. As Moses went up the mountain to receive the gift of the commandments for the people, Jesus had "gone up" and sent down the great Gift of the final age, the Holy Spirit. Seeing the sky as the dwelling place of God is ancient image and is used in the Hebrew Scriptures and in the New Testament.

12. *What does the term salvation history mean to you? Can you name some other events which play an important role in this special history?*

13. *How did the event of Pentecost affect the Apostles as individuals and as a group?*

The Images of Pentecost

Here are some of the images used by Luke to tell the Pentecost story, and what the images represent.

- **Noise**—God's might.

- **Strong, driving wind**—Spirit representing God's power.

- **Fire**—A many-tongued, burning (living?) light of consolation and understanding that rested on each individual. Though this was a community event, each disciple received the spirit individually.

- **Great enthusiasm**—The effect of God's touch could not be contained by human emotions. They were accused of acting as if they were drunk.

- **Bold proclamation**—Urgent sense of mission (see Acts 2:15).

Chapter 6   Rooted in Jesus, Formed by His Spirit

Catching the Spirit

As Christians we believe that God is Trinity. We are usually most familiar with Jesus, whose human character is evident from every page of the Gospels. But the Spirit is somewhat of a shadowy figure to most of us.

In the Hebrew Scriptures the Spirit of God appears in the very first pages of the Bible. In Genesis 1:1-31 and 2:1-25, God's Spirit moves over the waters bringing organized life out of the chaos that precedes creation. God breathes this Spirit into Adam.

In the New Testament, the Spirit becomes more personal as God's saving presence and action operating in Jesus, the apostolic community, and the Church. In the Gospels, the Spirit is active in Jesus (Mark 1:10-13). After Pentecost, all who are baptized receive the Spirit, and the Apostles are given special abilities by the Spirit in order to spread the Good News.

The Spirit is portrayed by various images and symbols in the New Testament, for example, as a counselor, a teacher, a bestower of gifts, and a force of new life. The Spirit is distinct from the Father and the Son, and acts as a guide for followers of Christ in all ages.

The Catholic faith teaches that the Holy Spirit is God, a distinct, eternal Person of the Trinity, of one substance with (and equal to) the Father and the Son. The Spirit will continue to provide us with guidance and knowledge as we continue our quest for faith and understanding.

Pentecost did not exactly "start" the Church. Just as your birthday does not commemorate your conception, but your visible appearance, Pentecost marks the moment when the outpouring of God's Spirit and power became an established reality for the disciples. On that day, all present, including Mary, experienced themselves as a Spirit-transformed people. Even though they were no longer alone in their mission to spread the news of the kingdom, the Apostles nevertheless needed time to assess the significance of all that Jesus had said and done, and to discover their role. They continued to pray and seek the Spirit's guidance. They searched the Scriptures and reflected on Jesus' ministry for direction. They continued to learn even as they went out to preach the Good News.

14. *Think about the word transform. What does this word mean to you? Has any person or event transformed your life?*

15. *What other experiences could you imagine in thinking about the images described above?*

Summary

- The Church evolved from what Jesus said, did, and was.
- The Apostles were chosen to complete the task of proclaiming the Good News of the kingdom.
- At Pentecost, the Apostles were transformed by the Spirit and empowered to praise God and teach all nations the Good News.
- At Pentecost, Jesus and the Father sent the Holy Spirit to guide the disciples of Christ in their mission.

SECTION 2
Checkpoint!

■ Review

1. What is the job of a founder?
2. What actions of Jesus established the foundation of the Church?
3. How did the Apostles react to the loss of Jesus?
4. What happened at Pentecost?
5. Why did Luke use images to describe the reception of the Spirit?
6. Words to Know: founder, Pentecost, salvation history.

■ In Your World

1. Using the images in Acts 2:1-18, 36-41, present the event of Pentecost either in drawings or music. Be prepared to explain the meaning of your drawings or pictures and the significance of each type of music.
2. Present a scene which reenacts the reaction of the Apostles on the day of the crucifixion. Read the passages in the Gospels and then use your own words to recreate the emotion felt by the disciples.

■ Scripture Search

1. Read John 14:16-17, 25-26; and 15:26-27. What functions of the Holy Spirit are described here? How does the Spirit act as a link between Jesus and his disciples in all ages everywhere?
2. Read the following passages: Luke 4:31-37; Luke 5:12-13; Mark 8:1-10; Matthew 17:14-20. What types of miracles does Jesus perform? How does the recipient respond to Jesus' actions? What do his actions reveal to you about his Person?

SECTION 3
Patterns in the Infant Church

If you have ever watched a younger brother or sister grow up, you know that babies already exhibit personality traits that will characterize them in later years. The infant community of the Church acted in ways that it would continue through the centuries. These patterns reveal that the Church was building on the foundation Jesus had laid in his life and teaching.

Core Characteristics

There are four characteristics—*kerygma, koinonia, diakonia, leitourgia*—which emerged early and expressed the personality of the Church. Today, when we take part in these actions, we are participating in the mission of the Church as it emerged in the time following Pentecost.

Kerygma—Proclamation

Like Jesus, the Apostles preached to people outside the immediate community of the disciples. Instead of centering on the coming of the kingdom, they spoke about salvation in Jesus, who had been crucified, raised from the dead, and exalted in heaven from where he sent his Spirit. Paul's letters proclaim this message very loudly, adapting this kerygmatic proclamation for the benefit of the Gentiles. *Kerygma,* from a Greek word meaning "proclamation," refers to the core action and message of the Gospel: the Good News of salvation through the Word of God. This

For Example

The *Didaché* (100) is the oldest known document of directions for catechetical instruction, worship, and ministry. It is titled "Teaching of the Twelve Apostles." A manuscript was found in 1873. The early Fathers of the Church refer to it in their writings.

teaching was the original form of what is now known as catechesis. The Christian message is fundamentally that (1) God loves with a universal and unconditional love, (2) God's love establishes new relationships (God is Father and people are brothers and sisters), (3) Jesus reveals this love and is the prototype of how our relationships should be lived, and (4) Jesus is Lord and Savior by His life, death, and resurrection. Upon this base the entire structure of Church teaching is built.

A People at Prayer

The Eucharist was the earliest form of Christian worship. This celebration of the Last Supper was the special event that linked all followers of Jesus to one another. In the early Church, this shared meal brought Christians to the table fellowship of Jesus. The Eucharist usually took place in a private home. Most followers of Jesus still attended worship at the Jewish Temple before assembling for the Lord's Supper.

The words which turned this communal meal into a holy celebration of Eucharist are called the words of institution: "Take it, this is my body... This is my blood of the covenant, which will be shed for many" (Mark 14:22, 24). The Christian worship service, which centers on the Eucharist, has its beginning in these words.

Koinonia—Community

As Jesus had done, the Apostles gathered together a community of faithful people. This group of human beings struggled to know and do God's will. Of "one ear and one mind," and centered in Jesus, the community shared all their possessions and worshiped in common (Acts 4:32).

The Church still witnesses through community. God saves us as a community of people who live, work, celebrate, and worship together, giving credibility to the *kerygma*.

Diakonia—Service

People carried their sick and those troubled with unclean spirits to the Apostles as they had brought them to Jesus. In the name of Jesus, they worked many wonders (Acts 5:15). Faith in Jesus was a matter of deeds, not merely of words. From them the community of disciples learned to minister to one another in Jesus' name.

Ministry means rooting out injustices and promoting the common welfare; clothing the naked and comforting the sick; challenging sinners and forgiving them as well. In the words of Pope Paul VI: "When the Gospel comes to a place, charity comes with it, bearing witness to the human validity of Christ's message and taking the form of schools, hospitals, social assistance, and technical training" (Pope Paul VI's World Day Message, 1970).

The Church: A Spirit-Filled People

Leitourgia—Worship

At first, the community prayed in the Temple as Jesus had done with his disciples. They also gathered in their own meetings, to celebrate the breaking of the bread as the form of worship bequeathed to them by Jesus at the Last Supper. *Leitourgia*—worship, the sacraments, and primarily the Eucharist—remains the core of the Christian community. In *leitourgia*, the *kerygma, koinonia,* and *diakonia* are united and find expression. There we offer everything we are, our life and service to the Lord. In turn, our celebration enriches us and send us into the world.

---

16. *How has your Church community reflected these four characteristics?*

Christ returning to judge the world is an apocalyptic figure taken from the Book of Revelation. The second coming is part of the Church's Koinonia.

Chapter 6   Rooted in Jesus, Formed by His Spirit

Additional Characteristics

In addition to the four key characteristics of *kerygma, koinonia, diakonia,* and *leitourgia,* other important characteristics were apparent in the early Church.

- **Authority**— *Like Jesus, the community looked to heaven for their authority and guidance. The teaching of the Apostles was held in special regard because they had personally witnessed Jesus from the beginning of his public life. They took Jesus' message into the entire community. There were heated meetings between the Apostles and the other elders— sometimes very heated meetings. Peter emerged at the center of the community and was instrumental in making the final decisions. Sometimes the Holy Spirit intervened dramatically to point a new direction. At other times, they had to rely on their own Spirit-guided judgments to interpret Jesus' life and teachings. Authority was always exercised as service to the Church (see Acts 10:44-48; 11:15; 15:4-12, 18-21).*

- **Sense of Mission**—*Compelled to spread the Good News, the Apostles shared the gift of the Spirit with all sincere seekers through Baptism and the laying on of hands. At first, all converts were Jews. After the martyrdom of Stephen in 42 and of James, bishop of Jerusalem, in 62, the Church recognized the universality of Jesus' mission and began to spread out beyond the borders of Jerusalem.*

- **Tradition**—*The questions, doubts, and objections of converts forced the early Church to think through its faith. The community recalled what Jesus had said or done, and used his sayings, parables, or stories as authority for their teaching and decisions. As different problems arose in communities outside Jerusalem, they called upon Jesus' teachings to provide practical solutions. The heritage of Jesus, shaped by the first generation of the Church community, was later captured in the New Testament, especially in the Gospels. Other early teaching and preaching, liturgical prayers and practices, and Church decisions on faith and morals found their way into writing and were transmitted through the centuries.*

    Tradition refers to the body of revealed truth handed down from the Apostles through the ages. It is contained in the doctrine, teaching, and practice of the Catholic Church. It occurs in both written and oral forms and in its widest sense includes the Scriptures.

Early writer-theologians are called "Fathers of the Church."

- **Goods Held in Common**—*By holding their property and goods in common, early Christians formed a community of love and made sure that no one was ever in need (Acts 4:32-35).*

- **Expectation of the Second Coming**—*Although the kingdom had arrived, the early Christians expected Jesus to come again at "the time of universal restoration" as Peter said in his sermon. They were filled with hope. This waiting for Jesus to return is known as an eschatological hope.*

- **A Share in the Paschal Mystery**—*The Apostles were full of joy when they were judged worthy of ill treatment for the sake of "the Name." "The Name" was used to refer to Jesus, whose name was accorded the respect due to divinity (see John 1:7). This initial period of the Church has been studied often in order to probe its meaning for future generations of the Church.*

---

17. Which of the characteristics listed above can be applied to the Church today? Which do see working in your own parish?

18. Of the five models of Church—institution, community, sacrament, herald, and servant—which apply to the Church as described above? Explain your answer.

Necessity of Church Membership

Is membership in the Church necessary for salvation? The Catholic Church teaches that Jesus founded the Church as part of God's plan for the salvation of the human race and that, for those acquainted with that plan, it is necessary to belong to it. The *"Dogmatic Constitution on the Church,"* #14 says, "They could not be saved who,

Eschatology: the part of theology that deals with the final things, especially the Second Coming of Christ.

Poverty and Wealth

The early community of the faithful found itself facing many important and pressing questions. Besides proclaiming the Good News, the Apostles had other jobs that needed to be done in order to support the small, but growing, community. One of the questions had to do with the use of money. Followers of Jesus came from all walks of life. Many poor slaves and servants, widows and orphans, and also wealthy landowners were baptized and became part of the Body of Christ. Some asked how wealth was to be used. Should the wealthy give away all their money?

Clement of Alexandria, a Church Father from what is now Egypt, was one of the first Christians to write about the responsibility of those with money. He stated that rich and poor exist together and can benefit from one another. Clement said that the rich can certainly retain their money as long as they stay detached from it and always are willing to share it with the poor. He warned of the temptations that money brings.

Almsgiving (charity) was a responsibility of all who had more than they needed. Money was collected especially for widows, orphans, and those imprisoned. Almsgiving, along with fasting and prayer, was regarded as penance for sin.

♦

knowing that the Catholic Church was founded as necessary by God through Christ, would refuse to enter it or to remain in it." Yet those of good will who are unaware of God's plan or who have not recognized its truth may likewise find salvation. The faith of Christians is a blessing that brings with it greater responsibility.

19. *How do you think the view expressed above demonstrates the presence of God everywhere?*

The Church as Guardian of Revelation

The U.S. Constitution was established in 1789. Yet we need the Supreme Court to interpret its meaning for each generation, while also working to retain the original intentions of those who wrote the document. In the same way, even though public revelation closed with the death of the last Apostle (John, late first century), Christ's community needs authentic, ongoing interpretation of his teachings. Responsibility for this interpretation rests with the bishops

Ravenna—"St. Matthew the Evangelist"—VI century
Early Church art tried to capture how the evangelists were inspired by God. Here an angel is seen with the evangelist Matthew.

Chapter 6   Rooted in Jesus, Formed by His Spirit

and the pope, the official teachers of the Church—the magesterium ("*Dogmatic Constitution on Divine Revelation,*" #10). The Church, recognizing the indwelling of the Spirit within its members, credits them with having the spiritual balance needed to interpret Scripture and Church teaching, and often relies on its people for new insights. Only seven passages of Scripture have been officially interpreted in 2,000 years!

20. *What would you say to someone who tried to convince you that either the Constitution or Scripture is a document tied to the past which has no meaning for the present?*

Summary

- There are four core characteristics of the early Church: proclamation, community, service, and worship.

- Each characteristic is still evident today in the life of the Church.

- Other characteristics include authority, mission, tradition, holding goods in common, expectation of the end, and sharing in the paschal mystery.

- For those who know of God's plan, membership in the Church is necessary.

- The Church is a guardian and interpreter of revelation for all time.

SECTION 3
Checkpoint!

■ Review

1. What is the ancient and modern significance of each of the four core characteristics of the Church?

2. What is the content of the Christian message today?

3. Explain the meaning of the word *"kerygma."*

4. Describe two characteristics of the early Christian community.

5. What does the Catholic Church teach about the possibility of salvation for those who have never heard its teachings?

6. How can the Church continue to make revelation understandable and important?

7. Words to Know: *kerygma, koinonia, diakonia, leitourgia,* tradition, eschatology, magesterium.

■ In Your World

1. Participate in an exercise of interpretation. Have your teacher help you find the record of a recent Supreme Court decision. Read some of the decision and determine how the justices try to apply the essence of the Constitution to a new situation. Then, do the same for a passage in Scripture. For example, read Genesis 22:1-19. Take the events described and try to apply them to a modern situation which might be similar. What lessons are learned from the passage? How can it be made relevant for today?

2. Choose visible, material images for some or all of the characteristics of the Church described in this section of the chapter. Explain your choices.

■ Scripture Search

1. The book of Acts provides us with the earliest history of the Church community. Read Acts 1-6 and mark out those sections which illustrate the characteristics of the early Church.

2. Read the following passages: Matthew 24:1-36; Mark 13:3-37; Luke 21:5-28; Daniel 11:1-13, 12:1-4. What images are used to describe the events at the end time? How do you think the Apostles reacted upon hearing this? What can these passages teach us?

Chapter 6   Rooted in Jesus, Formed by His Spirit

CHAPTER 6 Review

■ Study

1. What is meant by the statement, "the Catholic Church like a family"?
2. Of what benefit is knowledge of the past for you individually and as a member of the Church?
3. Why might people ask if Jesus really founded the Catholic Church?
4. What are two reasons people might give for rejecting the necessity of membership in the Church?
5. In what sense is it correct to say that Jesus founded the Church?
6. Why do Jesus' actions have universal value?
7. When did the work of organizing the Church begin, and by whom?
8. What has always been the function of the Spirit in the continual formation of the Christian community?
9. What were some of the experiences of the Apostles at Pentecost?
10. Explain Luke's use of images to describe the Pentecost event.
11. How do the four core characteristics of the Church act to assure continuity between the ancient Church and the modern Church?
12. What is tradition?
13. For whom is Church membership necessary for salvation?
14. How do all members of the Church participate in the ongoing interpretation of revelation?

▪ Action

1. Plant a seed and let it grow in your classroom. Make sure everyone has some responsibility for the care of the seed. Keep a careful and detailed record of the growth of the seed. How does its growth parallel the growth and development of the Church? Refer to Matthew 13:24-30 and Mark 4:6-29.

2. Conduct live interviews with followers of Jesus for an ancient news program. Interview several followers of Christ over a period of time from the day after the crucifixion to the period after Pentecost. Be sure to ask questions about the reactions of that individual, the organization of community, and its future.

▪ Prayer

The Holy Spirit was sent to us as the gift of God's abiding presence that offers us comfort, guidance, and knowledge. Yet, we seem to know and say very little about the Third Person of the Trinity.

The Holy Spirit touches each of us in a personal way. Through prayer, we can become more aware of the working of the Spirit in and through us. We often direct our prayer to God. But recognizing the strength of the Spirit within us can help us in our communication with God and in our mission to the world as followers of Christ.

As you begin your time of private prayer or contemplation each day, add a prayer to the Spirit. Ask for the Spirit's help in determining God's will for you. Here is an example of a prayer, or compose one especially for yourself:

Holy Spirit, fill my heart with your love. Renew my love for God and humanity daily. Help me to be wise and to come to know God's will for me. Bring to mind the teachings of Jesus and give me the strength to continue learning and growing in faith. Amen.

CHAPTER

7

Independence in the Spirit: The First Century

OBJECTIVES

In this Chapter you will

- Learn about the early history of the Church as it is related in the Acts of the Apostles.

- Examine the martyrdom of Stephen and its effects on the Jerusalem Church.

- Discover the meaning of Saul's conversion for the conversion of the Gentiles.

- Read about the first Church Council and Peter's role in leading it.

- Follow the emergence of Rome and the written Scriptures as the first century comes to a close.

The Church, endowed with the gifts of her founder and faithfully observing his precepts of charity, humility, and self-denial, receives the mission of proclaiming and establishing among all people the kingdom of Christ and God.
— "Dogmatic Constitution on the Church," #5

The Church: A Spirit-Filled People

SECTION 1
The Church After Pentecost

Because you are a part of the Church, its story is your story. And because Christianity is a religion that dates back to Jesus, its growth and development can be traced back to him. But how can we discover what happened to the Church in the important years after Pentecost?

If you were writing the history of your town, you would look for primary sources of evidence: land deeds, old letters, newspapers, birth records, photographs, and legal documents. Anyone trying to write the history of early Christianity, however, discovers that time, wars, persecutions, natural disasters, and Roman imperial policy of destroying Christian books have destroyed most of the historical records that the first-century Christians may have left. The best information we have comes from Luke's Acts of the Apostles.

Acts of the Apostles

Acts is a stylized account of events in the primitive Church, from the ascension of Jesus (c. 30) to Paul's imprisonment in Rome (c. 62). It was written more than a generation after the events referred to actually happened. Chapters 1-12 detail the ministry of Peter. Chapters 13-14 and 16-28 follow Paul on his great missionary journeys. In Chapter 15, Luke places the momentous event that determined the future history of the infant Church—the Council of Jerusalem. To stylize means to make something conform to a design rather than flow in a natural pattern. The design of Acts is not a strict history. It is a theological essay that shows the early Church's internal and external development, especially in its mission to the Gentiles.

c. 30: c. before a number means *circa,* or "around that time." Used when historians are not exactly sure of the date of an event.

Chapter 7   Independence in the Spirit: The First Century

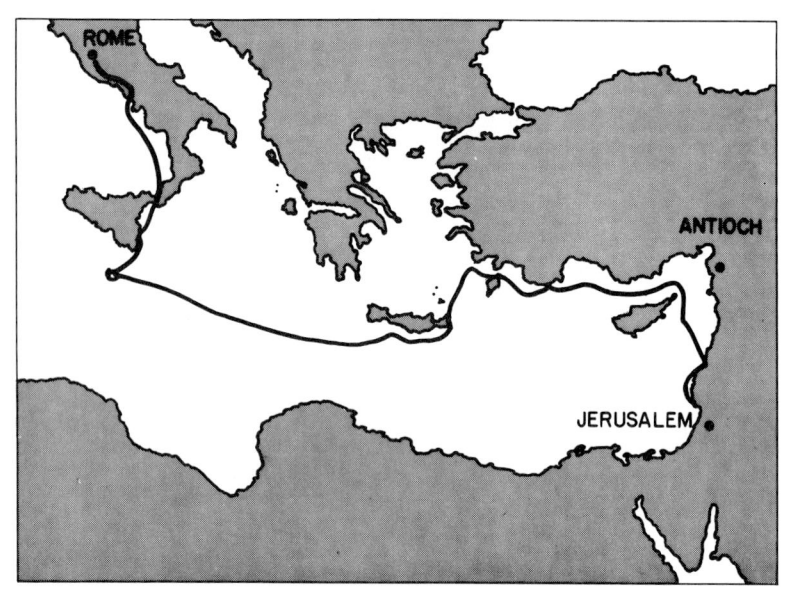

As he proclaimed the Good News, Saint Paul made four journeys. This map traces Paul's final journey to Rome.

The Church that emerges in Acts is essentially the same as the Church today—a people faithful to the teaching of the Apostles and to prayer and breaking bread together, while being mindful of others' needs in their daily lives (Acts 1-8, 15:28). But Acts provides only a sampling of events. It is not a textbook, but an account of the evolving relationship between God and God's people. Acts tells part of the salvation history of Christianity. It demonstrates how Peter and the community dealt with problems. It describes the persecution of the young Church. There is a sense of pioneer excitement as the Apostles create new ministries and as wonders and signs confirm their preaching.

Acts helps to clarify the relationship of Christianity to Judaism and to the Gentile (non-Jewish) world. Peter and Paul were the dominant figures of the early Church. Jerusalem, Antioch, and Rome were the primary churches. Woven throughout all these events and developments is the powerful influence of the Holy Spirit.

This chapter will explore the six major events of first century Christianity: (1) the martyrdom of Stephen (c. 36); (2) the conversion of Saul (c. 37) and his missionary role; (3) the Council of Jerusalem (49); (4) Peter's role and his martyrdom in Rome (c. 67); (5) the destruction of Jerusalem (70); and (6) the writing of the Gospels.

The Church: A Spirit-Filled People

1. *If you were to write your own autobiography, what primary sources would you consult?*

2. *How is the study of the history of the Church unlike the study of other periods in history, like the Civil War, or of other institutions, like the Roman Empire?*

Events in Jerusalem Before Stephen's Death

Immediately following Pentecost, the followers of Jesus considered themselves members of the Jewish community in Jerusalem. Peter's role of spokesman for the Twelve, as well as his habit of taking charge, continued as he guided the community in its choice of Matthias to replace Judas. Luke tells us "the community of believers was of one heart and one mind . . . With great power the Apostles bore witness to the resurrection of the Lord Jesus . . . There was no needy person among them" (Acts 4:32-34).

The Spirit did not isolate the young community from problems. The first indications of trouble came the day crowds gathered following Peter's miraculous cure of a lame man at the Beautiful Gate of the Temple (Acts 3:1-10).

Scale model of the Jerusalem Temple. The original Temple was destroyed by the Romans in 70 AD.

Chapter 7 Independence in the Spirit: The First Century

Peter used the occasion to preach salvation through the crucified and risen Jesus, and invited his fellow Jews to believe and repent. The Sadducees, some of whom were members of the Jewish court called the Sanhedrin, had the Temple guard arrest Peter and John. Peter used this arraignment before the leaders, elders, and scribes as another opportunity to preach salvation in Jesus' name alone (Acts 4:5-12). Later, a second imprisonment of all the Apostles resulted in a miraculous deliverance and another testimony by Peter. This time, the Sanhedrin's official decision was prompted by a prophetic statement of Gamaliel, the revered teacher of Paul, "if this endeavor or this activity is of human origin, it will destroy itself. But if it comes from God, you will not be able to destroy them . . ." His reasoning won the day, and the Apostles were released (Acts 5:34-39).

3. What do you think about Gamaliel's statement? Can it be applied to other groups today?

4. Why do you think there was tension between the Jewish officials and the Christian leaders?

Peter's curing of the lame man led to trouble with the Sadducees. Peter and John were arrested.

The Church: A Spirit-Filled People

Simon the Magician

Acts 8 tells the story of Philip's experiences in Samaria, an area north of Jerusalem. Philip went to Samaria to avoid the persecution in Jerusalem, and preached the word of Christ while he was there. Acts tells us that he was successful in his mission. He healed many sick people, and many became followers of Jesus.

This chapter also tells the strange story of a man called Simon who had practiced magic in Samaria. He was followed by many people because of his powers. But the proclamation of the Good News by Philip was even stronger. Simon himself was baptized but later offered the Apostles money in order to buy the power they had. The Apostles expressed their anger with him and he repented.

You may be asking yourself about this magician. What kind of magic did he practice? Is there even such a thing as magic? Simon is an interesting character. The information in Acts doesn't tell us much about what Simon was doing, but it does tell us that he had a lot of influence over the people. But, apparently, even more people recognized that Philip's power was greater. Simon saw that, too. We also see from this story that it is impossible to buy the power of the Holy Spirit. It is a free gift from God.

Simon wasn't alone in calling himself a magician. At this time, many people claimed to have the ability to heal or perform other miracles. Perhaps they were more familiar with methods of curing illness than the common people. Their apparent power made them respected and feared wherever they went, that is, until the Good News was revealed as the real source of all power. The Holy Spirit was bestowed on those who heard it and believed.

Simon the Magician was looking for worldly power from the Apostles. Why was he disappointed?

Chapter 7　Independence in the Spirit: The First Century

On This Rock

Baptism and the Eucharist were the primary sacraments of the early Church. As early as 100, the *Didaché* offered regulations for baptisms. Here is part of what it says: "The procedure for baptizing is as follows. After rehearsing all the preliminaries, immerse in running water, 'In the Name of the Father, and of the Son, and of the Holy Spirit.' If no running water is available, immerse in ordinary water. If neither is practicable, then sprinkle water three times on the head, 'In the name of the Father, and of the Son, and of the Holy Spirit.' Both baptizer and baptized ought to fast before the baptism, as well as any others who can do so; but the candidate himself should be told to fast for a day or two beforehand." The instructions take into account a number of possible situations. Fasting was seen as a form of purification for everyone involved in the sacramental rite. Running water was important because it was seen as a symbol for the "living water" Christ promised the woman at the well in John 4:4-42.

The Witness of Stephen

Stephen, Christianity's first martyr, died in Jerusalem at the hands of his fellow Jews c. 36. Acts identifies Stephen as one of the seven Hellenist deacons appointed to help the Apostles in caring for the Greek widows. His preaching and wonder-working put him in the spotlight. Some of the Jews, unable to win in open debate with Stephen, accused him of blaspheme before the Sanhedrin. Dragged before the Jewish leaders, Stephen fearlessly delivered an apology for the Christian Faith. He pointed out Christianity's obedience to the Holy Spirit, its continuity with Judaism, but also its independence from it. Enraged at this new teaching, which seemed to bypass the tradition of Judaism, the Sanhedrin condemned Stephen and ordered him stoned to death (Acts 6, 7). It was a crucial time in the life of the infant Church.

Jewish persecution of the people who believed in Jesus followed Stephen's death. A large part of the Christian community fled to Samaria, Syria, and Cyprus. This dispersion caused the Christian movement to expand from Jerusalem to Antioch, the Roman Empire's third largest city. The new faith was opened to Samaritans and Gentiles.

St. Stephen's Gate, in Jerusalem, is the traditional sight where Stephen, the first martyr, was stoned to death in 36 AD.

The Church: A Spirit-Filled People

As believers spread throughout society, they became witnesses of the Good News. There were so many miracles performed in Samaria that a certain magician, Simon Magus, tried to purchase this mysterious power. Philip and Peter's condemnation of Simon (Acts 8:9-24) once and for all disassociated Christianity from the many magic cults prominent throughout the Empire.

By surrounding the account of Philip's baptism of the Ethiopian court official with several supernatural elements (Acts 8:26-40), Luke shows that Christianity was meant to break out of Jerusalem. Two event show this most clearly: The baptism of the pagan centurion Cornelius and the conversion of Saul.

5. Why do you think people are intolerant and suspicious of things that are new or unfamiliar? How have you experienced this type of behavior?

6. Read the account of Stephen's death in Acts 7:54-60. What parallels do you find with Jesus' death?

7. What would Simon Magus' failure to buy the power of the Spirit have revealed to the Samaritans about Christianity?

Summary

- Acts of the Apostles is a stylized account of early Christian history.

- The early Christians remained members of the Jewish community amidst growing tensions.

- Stephen was the first Christian martyr, killed for preaching Jesus' resurrection.

- After Stephen's death, many Jewish-Christians fled to other cities.

- Miracles in Samaria and conversions of Gentiles showed that God's salvation was offered to all people everywhere.

Hellenists: Greek-speaking Jews dispersed throughout the Roman Empire.

Apology: a spoken or written defense of some idea, religion, or philosophy.

Chapter 7 Independence in the Spirit: The First Century

SECTION 1
Checkpoint!

■ Review

1. What is a stylized history?
2. What period of time does the book of Acts cover?
3. Why were Peter and John arrested?
4. How did Stephen defend Christian Faith from his accusers?
5. What were some of the effects of Stephen's martyrdom?
6. Who was Simon Magus and what did he try to do?
7. What important changes were initiated by the baptism of the Ethiopian official?
8. Words to Know: stylize, circa, Antioch, Sanhedrin, Simon Magus, Samaria.

■ In Your World

1. Dramatize the conversion of Saint Paul as it is recorded in Acts 9:1-19, 22:3-16, and 26:4-18. What emotions do you think Paul and his companions feel? How did they react to the situation? How did he?
2. Talk to a Jewish friend about the beliefs and practices of Judaism. Ask the rabbi of a nearby temple if it is possible to attend a service. Note the similarities and differences between a Jewish and a Christian worship service.
3. Read the account of Stephen's martyrdom in Acts 7:54-60. Present a pictorial or musical account of this event.

■ Scripture Search

1. Read Acts 10. How does God show Peter that salvation is meant for Gentiles as well as Jews? Where does the account take place and who is involved?
2. Trace one of Paul's journeys: (1) Acts 13:4-14:28; (2) Acts 16:1-18:22; or (3) Acts 18:23, 21:16. Where did he travel? What do you know about his activities from the account? What reception did he get? How was he changed?

SECTION 2
The Missions of Paul and Peter

The lives of Paul and Peter changed the shape of the Church dramatically. The mission of Paul to the Gentiles, and his ability to mediate disputes, contributed to the spread of Christianity far beyond Jerusalem. Peter and Paul's leadership guided the Christian community through its first crisis.

Saul's Vocation and Mission

Apart from Pentecost itself, Saint Paul's conversion is probably the most significant event in the entire Book of Acts. It is narrated three different times. The role of the Holy Spirit is evident. Saul—Saint Paul's name prior to his conversion—was still breathing the fire of persecution against those who followed "the new Way," when God said to Ananias, "Go, for this man is a chosen instrument of mine to carry my name before Gentiles, kings and Israelites" (Acts 9:15).

For a long time after his baptism and even after preaching about Jesus in Damascus, suspicion lay heavy on Paul. To many he appeared to be a traitor. There were followers of Jesus who remembered his zealous efforts to drag them off to prison. The Jews who had not yet been converted to "the Way" found his emphasis on freedom from the laws of the Mosaic covenant not only foreign, but also a threat to their religious traditions and culture. Barnabas saved the situation. He eased Paul's transition from persecutor to preacher of the Good News by accepting and sponsoring him in Jerusalem and by inviting Paul to work with him in Antioch.

There the followers of Jesus first came to be called Christians (Acts 11:26). It was also at Antioch that Greek converts to Christianity produced the first mixed Christian communities of Jews and Gentiles as "a great number who believed turned to the Lord" (Acts 11:21).

Paul labored there for a year and a half. Then, with Barnabas, he undertook a relief mission to the Christian community at Jerusalem. Upon their return, both men were commissioned for a missionary journey. Luke makes it clear that the mission was the work of the Spirit. "While they were worshiping the Lord and fasting, the Holy Spirit spoke to them: 'Set apart for me Barnabas and Saul for the work to which I have called them' " (Acts 13:2). The two traveled first to Cyprus, then north to Asia Minor, where they preached at Antioch in Pisidia, Iconium, Lystra, Derbe, and the surrounding towns. Everywhere they "appointed presbyters for them in each church and, with prayer and fasting, commended them to the Lord in whom they had put their faith" (Acts 14:23). They continually gave thanks to God for having "opened the door of faith to the Gentiles" (Acts 14:27).

Paul's first missionary journey was already completed when the question of the Gentiles and their relationship to Judaism came to be settled. So strong were the emotions of all involved that only a meeting at Jerusalem was capable of restoring order. This one meeting, known as the Council of Jerusalem, decided the course of Christianity. Here again, the Spirit was at work.

8. *What do you think is significant about Saul's changing his name after his conversion? What does it mean?*

Paul of Tarsus—An Autobiography

Through Paul's preaching and letters, we can understand this fiery and zealous Apostle of Jesus better. He traveled far and wide and was both hated and loved. Here is what he has to say:

- **About himself**— "I am a Jew, born in Tarsus . . . I was educated strictly in our ancestral law . . . I persecuted this Way to death" (Acts 22:3-4).

- **About his mission**— "I had been entrusted with the gospel to the uncircumcised, just as Peter was to the circumcised" (Galatians 2:7). "(I) will most gladly spend and be utterly spent for your sakes" (2 Corinthians 12:15).

- **His teachings**— "Christ died for our sins in accordance with the Scriptures" (1 Corinthians 15:3-4). "For through faith you are all children of God in Christ Jesus. There is neither Jew nor Greek, there is neither slave or free, there is not male or female; for you are all one in Christ Jesus" (Galatians 3:26-28).

- **Christian conduct**— "Live in a manner worthy of the call you have received . . . Be kind to one another" (Ephesians 4:1, 31-32).

- **His death**— "Just one thing: forgetting what lies behind but straining forward to what lies ahead, I continue my pursuit toward the goal, the prize of God's upward calling, in Christ Jesus" (Philippians 3:13-14).

Presbyters: people who presided at the Eucharist, preached, taught, led prayer, and anointed the sick.

The Council of Jerusalem

The first serious indication of a break between Christianity and the Jewish community, a break already hinted at in Stephen's final sermon, involved the issue of whether Gentile converts should be required to observe Mosaic Law. The Jewish-Christians in Jerusalem were circumcised Jews. They believed in Jesus who himself had accepted circumcision and the Law. For them it seemed obvious that non-Jews who accepted salvation through Jesus must likewise be circumcised and observe the Law of Moses. Yet at Antioch, Paul and Barnabas were openly preaching that Gentile followers of Christ were not bound by the Law. When Judeans came to Antioch and told the Greeks, "Unless you are circumcised according to the Mosaic practice, you cannot be saved" (Acts 15:1), the Greeks became very angry. Paul, Barnabas, and some others decided to "go up to Jerusalem to the Apostles and presbyters about this question" (Acts 15:2).

In Jerusalem, the Apostles, the presbyters, and the group from Antioch arranged a meeting. After much discussion, Peter, whose experience with Cornelius had prepared him for this moment, spoke up. "My brothers, you are well aware that from early days God made his choice among you that through my mouth the Gentiles would hear the word of the Gospel and believe. And God, who knows the heart, bore witness by granting them the Holy Spirit just as he did us . . . we believe that we are saved through the grace of the Lord Jesus, in the same way as they" (Acts 15:7-11). James, as leader of the Jerusalem community, proposed sending a letter to the Gentile communities to explain their freedom from the Law and to ask only some minimum observances in order to avoid scandal to Jewish believers (Acts 15:3-30). The break with Judaism occurred because of the Council's decision to define Christianity in terms of union with Christ, independent of the practice of the Jewish law.

In Galatians 2, Paul has this to say about the Council of Jerusalem: "Then after fourteen years I again went up to Jerusalem . . . I went up in accord with a revelation, and I presented to them the gospel that I preach to the Gentiles . . . to them we did not submit even for a moment, so that the truth of the gospel might remain intact for you. But from

The Church: A Spirit-Filled People

those who were reputed to be important . . . those of repute made me add nothing. On the contrary, when they saw that I had been entrusted with the gospel to the uncircumcised . . . James and Kephas (Peter) and John . . . gave me and Barnabas their right hands in partnership . . . And when Kephas came to Antioch, I opposed him to his face because he clearly was wrong" (Galatians 2:1-11). As you can see, this was an issue that was of great importance to the early Church.

Paul and Barnabas at Lystra—Cartoon of Raffaelle
Paul and Barnabas, the Apostles to the Gentiles, proclaimed the Good News throughout the Middle East.

Consequences of the Council

In spite of the Council's decision at Jerusalem, Paul continued to suffer at the hands of the strict Jewish Christians, who were sometimes called Judaizers. At Philippi he was flogged and imprisoned. At Thessalonica he was the cause of demonstrations and violence. Finally in Corinth, insulted and opposed, Paul stopped trying to convert the Jews. "Your blood be on your heads! I am clear of responsibility. From now on I will go to the Gentiles" (Acts 18:6). And so the dissociation from Judaism, begun at the Council of Jerusalem, was carried forward by Paul. Not that he thought God had abandoned the Jews in favor of

Mosaic Law: contained in the biblical books of Exodus, Leviticus, Numbers, and Deuteronomy.

Judaizers: Jewish-Christians who continued to observe Jewish law and required other members of their communities to do the same.

Chapter 7   Independence in the Spirit: The First Century

the Gentiles. Clearly he had not. Nor had his love for his fellow Israelites diminished. Quite the contrary. Writing to the Romans, he says, "I could even wish that I myself were accurse and separated from Christ for the sake of my brothers, my kin according to the flesh. They are Israelites; theirs the adoption, the glory, the covenants, the giving of the law, and the promises; theirs the patriarchs, and from them, according to the flesh, is the Messiah" (Romans 9:3-5). "I ask then, has God rejected his people? Of course not! . . . Now I am speaking to you Gentiles: . . . If the first fruits are holy, so is the whole batch of dough; and if the root is holy, so are the branches. But if some of the branches were broken off and you, a wild olive shoot, were grafted in their place and have come to share in the rich root of the olive tree, do not boast against the branches . . . you do not support the root; the root supports you" (Romans 11:1,13, 16-18). Paul explained the mystery to the Gentiles in this way: "a hardening has come upon Israel in part, until the full number of Gentiles comes in, and then all of Israel will be saved . . . For the gifts and the call of God are irrevocable" (Romans 11:25, 29).

The Church's Loss of Privileges

The Romans believed in the existence of many gods, and also worshipped the emperor as divine. They allowed the Jews to continue to worship Yahweh. As long as Rome saw Christianity as a sect within Judaism, it enjoyed the same freedom of worship granted to Judaism. But when Jewish communities split over the identity of Jesus and the Gentile observance of the Law, the followers of "the Way" — "the saints," "the elect," or the "Church of God" as they were sometimes called—were driven from the synagogues.

To accept Jesus as God's Son seemed to undermine the whole foundation of Judaism's belief in God's oneness. These conflicts were interpreted by Roman authorities as in-house squabbles among the Jews. In at least one instance in Rome in A.D. 49, riots caused the police to expel all Jews from the city whether they accepted Jesus or not. When the break between Christians and Jews became evident, Christians lost their exemption from participating in Roman worship. Persecution was inevitable.

Saint Paul suffered for his faith, spending much time in prison. Much of his legacy, the Epistles, were written while he was in prison.

Until its destruction in 70, Jerusalem served as the main church of Christianity. Paul acknowledged its special role by reporting to that community after each of his missionary journeys. From there, too, the decisions of the Council of Jerusalem were carried to all the other churches for observance. As long as the Apostle James, son of Alpheus, was the leader of this community, he managed to keep a relative peace between converts from Judaism and Jewish authorities, as well as between the more conservative, Hebrew-speaking and the more liberal, Greek-speaking groups of Jews. His martyrdom under King Herod Agrippa in 62 opened the door to unbridled dissension.

9. How would you have settled the dispute between the two sides?

10. How were both Christianity and Judaism changed by the decision of the Council of Jerusalem?

11. Were you aware of the roots of your Catholic faith in Judaism? Do you think most Christians are? How is that knowledge valuable?

12. Why would participating in Roman worship be impossible for either a Jew or a Christian?

Irrevocable: not capable of being changed.

Chapter 7 Independence in the Spirit: The First Century

Communion of Saints

You may have already noticed that martyrdom, or witnessing for Christ, became the fate of many of the faithful. The history of the early Church is filled with heroic accounts of the painful deaths of those who refused to renounce their faith. One such martyr was Saint Polycarp of Smyrna, who died c. 155.

Smyrna was an ancient city, now known as Izmir, Turkey. Saint Polycarp was the bishop of Smyrna. He had known Saint John the Evangelist. During a period of persecution, he was turned over to the authorities. They tried to persuade him to give up his faith, but he refused.

Polycarp remained firm in his faith, and he was condemned to die at the stake. But when the fire was set, it formed an arc above his head and left him unharmed. The crowd of spectators then attacked him and stabbed him to death. The written account of Saint Polycarp's martyrdom is one of the earliest texts we have which describes this challenge faced by the Church.

The Spirit Acts in Peter

Although the ministry of Paul was of crucial significance in shaping the first-century community, leadership of the Church clearly fell to Peter (John 18:17,25,27). Humbled by his threefold denial of Jesus, strengthened by Jesus' commission to feed his sheep (John 21:17), and empowered by the Holy Spirit, the man who emerged from the Pentecost experience had been reborn. Acts portrays him as no longer hesitant or doubting, but fearless in directing the destiny of the infant Church in Jerusalem. It was Peter who preached the first sermon, converting more than three thousand. It was Peter who worked the first miracle—the cure of the lame man at the Beautiful Gate of the Temple—and then acted as apostolic defense attorney before the Sanhedrin. It was Peter also who judged and condemned Ananias and Sapphira for their deceit in holding back part of their property. He converted thousands to belief in Jesus (Acts 2-4).

Saint Peter, considered the first pope, took the message of Jesus Christ to Rome, where he was put to death for his beliefs.

The Church: A Spirit-Filled People

He cured those sick or troubled with unclean spirits. He ordained new ministers and calls down the Holy Spirit on the Samaritans. In Caesaria, it was Peter who baptized the first Gentile convert, Cornelius, together with his entire household, and handled the opposition his actions stirred up in Jerusalem (Acts 5-8). Later, in Antioch and throughout Judea, Peter was there teaching, working miracles, and confronting people (Acts 10). At times he suffered imprisonment (Acts 9:32-43); at other times he received heavenly visions or won miraculous escapes (Acts 12).

13. How are the activities of Peter still being carried out, and how can you be involved in them?

14. What kind of person do you think Peter was to have been able to accomplish all that he did?

Summary

- Saul's conversion led to a change of name and a new mission to the Gentiles.
- Paul undertook many journeys.
- The Council of Jerusalem tried to resolve the dispute over observance of Mosaic Law and Gentile converts.
- Gentiles were not required to observe the Law and a split between Jews and Christians resulted.
- After the split, there was persecution by both Romans and some Jews.
- Peter acted as leader, preacher, healer, and baptizer.

SECTION 2
Checkpoint!

■ Review

1. What was the special mission of Paul?
2. What important events occured in Antioch?
3. Name some of the places Paul and Barnabas visited on their missionary journies.
4. Explain the conflict which led to the Council of Jerusalem.
5. Which side was victorious at the Council, and what were the consequences of its decision?
6. Why did Christians lose their privileges with the Roman government?
7. How did Peter demonstrate his leadership abilities?
8. Words to Know: Saul/Paul, Mosaic covenant, Council of Jerusalem, Judaizer.

■ In Your World

1. After reading Acts 15, reenact the Council of Jerusalem. Choose a team to represent those who accepted circumcision for all converts, and a team to represent Paul's side. What arguments does each side use? Which side is more convincing?
2. Choose one event from the ministry of Peter and present an artistic interpretation. Read through the passages noted in the text and choose the event which you think best illustrates Peter's contributions to the Church.

■ Scripture Search

1. Read Exodus 22:1-15, 21-27 and Leviticus 19:11-18. These are just two sections from the many chapters which comprise the Mosaic Law. What problems and situations do these passages address? What do they tell you about life for the ancient Israelites?

2. Read the following passages: Acts 3:1-11, 12:1-19. What events do they recount? Where is the action of the Holy Spirit evident? Can you think of a modern day parallel?

The Church: A Spirit-Filled People

SECTION 3
Ends and Beginnings

Peter's decision to leave Antioch in order to work among the Jewish communities at Rome had long-range effects. It made Rome the only Church in the West of the Empire with apostolic roots. Mark's Gospel is thought to have been written in Rome (Mark is considered to be a follower of Peter.) Both Peter and Paul were martyred in Rome. At this time Jerusalem was destroyed by the Romans. The destruction of the city forced Christianity into a new direction which led to many important developments, especially how the words of Jesus were to be transmitted to all Christians.

Shifting Westward

Although Antioch remained the hub of Eastern missionary activity, the name of Peter, his successors in Rome, the growing numbers of Gentile Christians, and the importance of Rome itself caused a Westward shift in thinking for the fast growing religion.

The Destruction of Jerusalem

The Church had not yet recovered from the loss of its two giants, Peter and Paul, when another event shook its foundations and changed the relationship between Christianity and Judaism forever. That event was the Jewish revolt during the years 66–70.

Most of the Jewish and Gentile Christians of Palestine separated themselves from this uprising against Rome and left the area early in the conflict, before the destruction of Jerusalem. The flight of the Christians sealed forever the division between Judaism and Christianity because it was interpreted as desertion by the Jews.

An account of Jerusalem's fall was recorded by the Jewish historian Josephus. As a Roman prisoner captured during the war, he witnessed the events from behind the Roman lines. Jerusalem was blockaded and left to starve. The Romans took revenge on those who fled the dying city by making the hill outside Jerusalem a forest of crosses—five hundred crucifixions daily. The corpses of those who died of starvation were thrown over the city walls and left to rot unburied. Half the city finally fell into Roman hands and still the Jews refused to surrender. Caesar ordered the city and Temple razed to the ground. In the end, the entire Jewish population was massacred or sold into slavery. The Temple and the local synagogues were destroyed. In fact, after 70 no material evidence of Israel's existence remained in Palestine. The emperor Hadrian built a new Roman city where Jerusalem had been and called it *Aelia Capitolina.*

The End of the Temple

The total destruction of Jerusalem was not only a severe blow to the Christian Church of Jerusalem. It had a profound affect on Judaism as well. Jewish worship centered on Temple sacrifice. Without the Temple in Jerusalem, the local synagogues became the centers of

The ruins of the synagogue of Zazrin provide some idea of the destruction which took place in Jerusalem.

The Church: A Spirit-Filled People

Masada—Place of Martyrs

The Jewish Revolt which lasted from 66-70 resulted in the loss of many thousands of lives and the complete destruction of Jerusalem. Jewish worship and religious life were drastically changed by the war. Josephus gave us graphic descriptions of the ravages of the fighting. We also know of one place where Jewish martyrs refused to surrender to the Romans.

Masada is a mountaintop fortress in the Judean desert, not far from the Dead Sea. It was built on top of a flat mesa, or large rock. King Herod had built a palace there, but by 66, a small group of Jews captured it and turned it into a fortress. There were 1,000 Jews, including women and children, fighting a force of almost 15,000 Roman soldiers.

The battle for Masada raged on for almost two years. When the Romans finally scaled the mountain on April 15, 73, they found that the Jews had taken their own lives rather than be captured by the Romans. Only seven people survived.

Masada has become a symbol of heroism for all people. It is possible to make the climb and to see the ruins of both Herod's palace and the more modest structures built by the Jews. Both Jews and Christians can take pride in the strength of the faith of their ancestors. Faith in God has helped them overcome temptation, compromise, or surrender.

---

worship. Without Temple sacrifices, the Jewish priests became unnecessary and were replaced by the rabbis, or teachers of the Law. The Jews became a "people of the book"—the Torah. In retaliation for the desertion of the Jewish Christians, some Jews launched a persecution against them.

Gradually, the followers of Jesus adopted the Hebrew Scriptures and transferred the rights and claims of the

Chapter 7 Independence in the Spirit: The First Century

Chosen People to the Church, the New Israel. Conversions to Christianity from among the Jews diminished. Gentile converts increased, and many of these converts read into the Christian Scriptures an anti-Semitism that had originally appeared to separate one segment of Jewish belief from another. For example, the use of the word "Jews" in John's gospel is addressed only to the Pharisee branch of Judaism. Jewish-Christian relations have been strained ever since. Once they gained political power, Christians began to persecute Jews. This became known as anti-Semitism—any form of prejudice, hostility, or persecution against Jews—which reached its climax in the Holocaust—the extermination of six million Jews by Nazis—during World War II.

15. *What would happen to you and your family if your town were to be totally destroyed?*

16. *Discuss your feelings about the Jews and anti-Semitism.*

Preserving Tradition in Written Form

The message of Jesus was kept alive through the Apostles in the communities they founded. As persecution, calamities, and natural death claimed these living witnesses to the Lord Jesus, the need to preserve and safeguard the oral traditions from corruption and loss became immediate. Collections of sayings, reports of miracles, the parables, the sermons, and the detailed accounts of Jesus' passion and death were already being shared within the Christian community. Now it became necessary to gather and shape these materials into an understandable whole. This process resulted in the compilation of what is today called the New Testament or Christian Scriptures. Its four Gospels reflect the traditions evolved from the faith view of the community for which each was written.

The definitive list of twenty-seven books the Church recognizes as inspired was officially drawn up in the late fourth century. The Muratorian fragment (a biblical manuscript from c. 150) lists the four Gospels, thirteen Pauline letters, John 1 and 2, and Revelation.

Mark, Luke, Matthew

Mark's Gospel was the first to be compiled, c. 65, probably written in Rome, and is thought to contain Peter's teachings. In this Gospel, Jesus is presented as the Son of God overcoming evil to give life. He is the great exorcist and healer. The crucifixion is seen as his most powerful act of healing and life giving. Mark's version of the Good News comforted and consoled the Gentile community then undergoing persecution in Rome.

Luke shows the influence of the Pauline tradition of Jesus. His Gospel emphasizes the role of the Holy Spirit. It also extends a welcome to the Gentile world in its emphasis on universal salvation. It reflects a concern for social justice and is characterized by mercy and compassion. It is thought to have been written in Greece about 75 and portrays Jesus as a Spirit-filled prophet and martyr. Acts (also written by Luke) records the life of the Church driven by the same Spirit.

Matthew's Gospel comes from Syria (then part of Palestine) and was written for a mixed community of Jew and Gentile Christians. Its final version dates from c. 80. In this Gospel account, Jesus fulfills the prophecies and is held up as the great teacher, rabbi, healer, the true Israelite, and a New Moses. Those who believe in him are the New Israel.

The Gospels of Mark, Luke, and Matthew are called "synoptic" because they share so much in common.

Chapter 7   Independence in the Spirit: The First Century

A People at Prayer

The Gospels and Paul's letters contain the earliest prayers and statements of faith of the followers of Jesus. Many of those prayers have their roots in Judaism. Others reflect a new-found faith in Jesus as Lord. These prayers are often confessions of faith. A confession is a statement of religious beliefs. These confessions are important because they show us the earliest forms of Christian worship.

At worship, the congregation might say in unison, "Jesus is Lord" (1 Corinthians 12:3). Or it might proclaim that "Jesus died and rose" (1 Thessalonians 4:14).

These two professions of faith reflect the beliefs of the earliest followers of Jesus. They form the very foundation of Christian faith. For the early Christians, prayer became a vehicle for emphasizing their basic beliefs as a community.

John and Paul

The Gospel according to John—the last to be written, c. 95—originated in Asia Minor, probably in Ephesus. John's emphasis is on Jesus as the great revealer of God, the Logos or Word, the authentic sign and Image of God. It is the most controversial of the Gospels and was the last of the Gospels to be placed among the inspired canon of Scripture because of its apparent Gnostic themes. The book of Revelation was compiled by disciples of John. It is highly symbolic and was meant to encourage the Christians undergoing persecution under the emperor Domitian, 81-96.

Paul's letters to the various Churches, as well as those of Peter and John, were shared among the Christian Churches. It is good to recall that all the books of the New Testament were shaped by the life situations in which they were written. The hard sayings they contain were not merely abstract ideals. Debates as to whether members of the community could own private property, whether the rich could belong to the Church, whether Christians could take oaths and go to law courts were practical, moral problems that confronted the early Christians. They found their way into the Gospels and Acts in open or disguised forms. Anti-Semitism is also there, probably caused by the persecution Christians were suffering at the hands of the Jews.

The Gospel of John and the Letters of Paul show the strong theology which developed within the early Church.

The Church: A Spirit-Filled People

17. *How do the different times and places of the compilation of the Gospels contribute to the richness of our knowledge of Jesus and the early Christian community?*

18. *Why is it important for a letter to address the concerns and use the language and images of the people for whom it is written?*

19. *What modern problems or dilemmas do you think the Apostles would have struggled with?*

Saint Peter's Square in Rome is a sign that the Church reaches ever outward to the world to proclaim the Good News.

Moving Onward

As Christianity entered into the second century, it had already been tested and strengthened by persecution. Under the guidance of the Spirit, it was becoming a universal religion in its own right—no longer Jewish but open to all. With the Spirit's inspiration, its major teachings had been set down in writing. Already Christians were beginning to question whether the time of the Lord's Second Coming was to be much later than expected.

Canon: an official list, here referring to the books of the Bible.

Gnosticism: a heresy of the first centuries that claimed salvation could be attained through secret knowledge.

Chapter 7   Independence in the Spirit: The First Century

Amidst all that had been accomplished there were still problems, of course. Conflicts between Christians and non-Christian Jews continued. False rumors regarding Christian beliefs and practices were still believed by the Romans. But amid the divisions and tensions, the number of converts continued to increase. Christianity was making gradual inroads into even the more sophisticated levels of Roman society. It would be from Rome, the imperial capital, not Jerusalem, that the Church would spread out around the world, connecting Jesus and his Apostles and the Church of today.

Summary

- Rome emerged as the center of Christianity with Apostolic roots in Peter.

- With Jerusalem's destruction in 70, the split between Judaism and Christianity was finalized.

- Christians continued to read the Hebrew Scriptures and slowly added written collections of Jesus' sayings and actions to it.

- Each Gospel was written for a specific audience and focuses on different issues.

- All the books of the New Testament are part of the canon of inspired Scripture.

SECTION 3
Checkpoint!

■ Review

1. How did Rome become the center of Christianity?
2. What does Josephus tell us about the war which ended in the destruction of Jerusalem?
3. How did the relationship between Jews and Christians become even more strained as a result of the failed revolt?
4. Why are the Jews called "people of the book"?
5. What are some of the differences between the four Gospels?
6. Describe the community to whom each Gospel writer directed his writing.
7. Words to Know: Jewish Revolt, Josephus, Temple, canon, anti-Semitism.

■ In Your World

1. Create a timeline of events discussed. Be sure to include as many as possible. For example, Jesus' crucifixion, Saul's conversion, the Council of Jerusalem, the date of each Gospel. Try highlighting the dates you think are most important in red.
2. Create your own Gospel parallels. Using Matthew, Mark, and Luke, have three groups read an account of the same event in all three Gospels. How are the accounts the same, and how do they differ? From what you now know about each Gospel, what do you think may have caused the differences?

■ Scripture Search

1. Read the following passages: 1 Corinthians 9:1; Galatians 1:1; 2 Corinthians 1:6, 12:9, 12:12. On what grounds does Paul claim to be an apostle of Christ? Do you think he can be an apostle without having been with Jesus during his earthly life?
2. Choose one Gospel or one letter of Paul and read it. Was it hard to read? Why do you think these inspired documents have remained so important to Christians through the centuries without seeming old-fashioned?

Chapter 7   Independence in the Spirit: The First Century

CHAPTER 7 Review

■ Study

1. What period of time is covered in Acts?
2. What is accomplished in the history that is recounted in Acts?
3. What happened when Peter was brought before the Sanhedrin in Jerusalem?
4. Why was Stephen martyred?
5. Name two consequences of Stephen's death.
6. Describe Paul's work as a missionary. Where did he go, and who sent him?
7. What conflict did the Council of Jerusalem set out to resolve, and what were the results?
8. How did Jewish-Christian relations change after the Council?
9. What does Paul say about the status of the Jews in the eyes of God?
10. Why did the tension between Jews and Christians anger the Romans?
11. Explain the importance of Peter in the shifts from Jerusalem to Antioch to Rome.
12. What happened to Judaism when Jerusalem was destroyed by the Romans?
13. Describe the particular focus of each Gospel, and explain where and for whom each was written.
14. How do the Gospels differ from the letters of Paul?

■ Action

1. Each person in class ranks the six events discussed in this chapter in order of importance. Compare all the lists. Are there any patterns? What reason do people give for their rankings?

2. Do some reading about a Jewish holy day or feast such as Passover, Succoth, Yom Kippur, or Hanukkah. Why is it celebrated? What special actions are made, prayers said, or food eaten? Are there any passages from Scripture which mention or describe this celebration? Share your new knowledge with someone else and let each person tell you about what they have learned.

3. Draw an illustration which could be used as a front page for one of the Gospels. Use an event described in the Gospel, or a scene which represents the Gospel audience.

■ Prayer

Often prayer comes in response to an event. When earthquakes or floods strike, we pray for both the victims and the survivors. When a person recovers from an illness, we pray in thanksgiving.

Choose one or more of the following miracle stories from the Gospels and use it as a help for your meditation and prayer:

Luke 5:12-16 (the leper);

Luke 5:17-26 (the paralyzed man);

Luke 18:15-17 (the blind beggar);

John 11:37-45 (Lazarus).

How would you give thanks to God if you witnessed such a miracle? Write down your own prayer to God. Think about your response in faith to God's actions.

Chapter 7   Independence in the Spirit: The First Century

CHAPTER

8

From Persecution to Power: A.D. 100–800

OBJECTIVES

In this Chapter you will

- Learn about the early history of the Church.

- Discover the role of the martyrs in the development of the Church.

- Observe the evolution of the Church as it gained favor in the Roman Empire.

- Learn about the beginning of monasticism.

- Study how the Church protected itself from heresy and made contributions to the society around it.

The Church, "like a stranger in a foreign land, presses forward amid the persecutions of the world and the consolations of God," announcing the cross and death of the Lord until he comes. But by the power of the risen Lord she is given strength to overcome, in patience and in love, her sorrows and her difficulties, both those that are from within and those that are from without.
— "Dogmatic Constitution on the Church," #8

The Church: A Spirit-Filled People

SECTION 1
The Big Picture

If you examine a tapestry, you will find that the underside is ugly—a tangle of crisscrossed colored threads and knots. But when you turn it over to the other side its beauty may delight you. The history of Christianity in the second to eighth centuries is like a tapestry. There is both messiness and beauty depending on which side you are examining. The underside contains accounts of persecutions, division, heresy, enemy invasions, and a divided empire. On the beautiful side, you will see the stories of heroism in martyrdom, gallant efforts to bring Christianity to the empire, great intellectual minds defending and explaining the Faith, the rise of monasticism, and the rise of the Church as a temporal power filling the void left by the collapse of the Roman Empire. All of these elements together, the messy and the beautiful, make up the big picture of the early history of Christianity.

The Earliest Opposition

From the Emperor Nero, 54-68, to the Edict of Milan, 313, being a Christian required a readiness for martyrdom. More than a million Christians gave their lives for their faith during this time. Their courage and steadfastness was a marvel to the Romans, and caused many of them to convert.

It would not be accurate to think that every Christian who lived during the first three centuries hid and worshipped in fear. The persecutions were sporadic. Early persecutions reflected a pagan society's hatred for a minority group it could not understand. Romans honored the gods and goddesses whom they believed were responsible for peace and prosperity. They believed it was their civic duty to offer

Martyr: from the Greek word for "witness," someone who sacrifices his or her life for the sake of a principle or religious value.

Chapter 8 From Persecution to Power: A.D. 100–800

incense or a prayer to a statue, or image, of the Emperor during public ceremonies. A Christian's refusal to take part in such activities could only be seen as an act of disrespect or treason, or both.

Hubert—Nero watches as Rome burns.
Historians believe that Nero set Rome afire, and then persecuted the Christians as scapegoats.

Nero: The First Challenge

The first and perhaps cruelest of the imperial persecutions occurred under Nero. Saint Paul was beheaded and Saint Peter was crucified during his reign. Some Christians were drowned in the Tiber River, others were burned at the stake, and still others were wrapped in animal skins and hunted by ferocious dogs.

The reasons for the outbreak of this first persecution are obscure. Nero, whom some historians believe was insane, exploited public opinion which depicted Christians as moral monsters. During the first hundred years of Christianity, services were often held at night and in secret. Because only the baptized could attend the Eucharist, what took place when Christians gathered was very mysterious. Charges of cannibalism and other evil deeds seemed confirmed by rumors that Christians ate and drank flesh and blood at their secret services. When a fire destroyed large areas of Rome, the Christians became Nero's scapegoats.

Whatever the cause of this fury, a pattern of blaming the Christians for what went wrong in the Empire was established. Later, Tertullian wrote: "If the Tiber rises above its banks, if the Nile does not overflow, if the skies are not clear, if the earth quakes, if there is a famine or plague in Rome, up goes the cry, 'The Christians to the lions.'" Nero's law, "It is forbidden to be a Christian," remained on the books after his death.

Bread of Christ

Although Christianity was outlawed, Christians were not hunted. They were at risk from informers, especially during festivals in which Christians refused to participate, or from personal enemies or local magistrates who would denounce them. Martyrdom was the sentence for their supposed crime. Highly revered Church leaders became witnesses for Christ. Ignatius, third bishop of Antioch (50?-110?), was one of these leaders. He had served his flock for forty years when he was ordered to Rome to be torn apart by beasts. During his journey toward Rome, he sent letters to various Churches thanking them for their sympathy and encouraging them to be faithful. Ignatius begged the Christians in Rome not to try to prevent his martyrdom. "I am afraid of your love, lest even that do me wrong. Grant me nothing more than that I be poured out to God while an altar is still ready," he begged. "I must be ground by the teeth of wild beasts to become the pure bread of Christ."

---

1. Why do people often hate or persecute minority groups? In what ways does society here and in other countries persecute religious and other minority groups?

2. A martyr is willing to die rather than compromise a belief. Who would you identify as a modern martyr? For what beliefs and ideals of yours would you be willing to die?

3. Have you ever been a scapegoat? How did that make you feel? Why do people (or societies) create scapegoats?

> **Scapegoat:** a person or thing blamed for the mistakes or crimes of others.

Chapter 8   From Persecution to Power: A.D. 100–800

4. *Think about the vivid imagery Ignatius uses in his description of his own martyrdom. What Christian symbols does he use? How do they add to the strength of his request?*

On This Rock

Saint Ignatius of Antioch's importance for the Church comes from his courageous martyrdom and from the letters which he wrote while on his final journey to Rome. In those letters he tried to give Christians throughout the Empire a vision of a united Church. Here is a part of the letter Ignatius wrote to the Christians of Ephesus:

"Pray, then, come and join this choir, every one of you; let there be a whole symphony of minds in concert; take the tone all together from God, and sing aloud to the Father with one voice by your good works that you are indeed members of His Son's Body. A completely united front will help to keep you in constant communion with God." Ignatius' valiant witness tells us much about the early Church and the length Christians were willing to go for their faith.

The Empire Versus the Church

In the third century, Christians faced the threat of persecution from the Imperial level rather than the local level. In 202, Emperor Septimus Severus made conversion to either Judaism or Christianity illegal. The reception of Baptism became a criminal act, and many catechumens and newly baptized Christians were martyred. By the middle of the century, Emperor Decius devised a plan to destroy Christianity entirely.

An imperial law commanded all citizens to offer sacrifices to the traditional Roman gods. As evidence that they had complied, each person received a certificate. A council was set up in each town to verify certificates.

Caught unaware, many Christians panicked. In the face of certain death, many complied with the law and gave up their faith. Others, by means of forgery or bribes, obtained false certificates. Many others were imprisoned and executed. Even so, Decius did not succeed. Although records show that no citizens of Rome were Christian by the time Decius died, many had continued to practice their faith in secret, and countless others who had denied Christ repented and rejoined the Church.

5. *What would you have done during the persecution of Decius? What challenges to their faith did people who bought certificates face? How is faith strengthened by such events?*

The Church: A Spirit-Filled People

The Creed of the Catacombs

A catacomb is an underground burial chamber. Because Roman law forbade burial within city walls, the catacombs along the main roads leaving Rome were normal burial places long before and after the era of Christian martyrs. They contain about 500,000 to 750,000 tombs and from 70 to 90 miles of corridors.

Despite the ravages of time, robberies, and removal of relics, the thirty-five known Roman catacombs still testify to the faith of the early Christians. Artwork, including inscriptions, paintings, mosaics, and statues reveal much about the beliefs and hopes of the people.

The passion of Jesus is presented in mosaic or sculpture as a triumphant procession, and Christ is most often shown as the Good Shepherd. The orant, or figure with uplifted arms, depicts the early Church's posture for prayer. Scenes of the Magi and the baptism of the Roman centurion Cornelius reflect an emphasis on the new Gentile orientation of Christianity in Rome.

Images of Paul show him as Christ's companion, a fisherman and shepherd. Baptism and the Eucharist are frequently pictured, the latter symbolized by fish and bread. Mary is usually shown with her divine Son and depictions of his work of redemption.

Many of the tombstone inscriptions speak of hope for eternal life. "May you live among the saints." "May you live in the peace of God!" "Januria, enjoy your happiness and pray for us." Others describe the lives of those who have died.

Early Christians wrapped their dead just as Christ had been prepared for burial. Visitors today still find small clay lamps and vials of perfume left as memorials at the tombs. The custom of placing stones containing relics of saints in church altars originated from the early Church practice of offering Mass on the tombs of martyrs.

The Final Persecution

The final and most far-reaching persecution by the Roman Empire occurred under Diocletian and his successors from 303-311. It called for the destruction of church buildings, confiscation and burning of all church books, dismissal of Christians from government jobs, and imprisonment of clergy.

For more than nine years, the persecution raged throughout the Empire. Tens of thousands of people were martyred and a town in Asia Minor was destroyed. Christians were burned at the stake, thrown to wild animals, stoned, or put into dungeons. It was said that the prisons were so full of Christians that there was no room left for thieves and murderers. In addition to the martyrs, many others were forced to leave their homes, give up their businesses, and separate their families.

These heroes of the last persecution came from all segments of society. Agnes gave her life for Christ when only twelve or thirteen years old. Agatha died in prison after being sent to a house of prostitution to induce her to give up her faith.

After escaping suffocation in a steam bath, Cecilia lingered three days with her head partially severed. Her fiance, Valerian, whom she converted to Christianity, also died for the faith.

During the persecutions, Christians were hunted down in the catacombs where they had gathered to worship in secret.

The Church: A Spirit-Filled People

Sebastian, a favorite soldier of Diocletian, became a target for archers, and the African bishop Cyprian died publicly before his people at Carthage. The Roman deacon and lover of the poor, Lawrence, was roasted on a metal grid over live coals and died jesting, "Turn me over, I'm done on this side."

6. How would Diocletian's laws affect you and other members of your parish?

Christians in the Roman World

The witness of the martyrs brought about many conversions. By the end of the second century, Christianity had spread into North Africa, France, Spain, Mesopotamia, Germany, and Yugoslavia. By the end of the third century, Christians could be found in every corner of the Empire. Tertullian's boast was prophetic: "Kill us, torture us, condemn us, grind us to dust . . . the oftener we are mown down by you, the more in number we grow; the blood of martyrs is the seed of Christians."

The courage and moral strength of the Christians during this time are reflected in this anonymous letter to Diognetus: "The Christians show love to all people—and all people persecute them. They obey all the appointed laws and go beyond them in their own lives. They are mocked and bless in return. Christians are in the world but not of the world."

Summary

- Early Christianity is filled with both beauty and messiness.
- Persecution was caused by hatred and fear of Christians.
- Many Christians were courageous witnesses of their faith and died as martyrs.
- Christianity withstood two centuries of persecution and emerged strengthened.

SECTION 1
Checkpoint!

■ Review

1. What events or occurrences contributed to the tapestry image of early Christianity?

2. What were Christians accused of during Nero's persecution?

3. How did the Roman Emperors try to destroy Christianity?

4. What was the status of Christianity at the end of the Age of Martyrs?

5. Words to Know: martyr, Nero, Diocletian, scapegoat, persecution.

■ In Your World

1. Read one of the accounts of an early martyr's death. Think about the images the description brings to mind, and why these often gruesome events were written in so much detail. Write a sample newspaper article describing the event itself and its effects on the people who saw it, both Christian and non-Christian.

2. Think about the ways artwork reflects the beliefs of a society. What images and words are placed on modern graves, and what feelings do they express? Design a symbolic plaque for one of the early Christian martyrs buried in the catacombs.

■ Scripture Search

Look up the following Scripture passages: Acts 7:51-8:3; Acts 16:16-34; 1 Timothy 2:1-4; 1 Timothy 3:1-13. How is the early Church pictured as an organization in these passages? What obstacles did early Christians face? What do you think of the guidelines for the behavior of Church leaders and lay people?

SECTION 2
From Persecution to Power

The rise of Christianity from a persecuted minority group to a group which had political influence and power was sudden and unexpected. This shift brought many converts into the Church and resulted in many changes for Christianity in its structure and order. For these reasons, the fourth century is one of the most important in the history of Christianity.

Constantine's Conversion

Tradition reports that the Emperor Constantine, although not a Christian, called on the God of the Christians before going into battle against Maxentius for control of the Empire. He saw a huge cross in the sky with the Greek inscription, "In this sign, you will conquer." Believing the sign, Constantine was successful in battle. The following year, 313, Constantine issued the Edict of Milan which ended the persecution of Christians and guaranteed them liberty of worship. As a result, by the year 400 Christians comprised more than one-half of the population of the Roman Empire.

Constantine was baptized on his deathbed in 337, but long before that, the new status of Christianity was noticeable throughout the Empire. Christian symbols appeared on coins, Church courts were recognized as valid, clergy were exempt from taxes, Christians took political offices, and royal buildings were donated for Church use.

By the end of the fourth century, Emperor Theodosius declared the formal and legal alliance between Church and state: "All peoples subject to the government of our clemency shall follow the religion which Holy Peter delivered to the Romans, as pious tradition from him to the present time declares, and as the pontiff Damasus manifestly observes it" (Codex Theodosianus XVI, 1, 2). Under Pope Damasus (366-384), Latin became the language used in the Church's worship. This alliance changed the face of the Church as well as that of the Empire. For example, divisions of the Church, such as parishes and dioceses, were designed to correspond to the political divisions of the Empire.

---

7. *What advantages and drawbacks for the Church could result from this alliance with government?*

8. *What are some examples of modern Church-state relationships in the United States or other countries?*

Rosselli—*The Baptism of Constantine*
It was the conversion of Constantine in 313 that led to the acceptance of Christianity within the Roman Empire.

A New Christian Lifestyle

During the third century, a new way of living was introduced into Christianity. It was called monasticism, and its first followers in the Empire were called hermits or anchorites.

The Church: A Spirit-Filled People

These men and women literally withdrew from society to live alone in parts of North Africa and Syria in order to nourish their relationship with God by prayer, penance, and solitude. In Egypt, Anthony gathered groups of anchorites for worship and instruction. Later, Pachomius, a Roman soldier who converted following the example of some Christians, developed Christian communities based on strict obedience to a superior. Monasticism spread quickly. However, with the growth of monasticism came the impression that monasticism was a superior form of Christianity and that "ordinary Christians" cannot aspire to holiness. While a false conclusion, this idea plagued the Church for centuries.

9. Why would a solitary life of prayer appeal to some people? Do you think that you would like a solitary life?

10. How does the impression that a person under religious vows is holier than "ordinary Christians" persist today? What are the advantages or disadvantages of both types of lifestyle?

These Trappist monks are a descendent of the monasticism which developed in the fourth century.

Monasticism: from the Greek word for "one."

Anchorite: from the Greek word meaning "to withdraw."

Chapter 8   From Persecution to Power: A.D. 100–800

Monasticism in the West

Benedict of Nursia (480-546) was only seventeen when he fled the corruption of Rome and went to Subiaco, a wilderness about thirty miles away from the city. He lived for three years in a small grotto, seeking God alone. Others came looking for him in order to form a community, and eventually one was formed at the abbey of Monte Cassino. When Benedict's first rules proved too strict, he developed a "little rule for beginners" that prescribed two courses at meals, a little wine, and sufficient sleep and clothing. It was a far cry from the harsh lifestyle adopted by the Eastern monks.

"All things must be done in moderation for the sake of those who are less hardy," the new rule said. Benedict's code governed every aspect of the monk's life. It was patterned on the Roman family, with the abbot taking the father's role. It allowed for a daily pattern of prayer and work. Benedict could hardly have known that his rule would become the foundation for monastic life throughout Europe for the next seven hundred years. The Benedictine motto is "Pray and Work."

Benedict of Nursia is considered the father of the monastic orders we know today.

Communion of Saints

Saint Anthony (251-356) lived as an anchorite in the Egyptian desert. He chose to practice an especially harsh form of monastic life, eating little, living isolated from society, and sleeping on the ground. In addition to prayer, Anthony constantly examined his own life in order to grow in virtue. He was a popular teacher and spiritual guide. His biography was written by Athanasius and contains vivid accounts of events in Anthony's quest for union with God. It is an important work of early Christian literature.

The Church: A Spirit-Filled People

Heresies and Councils: Problems and Solutions

Several of the most serious heresies threatened to divide the Church permanently. Each side in the disputes gathered supporters, circulated literature, and criticized the opposing view. Both the emperor and religious leaders became concerned about the negative effects of such tensions. Together, they decided to convene councils of bishops and other church leaders to try to resolve the problems. Details of the earliest council can be found in Acts 15. The doctrines which emerged from the negotiations of the councils (which often lasted months) form the backbone of Christian belief. Below you will find a list of some of the most important heresies and the councils or teachers that corrected them.

Heresy	Error	Correction
Nestorianism	Jesus is two persons; denies Mary's Divine Motherhood	Council of Ephesus, 431
Monophysitism	Jesus was one person with only one nature which is divine, not human	Council of Chalcedon, 451
Docetism	Jesus only appeared to be human	Council of Chalcedon, 451
Donatism	Sinners, or those who lapse, are no longer members of the Church	Augustine
Pelagianism	Denies original sin and grace; says the unaided human can achieve sanctity	Council of Ephesus, 431 Augustine

Each of these councils produced a set of canons, or rules, pertaining to various aspects of Christian living or doctrine. Vatican II was the twenty-first council of the Church.

Heresy: any deviation, distortion, or rejection of revealed truth or dogma.

Benedictine monks became known for their hard work, care of the fields and forests, and prayerful celebration of the liturgy. Many came from wealthy, educated families, and the communities they formed provided a model of stability for society. At a time when society was trying to assimilate many foreign peoples, Benedictine monasteries were models of order and centers of learning where books were copied, swamp lands cleared, and labor-saving devices invented. Benedictines are active in ministry still today. You may know some contemporary Benedictine monks who teach and serve in parishes.

11. *How do the activities of prayer and work complement each other in the lives of monks? What would be the challenges of a life of only prayer or only work?*

12. *With which forms of monasticism (religious communities) are you familiar? Use a Dictionary of Religion to identify at least ten groups.*

Disunity From Within

Guided by the Spirit of Jesus, the young Church learned to explain its faith when challenged by non-Christians as well as by heretics—Christians who taught ideas contrary to the faith of Christianity. Tertullian once wrote that the very purpose of heresies is to test the faith of those they tempt. The early Church had to stand firm against many heretical groups, such as the Gnostics, who taught that there were two divine principles, one of good and one of evil, which struggled with each other for control of the world. Their belief in dualism, which pits the body (considered evil) against the soul (considered good) has attracted many adherents throughout history, even the present. Before his conversion, Saint Augustine searched for truth in such a doctrine (Manicheism). When he became a Christian, Augustine rejected the empty teachings of Manicheism.

Saint Augustine of Hippo —bishop, scholar, and teacher.

Dispute Over Doctrine

The fourth and fifth centuries have been called the Age of Heresies. Most of them resulted from attempts to express and explain the mysteries of the Trinity and the Incarnation in doctrinal statements. The influence of Greek philosophy and the differences between the languages (Greek and Latin) contributed to the errors. Most dangerous was the error of Arius, a theologian from Alexandria (Egypt), who claimed that Jesus was merely an adopted son of God, created by God, and therefore not divine. Most of the Empire became involved in a war of words over this issue until Arianism was formally condemned at the Council of Nicaea in 325.

Backed by the Emperor, bishops who supported Arius remained in high Church positions. Athanasius, Patriarch of Alexandria and a foe of Arianism, was exiled five times by four different emperors. Pope Liberius even went into exile rather than denounce Athanasius as ordered by Emperor Constantius. On one occasion, in an attempt to kill Athanasius, imperial troops broke into the church where he was presiding at evening prayer. Some of his congregation died, allowing him to disappear into the night.

Creed: a brief formal statement of religious teaching and belief.

Chapter 8   From Persecution to Power: A.D. 100–800

In addition to Arianism, numerous other heresies challenged the faith during the third and fourth centuries. A series of councils were held in attempt to resolve these heretical issues.

One benefit of the fight against heresy was the Nicene and Athanasian creeds—formulated by the Church to state its beliefs clearly. Another positive development was the increase in devotion to Mary resulting from the defense of her divine motherhood at the Council of Ephesus.

Since the Council of Ephesus, Mary has been honored as the Mother of God.

Dispute Over Practice

Besides the heresies of these early centuries, other internal disputes sometimes threatened to split the Church. For example, one centered on setting the date for celebrating Easter. The Eastern Church still held to the traditional Jewish Feast of Passover, while the Western Church moved Easter celebration to Sunday. The intense debate almost resulted in schism before the common sense of Saint Irenaeus saved the day. Each side kept its own date.

More serious than the debate over Easter was the controversy over how to deal with Christians who repented after they had abandoned the faith under persecution (apostates). In Africa, Bishop Donatus organized a parallel Church that excluded all who had lapsed from the faith. It lost power only after Augustine and an imperial edict condemned it. Through these difficult times, the Church continued to struggle to understand and proclaim the Good News of Christ.

13. *How does the Gnostic belief in dualism call into question the Christian belief about the goodness of the body and its relationship with the soul? What would dualists feel about marriage, pleasure, or creation?*

14. *What important role do creeds play in a religion?*

15. *Are heresies just a problem of the past for the Church? Why or why not?*

16. *How would you have dealt with the controversy over the date of Easter, or the problem with apostates?*

17. *Name some issues which are controversial in the Church today. How would you describe them?*

Summary

- Under Constantine, Christianity became a tolerated, and later, under Theodosious, a favored religion.
- Monasticism emerged as a new Christian lifestyle stressing a life of prayer and work.
- Divisions within the Church threatened its unity but were settled at councils.

Schism: a division or split within a religious body.

SECTION 2
Checkpoint!

■ Review

1. What important changes occurred to Christianity during the reign of Emperor Constantine?

2. What are some ways Christianity adapted to its new role in the Empire?

3. What was life like for monks in the East?

4. What is the purpose of a monastic lifestyle?

5. What did Benedict's rules provide for Western monks?

6. What is the danger of heresy, and how did Arianism threaten the unity of the Church?

7. Words to Know: Constantine, Edict of Milan, monasticism, heresy, Arianism, Nicene Creed, apostates.

■ In Your World

Design a code of conduct for a new monastic order you are founding. What is daily life like? What do the adherents wear? What is their diet like? When and how long do monks pray and work? Practice this code of conduct in your class for a week. How do you like living this way?

■ Scripture Search

Study the creation story in Genesis 1:26-31. Read 1 Corinthians 6:12-20. How are body and soul related? How could you use these passages to argue with the dualists of the third and fourth centuries?

SECTION 3
Growth and Change

Throughout the first three centuries, Christianity attracted converts from all levels of society, but in particular its teachings and doctrine caught the attention of many educated and dedicated thinkers. These people took on the responsibility of explaining and clarifying issues of the faith, and are considered to be theologians. The most brilliant of these men were called the Apostolic Fathers—Clement of Rome, Ignatius of Antioch, and Polycarp of Smyrna.

Early Centuries—The Golden Age

Following the Apostolic Fathers during the second and third centuries came the age of the Apologists. Scholars such as Justin Martyr, Tertullian, Irenaeus, Clement of Alexandria, and Origen wrote eloquently and passionately in defense of their faith. Lay people and clerics wrote great works which explained and defended Christianity in the face of Roman, Jewish, and Greek criticism. The writings of these men form the basis of the science of theology, and they provided a working vocabulary for future Christian theologians.

A third group of writers were those given the honorary titles of both Fathers and Doctors of the Church. They were individuals who were outstanding in learning and sanctity. The group in the East includes Athanasius, Basil, Gregory of Nazianzan, and John Chrysostom. They spoke and wrote in Greek. In the Latin West, Jerome, Augustine, and Gregory the Great are well-known writers. Most of these men were highly educated and had secular careers before dedicating their lives to the Church. Their lifestyles in the Church were pious and very ascetic. Their sermons and writings are still studied today. The title Doctor originally meant "learned."

Apostolic Fathers: men who had known the Apostles or their disciples personally.

Apologist: one who writes or speaks in defense of the faith.

It is still used by the Church. In 1970, Catherine of Siena and Teresa of Avila were the first women named Doctors of the Church.

Beginning with the second century, waves of barbarian peoples pressed into the Roman Empire and became both a threat and a challenge to the Church. In the fourth century many different groups such as the Goths, Vandals, Huns, Franks, and Saxons invaded the Empire, bringing violence and terror to its inhabitants.

The Roman Empire had gradually been splitting in two. Strong leaders on each side wanted to rule. There were language differences (Greek in the East and Latin in the West) and difficulties in communicating over long distances. Eventually, a political split caused the tensions between the Church in the East and the West to turn into a rift.

The Western part of the Empire was too weak to fight, and the Eastern part was struggling with internal divisions and invading north European and Eastern tribes. Finally, in 410, the capital of the Empire, Rome, was attacked and destroyed by the Visigoths, one of the invading tribes. Within seventy-five years, Western Europe fell and the civil government collapsed. The Church was the only institution with a strong enough organization to withstand the chaos.

Caravaggio—St. Jerome
Saint Jerome is thought to have translated the Bible from Greek into Latin.

The Church: A Spirit-Filled People

Arch of Titus, Rome
Rome was invaded and sacked by the Visigoths in 410.

Church leaders took on the responsibilities of feeding the hungry, caring for the sick and orphans, and even defending cities like Orleans. In Rome in 452, Pope Saint Leo the Great convinced Attila, leader of the Huns, to withdraw his troops and not invade the city.

Eventually, Church leaders and teachers were able to begin teaching and converting the barbarians. On Christmas Day, 498, Clovis, king of the Franks, and three thousand of his warriors were baptized and accepted the God of the Christians. This was the first step toward the Christianization of Europe.

18. What would you expect to find in the writings of these early theologians?

19. Can you name any other Christian thinkers (ancient or modern) whose names are not listed here?

20. What characteristics of Christian leaders and lay people do you think contributed to the ability of the Church to remain intact and influential during this period of instability?

Barbarian: the name given to any non-Roman.

A Restless Heart

No one could have predicted that the teenager from Tagaste who arrived in Carthage in 371 would change the world. At twenty, Augustine became a schoolmaster searching for knowledge and was hungry for love. Unbaptized, he led an undisciplined life and kept a mistress. His mother, Monica, prayed for his conversion.

He searched for answers, first in the dualistic teachings of Mani (which taught that two powers, one of good and one of evil, were in a continual struggle for supremacy) and then in secular philosophy. Augustine then thought he had found the answer in the birth of his son. Finally, in desperation, he prayed, "Father, let me find you," and the Scriptures spoke to his heart and he was converted. Five years of prayer and seclusion brought him maturity, wisdom, and strength. At thirty-seven he was ordained, and later he became the bishop of Hippo in North Africa. He addressed the problems facing the Church, engaged in public debate, wrote 232 books, and tended to his congregation.

His writings have guided the Western Church, contributing a rich Latin vocabulary to its theology and enhancing its reputation as an intellectual power. His sensitive, poetic nature comes through in his *Confessions*, the popular memoirs that are more prayer than confession. Augustine could say, "Before faith you must understand in order to believe; after faith you must believe in order to understand."

Augustine experienced uncertainty as a youth. He used that uncertainty, however, to strengthen himself. Instead of forgetting about the bad times, he chose to write down his memories of the pain, the loneliness, and the mistakes of youth.

The Sixth Century

The sixth century is perhaps best known for the contributions of Pope Saint Gregory the Great, elected in 590. He began his work by organizing the defense of Rome against the Lombards. He ransomed captives, negotiated peace, provided relief for the destitute, maintained communication with his people, and reformed the sees of Italy. He did not even hesitate to criticize the emperor when he got out of line. Even so, he was the first to use the title still used by the Holy Father today, "Servant of the servants of God."

Gregory was educated in civil service and diplomacy, and he prepared Rome to function as a kind of international supreme court. He reorganized the Church and canon law based on the pattern of the Empire. He reformed the liturgy, and the Georgian Sacramentary became a widespread official Church book used for directing worship services. He also introduced Gregorian chants, a type of singing.

In addition to organizational changes, Gregory believed that the conversion of the barbarians was the work of the whole Church and began a missionary program used for many centuries. Writing to Augustine, the Archbishop of Canterbury, he advised: "Do not destroy the pagan temples, but instead sprinkle them with holy water, set up altars in them, and place relics there. In the places where it has been the pagan custom to offer sacrifices to their diabolical idols, allow them to celebrate Christian festivals instead, in another form, on the same date."

The eastern part of the Empire withstood the barbarian invasions because of its military strength, good defenses, and strong imperial rule. But internal problems weakened it. The Council of 381 had elevated the Patriarch of Constantinople to a position of honor second only to Rome. The Council of Chalcedon in 451 further extended the prestige of Constantinople by declaring that it should have the same power as Rome in Church matters while remaining second to it. As a result, a struggle for primacy between the Eastern and Western churches began. Tensions were aggravated by distance, language and cultural differences, and external threats.

In the East, Christianity flourished. Additions to the liturgy included spectacular and distinctive art, music, and special

See: the official center of authority of a bishop; a diocese.

Canon law: the whole body of Church laws arranged into sections called canons.

Sacramentary: a book containing the prayers and directions for Mass, but not the Scripture readings.

Chapter 8   From Persecution to Power: A.D. 100–800

A People at Prayer

The early Councils provided creeds which are now part of the liturgy of all Christians. The Nicene Creed is a clear statement of Christian faith in the divinity of Christ. "We believe in One God, the Father of all things visible and invisible. And in one Lord Jesus Christ, the Son of God, begotten of the Father, Only-begotten, that is, from the substance of the Father."

The monastic movement nourished the Church as monks spent a great deal of their days in prayer and contemplation. Here, Gregory of Nyssa describes the process of prayer: ". . . coming close to God is not a question of simply changing the place where we pray. No, no matter where you may be, as long as your soul forms the sort of resting place in which God can dwell and linger, he will visit you. But if you fill your inner self with base thoughts, then you could be standing on Golgotha and you would still be as far from welcoming Christ into yourself as someone who has never begun to confess him."

liturgical garments. Monasteries multiplied, and the veneration of Mary as the Mother of God intensified. At the same time, veneration of the emperor also grew. He was called "the image of God, his representative on earth. Where did this leave the pope? The Patriarch of Constantinople became sort of a prime minister to the Eastern emperor and the Church received imperial favors. As a result, Eastern Christianity was more closely tied to the secular (nonreligious) government than its Western counterpart.

Christianity in the Eastern Empire had a great variety of expressions. Some of the best known mystics, learned theologians, monks, heretics, and bishops flourished during this time. It was a time when society suffered from inflation, taxation, and bureaucracy. It was also a time of magnificent building and artwork. Emperor Justinian (527-565) built the church of Saint Sophia to celebrate his military victories. It took five years and ten thousand workers to build this church. It is a brilliant example of Byzantine art and architecture.

---

21. What are the benefits and dangers of following the directive of Gregory concerning the pagan temple?

22. What problems might occur from too close a relationship between the government and the church?

End of an Era

One of the most serious threats to the survival of Christianity in the eighth century came from the spread of Islam across Asia, Africa, and Europe, almost engulfing the Roman-Christian world. Had it not been for internal divisions within Islam, and the victories of Leo the Isaurian at Constantinople in 718 and Charles Martel at Poitiers in 732, Islam might have been successful.

Islam originated in Saudi Arabia with Muhammad (570?-632). He accepted the one God of the Jews and Christians (whom he called Allah) and claimed to be the final prophet.

Muslims gather during yearly pilgrimages to pray at the holy shrines of Islam.

The creed of Islam is "There is no God but Allah, and Muhammad is his prophet." Within ten years, Muhammad had unified the wandering tribes of Arabia into a political and religious body. The revelations of the prophet Muhammad were collected in the Koran (Qur'an), the holy book of the Muslims.

After Muhammad died, leadership fell to Caliph Omar, who initiated the slow and steady spread of Islam. Within ten years it had spread to Persia, Egypt, Palestine, and Syria. Within fifty years, all of Roman Africa was under Muslim control, and within one hundred years, Spain and southern France were, too. Muslims controlled political as well as religious life. Not all the conquests were violent, but there were some wars of resistance.

Islam is considered a monotheistic religion (belief in one God) and its followers (Muslims) pray daily, make yearly donations to charity, fast, and try to make a religious journey to their holy city of Mecca at least once in a lifetime.

Islam's victories were swift. The Muslims were highly organized and were spurred on by their religious fervor. The Christians in southern Europe were loosely organized and economic conditions were poor as a result of the barbarian invasions of the previous three hundred years.

In the Eastern Empire, the patriarchates of Jerusalem, Antioch, and Alexandria fell to the Muslims. Constantinople expended its energy defending itself from Muslim pressure. Arab conquests of Europe isolated it from the East. Church leaders there turned to the ruling Carolingian dynasty for protection. The following chapters will recount the attempts of both secular and Church leaders to regain these lost territories.

23. *What do you know about Islam? Do you know any Muslims? What is your attitude towards them?*

Summary

- Many educated thinkers wrote great documents explaining and defending the faith.
- Barbarian invasions threatened the security of the Empire.
- The Church aided in defending the Empire and was successful in converting many of these enemies.
- Gregory the Great contributed to the Church by centralizing and evangelizing.
- Eastern Christianity grew further apart from the West and vied for primacy with it.
- Islam proved to be a new threat to the Church and society as it spread westward.

SECTION 3
Checkpoint!

■ Review

1. What was the function of the Apologists?
2. What kind of people are Doctors of the Church?
3. What factors led to the downfall of Rome in 410?
4. How did Gregory the Great revitalize the Church?
5. Why did the East and West grow farther apart in the sixth century?
6. Explain the results of the spread of Islam for the Church.
7. Words to Know: apostolic fathers, apologist, barbarian, see, Canon law, Sacramentary.

■ In Your World

1. Draw a map of Europe, northern Africa, the Middle East, and Asia. Put in all the countries and cities cited in this chapter and chart the movement of Christianity, the barbarians, and Islam over six hundred years. How many thousands of miles were covered? Consult a historical atlas and see if you can find out the population of these cities at that time.
2. Find a copy of the Koran (Qur'an) in the library. Read through some sections and note how it compares to the Bible. What are the similarities, and what are the differences?

■ Scripture Search

Read Matthew 4:18-22, 9:9. What professions did the disciples have before giving them up to follow Jesus? Do you think their lives and careers before meeting Jesus hindered or helped them in their discipleship? Why? How did the education and lives of the three groups of writers described in this chapter enhance their contribution to the Church? How will your education help you be a better member of the Church?

CHAPTER 8 Review

■ Study

1. What were some of the difficulties faced by the early Church?

2. What were some of the reasons for the persecutions during the first three centuries?

3. How did martyrs strengthen the faith of Christians?

4. Why were the persecutions instigated at the level of the emperor?

5. What meaning do the written accounts of the martyrs' deaths have for Christians today?

6. In what ways did life for Christians and the Church change after the Edict of Milan?

7. What is the purpose of monasticism, and how was it misunderstood by some?

8. What was daily life like for monks in the East? How was it different in the West?

9. What is a heresy? Why do you think the Church faced the challenge of heresy in the fourth and fifth centuries?

10. List two heresies and how they were addressed by the Church.

11. How do the three groups of writers discussed in this chapter reflect the development of the Church itself?

12. What were some of the contributions of Gregory the Great?

13. How and why did the Eastern and Western Churches begin to separate?

14. Describe the effects of the spread of Islam on Christianity in Africa and Europe.

■ Action

1. Create two new martyrs for the early Church and write the story of their witness for the faith. Give them a name, age, and family. How did they come to be martyrs? What were the circumstances of their death? How did family, friends, community, and enemies react to the courage and strength of these martyrs?

2. Give an illustrated presentation on early Christian art. Include the catacombs and any other types of artwork or architecture. Explain the purpose and symbolism of each item.

3. Make a time-line of important dates in history for the early Church between the years 50 and 732. Include the lives of Christian martyrs and theologians, the reigns of emperors, and dates of important councils.

■ Prayer

Try praying in different environments. Start first by finding a quiet and completely isolated spot. It could be your room, a calm corner of your Church, or a place outdoors. Sit quietly in contemplation for five minutes.

Next, pick a busy and noisy place. It could be your kitchen at home, the cafeteria, or a bustling street corner. Try to concentrate in prayer for five minutes. Which was easier, the quiet or the noisy place? Repeat this exercise until you are able to concentrate in the noisy place for at least a few minutes without being distracted.

Think about how a few minutes of prayer in the middle of a busy day makes you feel. If you are able to really concentrate and pray, you may want to try to do so at least once every day.

CHAPTER
9

Building Christendom: A.D. 800–1500

OBJECTIVES

In this Chapter you will

- Read about the unification of Christian Europe under Charlemagne.

- Learn how invasions, attempts at reform, and the Greek Schism weakened the Church.

- Examine the struggles between Church and state leadership.

- Observe advances and weaknesses in the Church through new orders, universities, power struggles, and plague.

- See how the Church reached the end of an era with an outburst of artistic expression and the resurgence of worldliness.

The Church is not blind to the discrepancy between the message it proclaims and the human weakness of those to whom the Gospel has been entrusted . . . Guided by the Holy Spirit, the Church ceaselessly "exhorts her children to purification and renewal so that the sign of Christ may shine more brightly over the face of the Church."
—"Dogmatic Constitution on the Church," #43

The Church: A Spirit-Filled People

SECTION 1
Looking Ahead

During the eighth to sixteenth centuries, the Spirit's creative power fashioned saints and nurtured piety. Along with this spiritual development, a network of buildings and institutions came to be built. But the history of the time reflected the church's pilgrim nature and constant need for reform as well as the agony and ecstasy of building a Christian Europe. Because of historical circumstances, the Church came to possess land and temporal power and became tied to feudal structures. This had consequences for the Church as these structures soon began the struggle of becoming emerging national states. It was also a time of great spiritual decline. Rivalry in the papacy, wars, disease, heresy, scandals, and worldliness among the clergy paved the way for the splintering of Christendom in the sixteenth century.

A Bright Light—Charlemagne

With the approval of the Holy Father, Saint Boniface anointed Pepin the Short as King of the Franks. In return, Pepin handed over to Pope Stephen II the extensive land holdings which later became known as the Papal States. With this acquisition, the pope became a temporal as well as a spiritual leader, and a new era of promise and problems began. The pope was to hold this temporal power until 1870, when Victor Emmanuel I seized the Papal lands. Today's 108 acres of Vatican City were agreed upon by Pius XI and Mussolini in 1929.

Pepin's oldest son, Charles the Great, or Charlemagne, imposed Christianity as the state religion of the West. He was farsighted, energetic, and intelligent, and he had already ruled as king of the Franks for thirty-two years before being crowned Emperor of the West by Pope Leo III on Christmas Day, 800.

Chapter 9   Building Christendom: A.D. 800–1500

Charles the Great's (Charlemagne) coronation in 800 marks the beginning of the Holy Roman Empire.

Franks: a group of people whose origin was in Germany.

Temporal: relating to earthly life.

Carolingian: the reign of Charles (Karl in German) and the Franks who followed him.

Renaissance: a period of rebirth; a revival in art, education, and architecture.

Tithing: the giving of ten percent of one's income or produce to the Church.

Saxons: a Germanic tribe who later invaded England with the Angles (Anglo-Saxon).

As Christian emperor, Charles took his duties seriously. With the strong assistance of the English churchman and scholar, Alcuin, the court became a center of the Carolingian renaissance. Imperial laws regulated everything from attendance at religious services, tithing, almsgiving, and Sunday rest to the daily recitation of the Lord's Prayer and the method of administering baptism. Lawbreakers were punished. With his organizational genius and vision, Charles unified smaller nations into a larger one and created dioceses. Establishing schools, seminaries, and libraries is considered possibly his greatest achievement.

It was Charles who added the "filioque" clause to the creed recited in the royal palace. This *filioque* clause stated that the Holy Spirit proceeded from the Father "and" the Son. The Eastern Church used "through" the Son. This theological issue was to become a major bone of contention in the schism of 1054. Charles also imposed the Benedictine Rule on all monasteries. He did not hesitate to massacre forty-five hundred Saxon warriors and march the remaining population into the rivers for baptism. He was a man of decision and action.

As emperor, he also handpicked his bishops and abbots, treating them as his personal civil servants. The question of whose authority was supreme, the pope's or the emperor's,

The Church: A Spirit-Filled People

became confused. Although the union of Church and state that Charlemagne established would unify the West, it would, nevertheless, plague the Church for centuries to come.

---

1. *What kinds of problems might a pope have if he was also head of a political state?*
2. *How do you think Charlemagne's policies changed the Church?*
3. *What was the difficulty in the way he picked and treated Church leaders?*

Problems and Solutions

How would people react if Pope John Paul II made one of his nephews head of papal finances, gave three other relatives the cardinal's red hat, and sold the Vatican Library to finance a business venture for a cousin? Just such abuses happened in the Middle Ages.

Most of the troubles that plagued the Church for the next seven hundred years were related to feudalism which grew out of the social, economic, and political anarchy brought on by the first barbarian invasions.

Feudalism

Feudalism is the system where all lands were held in the hands of the ruling lord—prince, baron, duke—and the people who worked on the land—serfs—were dependent upon the lord for everything. All that the land produced belonged to the feudal lord. These feudal lords had promised allegiance to the king. When the Church became owners of extensive land holdings, bishops and abbots became servants to the king. The king often appointed close friends and relatives to religious posts in order to safeguard his power, relying on their loyalty. Whether or not these

For Example

A nobleman of Provence bought the bishopric of Narbonne for his ten-year-old son.

Anarchy: the complete absence of law and order.

men had a religious vocation was seldom considered. This practice led to the following abuses:

- *temporal rulers appointed bishops and abbots, conferring on them the insignia of religious office (lay investiture—which caused a struggle that would last for centuries);*
- *Church offices were bought and sold (simony);*
- *relatives were appointed to Church positions (nepotism);*
- *marriages were arranged to keep benefices (special sources of income) in the family;*
- *the clergy kept concubines (nicolaitism).*

The invasion by the Vikings and others led to the collapse of government throughout Europe. The Church alone provided stability.

Invasions

Quarrels among Charlemagne's sons and grandsons caused a breakdown in his feudal empire. Political stability came to an end. People could no longer count on the kingdom to protect them. New barbarian invaders—Saracens, the Magyars, and especially the Vikings—plundered the rich abbeys, shrines, and churches and terrorized the countryside. By the end of the ninth century, Europe was in shambles. In the midst of political chaos, the Church alone represented the ideals of Christian peace, order, and unity. The Church alone intervened to stop wars between rival Christian factions.

Bernard: Bridge Between Two Eras

In the year 1112, Bernard had just turned twenty-one and he knocked at the door of the nearly empty Cistercian abbey of Citeaux, one of the strictest monasteries of Europe. More incredible, this young nobleman from Burgundy had brought his family and friends with him—thirty men in all. It was the rebirth of Citeaux. Bernard's call to the monastery was so strong, it was said that mothers hid their sons, and wives their husbands, when he came fishing for monks.

Four years later, the young Abbot Bernard left with twelve companions to found the monastery of Clairvaux. For ten years his love of poverty, silence, solitude, and contemplation were satisfied. His monastery was known for its emphasis on material poverty.

Eventually, Bernard became Father Abbot to sixty-eight monasteries, prophet, hero, counselor to popes and princes, and a preacher of the Second Crusade. Bernard was gentle, gracious, understanding, and was loved and welcomed everywhere. He is famous for fighting heresy, preaching, and writing poetry.

This Doctor of the Church bridged the feudal world of knighthood and crusades to the emerging world of towns, universities, and cathedrals. He renounced "everything but the art of writing well." His works mirror the humanity of Jesus and his deep and tender devotion to Mary. Bernard died at age sixty-three and was canonized within twenty-one years. Although Clairvaux no longer exists, its descendents number three hundred fifty monasteries, including the Trappist monasteries in the United States.

Concubine: a woman who lives with a man without being legally married to him.

Reform

With the establishment of the Benedictine Abbey of Cluny in 910, the Church began the process of reform. Cluny's charter guaranteed the monks the right to elect their own abbots and, by making them responsible only to the pope, freed them from the intrigues of the feudal system. As the reform spread, the monks were soon in demand both as bishops and even popes. Within a century, the Abbot of Cluny had become the second most important person in the Western Church.

4. Why do you think it is sometimes difficult to try to introduce reforms?

5. What effects do you think the Cluniac reforms had on the monks there?

6. What are some reforms that the Church is undertaking today?

The Greek Schism, 1054

The tensions produced by the modern-day divisions of Korea and Israel/Palestine are situations which compare with the trauma brought on by the division of Christendom into the Orthodox and Roman Catholic Churches at the end of its first thousand years. As the West battled with invaders and reform, the Eastern Church drifted away from the Church of Rome. In the eighth century, the veneration of sacred images had been a controversy. In the ninth, Photius, the Patriarch of Constantinople, had challenged Rome's primacy and orthodoxy. Distance, lack of communication, differences in psychology, language and liturgy, and scandals in Rome contributed to the division.

The immediate causes of the schism of 1054 involved the personal ambition of the Patriarch of Constantinople, Michael Cerularius, and a certain mishandling of the situation by papal legates. The "filioque" controversy surfaced once again. Western customs of using unleavened bread at the Eucharist, observing Saturday fasts, and ordaining celibate priests were rejected in the East.

The Patriarch of Antioch begged Cerularius to overlook externals: "We must not expect from these barbarians," he said, "the same perfect manners as we have among our own people. I beg you, I implore you to give way." A ceremonial burning of the papal bull with mutual excommunications completed the split. Only Cerularius was excommunicated, but his position as Patriarch of Constantinople meant that the entire East would eventually break away from Rome. Attempts at reunion were made at Lyon in 1274 and Florence in 1438, but were unsuccessful. Over nine hundred years later, in 1965, Pope Paul VI and Patriarch Athenagoras I lifted the excommunications of each other's representatives, but the tragic Greek schism of 1054 endures to this day.

7. Do you know anyone who is a member of the Orthodox Church? How does this person regard the pope?

Customs between the Catholic Church in the East and West are very similar, yet uniquely different. These Ukranian Orthodox Easter eggs, called *pysanky*, are an example of this uniqueness.

Veneration: honor paid to the saints as brothers and sisters of Christ in heaven.

Primacy: the state of being first in rank.

Orthodoxy: correct doctrine and teaching.

Schism: a formal split or division of a Church body into two.

Legate: an official representative of the pope.

Bull: an official document, edict, or decree issued by the pope.

Chapter 9   Building Christendom: A.D. 800–1500

On This Rock

One of the differences between the Eastern and Western Churches is the issue of the veneration of icons. Icons are religious images venerated as holy by Eastern Christians. In the West, it was feared that such images would turn into idols, or would overemphasize the human side of Jesus while ignoring his divinity.

The iconoclastic (image-breaker) controversy raged on for many years. The West forbade the veneration of icons in the 700s and 800s.

This controversy is often seen as one of the main factors in the eventual split between East and West. If you visit an Eastern Orthodox Church today, you will still see the beautiful, stylized icons decorating the interior. In the West, images are often used as ornaments and to reflect biblical scenes, but they do not have the status of icons.

Henry IV seeks entrance to Canossa Castle to beg absolution from Pope Gregory VII.

Pope Versus Emperors

The struggle over lay investiture continued to be a problem between Church and state in the West well into the fourteenth century. Our modern world reeled in shock when John Paul II was shot in 1979, but tenth century Christians must have been even more scandalized to see Christian kings and emperors deposing, insulting, and waging war against the Holy Father. In the tenth century, the popes could exert little or no direct influence on the Church because of political anarchy in Italy. Churchmen in other countries were often dependent on local rulers for assistance, a practice that led to abuses of power.

It was Gregory VII, 1073-1085, also known as Hildebrand, who led the reform to win freedom of episcopal elections, remove simony, and restore clerical celibacy. Under pain of excommunication, princes were forbidden to make appointments to Church offices. When the German Emperor, Henry IV, ignored this decree, Gregory deposed him and absolved all his servants from their oaths of allegiance. For three days, Henry stood in the snow outside the Castle of Canossa in Italy where Gregory had stopped, pretending to repent and begging for absolution. Later, Henry retaliated by finding flaws in Gregory's election to the papacy and deposing him. The pope died in captivity, declaring, "I have loved justice and hated wickedness, therefore I die in exile." In the end the emperor was forced to give up investing bishops.

Gregory had initiated badly needed reforms by centralizing authority, setting up papal courts, and codifying Church law. These reforms were an attempt to return to early Church policies, but with the political structure in place in 1075, no king could have accepted them without protesting. Unfortunately, these very reforms laid the groundwork for what later was to become the overly bureaucratic Church organization that Vatican II began to modify.

The Era of Antipopes

Until 1250, the Emperors Frederick Barbarossa and Frederick II tried to dominate the Church. "The law is whatever the emperor wills," Barbarossa's chancellor told the pope. Innocent III, 1198-1216, who represented the papacy at the height of its temporal power, and the only pope who might have been strong enough to deal with such attitudes, held the office almost entirely between the reigns of these two emperors.

In the battle between emperor and pope, imperial weapons included papal exile, the creation of antipopes, military troops, and the confiscation and destruction of Church property. Besides armies, the pope used excommunication, interdiction, papal bulls, and canon law. In England, the struggle centered on whether the government had the right to tax Church property and whether they had the right to use Church courts for trials. It destroyed the friendship of Henry II and Thomas à Becket, Archbishop of Canterbury. The king's exasperated remark, "Is there no one to free me from this turbulent monk?" resulted in Becket's murder in his own cathedral. The Archbishop's last words were, "For the name of Jesus and the defense of the Church I am ready to die." Thomas à Becket was canonized within three years, and Canterbury became a place of pilgrimage.

Antipope: a person, other than the one chosen by Church law, pretending to be pope.

Interdict: a church statement which excludes a whole parish or diocese from the sacraments and other Church privileges.

Pope Innocent III, represented the papacy at the height of its power.

The Church: A Spirit-Filled People

The Great Insult

The last great struggle between Church and state at this time involved the French king, Philip IV, and Boniface VIII, 1294-1303. When Boniface forbade the clergy to pay royal taxes imposed without his consent, French armies descended on the papal summer residence at Anagni and captured the Holy Father. If it is true that one of Philip's allies actually struck Pope Boniface in the face, it was a "slap heard 'round the world." One month later Boniface died as a result of imprisonment and shock. Papal prestige never recovered from this insult to the pope's dignity. The papal bull *Unam Sanctam*, 1302, which declared that the spiritual has power over the temporal, had little effect.

---

8. What tensions exist today between Church and state?

9. In what circumstances would you be willing to sacrifice a close friendship for the sake of what you believe is right?

Summary

- Charlemagne was a Christian ruler who regulated religious observance throughout the West.
- The "filioque" clause was a contributing factor to the schism between East and West.
- Feudalism led to tensions between Church and state in appointment of religious leaders and economic issues.
- In 1054, the East formally broke away from the West.
- Struggles between Church and state rulers led to excommunications, exile, antipopes, and even murder.

SECTION 1
Checkpoint!

■ Review

1. What policies did Charlemagne implement in his efforts to create a Christian Europe?

2. Explain lay investiture and discuss why it caused such problems between temporal and spiritual leaders.

3. How did Bernard help to restore a balance to the Church?

4. What were some of the causes of the Schism of 1054?

5. How did Gregory VII try to introduce reform and overpower the Emperor? Did it work?

6. Why was Thomas à Becket murdered?

7. Words to Know: Charlemagne, "filioque," lay investiture, simony, Cluny, schism, papal bull, antipope, Thomas à Becket.

■ In Your World

1. Attend a liturgy of the Orthodox Church. Observe the differences and similarities between a Catholic Mass and the Orthodox service. How is the building itself distinguished? What specific aspects of Eastern Christianity that you have learned about did you observe?

2. Have a round-table discussion about reform in the Church. Discuss the value of reforms which have been made, and other reforms you would like to see implemented. Let everyone contribute an idea and try to present criticism or suggestions. Choose someone to moderate.

■ Scripture Search

Read Matthew 22:15-22. What do you think this saying of Jesus means? What does it say about loyalty? How would you apply it to Christians throughout the world today?

SECTION 2
Crusades, Orders, and Pilgrims

The twelfth and thirteenth centuries brought many changes in the Church. The Church became involved in new activities, developed new structures, and faced new struggles. Great contributions to the life of Europe were made by educated and skilled Church members, both lay and religious. The dawn of the fourteenth century would bring crusades, dissent, and a new problem—the Black Death.

On the March for God

American soldiers in World War II were not the first soldiers to travel halfway around the world to fight. For nearly two centuries, 1100-1300, European soldiers traveled to the Middle East in a series of religious-military expeditions called Crusades. These campaigns were organized and blessed by the Church and were dedicated to regaining and defending the Holy Land from the Muslims. They were regarded as works of piety. This was a major change from the first three centuries A.D. when Christianity was non-violent. Jesus' command to love one's enemies was followed strictly. In the garden, Peter had been told to put away his sword. Augustine's "just-war theory," developed during the period of the barbarian invasions, was the start of this turnabout for the Church.

Historians have identified eight, or sometimes nine, specific Crusades. Idealism, chivalry, religious zeal, devotion to the faith, and a spirit of adventure were real during the Crusades, but so were the abuses that occurred at that time—political expediency, cruelty, and greed. This resulted in the shameless killing of Jews, Eastern Christians, and Turks as the crusaders moved west toward Jerusalem.

Chapter 9 Building Christendom: A.D. 800–1500

The Crusades, while failures militarily, brought a sense of unity to Europe, opening the continent to different cultures and trade.

Papal recruiters who preached the Crusades offered a variety of incentives for "taking the cross." Indulgences, granting full or partial remission of the punishment still due for a sin after forgiveness in the sacrament of Penance, similar to those granted to pilgrims traveling to the Holy Places, were among the enticing benefits for crusaders.

Kings, princes, noblemen, common soldiers, and peasants took the crusader's vow, sewing a huge cloth cross on the outside of their garments. Merchants and paupers tagged along. There was even the scandal of the so-called Children's Crusade of 1212, when thousands of adolescents who took the cross died on the journey or were captured and sold as slaves in Egypt. As the desire to participate in the Crusades weakened, some people took the vow and then paid others to go on the journey in their places.

From a military standpoint, the Crusades were a failure. The Crusades left Europe's most valiant men dead, the Church treasury depleted, and the East and West further from reunion than before. However, the campaigns were not without benefits. Pilgrims could again visit the holy places. The Crusades gave Europe a new sense of unity and brought about the meeting of different cultures and the exchange of trade. Crusaders who lost their lives were revered as martyrs.

10. *Do you think the Crusades were necessary? Why? What do you think about the idea of war (or some wars) as holy?*

The Flowering of Christendom

While much of the Church's story is told in terms of official Church leaders and outstanding saints and scholars, the Church is the whole People of God. The Spirit continued to live in the vast multitude of unnamed lay Christians who achieved all that was best in the medieval Church. They filled the monasteries, built the cathedrals, attended the universities, made pilgrimages, joined the new religious orders of mendicants, and went off as missionaries to Christianize northern Europe, Asia, Syria, China, India, and North Africa.

Monks, working at their scriptoriums, preserved the traditions of the past, and set the stage for the great revival of learning during the Middle Ages.

God's Mendicants

During this time, many of the clergy had grown wealthy and powerful. In order to restore the Church to Christian ideals of humility and poverty, the Holy Spirit gifted the medieval Church with a new form of religious life. Unlike the monks, who retreated from the world, groups of religious friars, or brothers, led by Francis of Assisi, Dominic, and others, carried Christ to the towns and marketplaces.

Mendicant: a beggar, one who lives on alms, or charity.

Medieval: The period between c. 600–1500, called the Middle Ages.

Chapter 9 Building Christendom: A.D. 800–1500

Communion of Saints

Catherine of Siena (1347-1380) joined the Third Order of Saint Dominic at the age of 16. Even during her childhood she had experienced visions. She was known for her care of the sick and poor, and she converted many. She was a deeply spiritual person, who became involved in resolving two of the serious crises of the Church.

At the age of thirty-three, in 1380, Catherine died. She was canonized in 1461 and declared a Doctor of the Church in 1970. Many of her letters and her work, *Dialogue*, remain to give us insight into the life of this member of one of the earliest orders of mendicants.

Franciscans

You're probably most familiar with Francis because of his Prayer for Peace. He was a soldier and the son of a wealthy cloth merchant of Assisi (Italy) when he was converted and then renounced all worldly possessions to depend completely on God's providence. Hidden beneath his coarse clothing, deceptive frailty, and poetic language was a will of steel and a heart on fire with love for God his Father. Christ had spoken to him from the crucifix, "Francis, go and rebuild my house; it is tumbling down." Francis went, changing the entire Church, and not simply the Chapel of San Damiano, as originally intended.

His devotion to "Lady Poverty" created an army of Friars Minor (Lesser Brothers) who carried the Gospel message of gratitude and joy throughout Europe, preaching Gospel poverty to lay persons in much the same way as Bernard had done for monks and clerics. The Poor Clares, his "little plant," as Francis affectionately called the Second Order, were the Friars' female counterparts under the leadership of Saint Clare.

Saint Francis and his followers challenged the world to return to a way of peace and spirituality.

The Church: A Spirit-Filled People

Dominicans and Other Orders

Dominic's Order of Preachers, with its emphasis on scholarship and preaching, attracted such quality thinkers and scholars that popes, cardinals, bishops, and university professors soon rose from their ranks. The Franciscans and Dominicans, together with the Augustinians and Carmelites, gave the Church a corps of preachers, teachers, and trained confessors who lived the Gospel and were ready to go wherever they were needed. Their Third Order of lay persons produced such saints as Elizabeth of Hungary, Saint Louis of France, and one of the two women Doctors of the Church, Catherine of Siena.

The Bible of the Poor

All the characteristics of medieval religion were typified in the abbey churches and cathedrals that were built from the eleventh to the thirteenth centuries. Massive walls, small windows, and rounded vaults of the Romanesque style gave way to the vaulted arches, stained glass windows, and towering spires of the Gothic cathedrals. Under the direction of the bishops, cathedral buildings became a corporate venture and towns competed with one another to build the largest structures. Contributions came from kings and princes, common folk and paupers, trade guilds, and penitents. The greatest examples of Gothic gracefulness are found in the four French cathedrals of Notre Dame (1163-1260), Chartres (1194-1260), Rheims (1214-1300), and Amiens (1194-1270).

A cathedral was not only the church of the bishop and the depository of a town's store of precious relics, but also an ideal place for town meetings, dramas, commercial exchanges, and pilgrim overnights. Sculpture, painting, and stained glass gave a visual representation to the mysteries of faith, society's structure and hierarchy, angels and demons, virtues and vices. For the benefit of most of the population, which could not read, Bible stories and Church teaching were taught through art work in the Cathedral. This made every cathedral an art gallery, school, and library as well as a place of worship.

Medieval Pilgrimages

In addition to creating Gothic masterpieces, common folk expressed their piety and faith by means of local and international pilgrimages. The Christian practice of pilgrimage has its roots in the days of the early Church, when believers went to Rome to pray at the tombs of the Apostles Peter and Paul. By the fourth century, pilgrims from the West were journeying to the Holy Land. Some visited shrines to obtain special favors, others to atone for a moral failing, to fulfill a sacramental penance or private vow, to gain a special indulgence, or simply as an expression of faith and devotion.

Those who were brave, or rich, followed the crusade routes to the Holy Land, often a three-year roundtrip, with the constant danger of being massacred or sold into slavery. Enticed by indulgences and many shrines, large numbers of people descended upon Rome. Multiple routes led to Compostello in northeastern Spain, where Saint James was said to have labored. From England, Canterbury beckoned. In addition, every nation had its own local shrines.

Medieval Architecture attempted to capture the greatness and glory of God.

The Church of the Middle Ages

The Church was one of the most important institutions of the Middle Ages. It had a great influence on all aspects of society, including art, architecture, literature, faith, medicine, law, economics, and even etiquette (the proper way to behave).

- *During the Middle Ages, mysticism flourished. The mystic attempted to experience more direct communion with God. Three of the most famous mystics are Saint John of the Cross, Hildegard of Bingen, and Saint Teresa of Avila. Mystics have left us beautiful poetry and accounts of their experiences which help us in our own lives of faith.*

- *Christian principles of justice and charity characterized the fraternities of workmen called guilds. Each guild was devoted to a particular trade, and they guaranteed fair prices, good workmanship, and work for all members. They also contributed to the building and upkeep of churches and cared for the sick, widows, and dependent children.*

- *Our idea of the ideal gentleman owes a lot to the image of the medieval knight. Knights practiced chivalry, which was a code of conduct that incorporated many Christian ideals. True knights defended religion and the king, protected the poor and oppressed, and fostered good manners. The Church introduced knighting ceremonies and encouraged knights to practice not only courage and loyalty, but also faith, humility, and charity. Many knights participated in the Crusades.*

- *In every period of history, the Church has been close to the people by being involved in all aspects of their daily lives. Christian ideals of behavior and faith have influenced professions, individuals, and institutions since the time of the Apostles.*

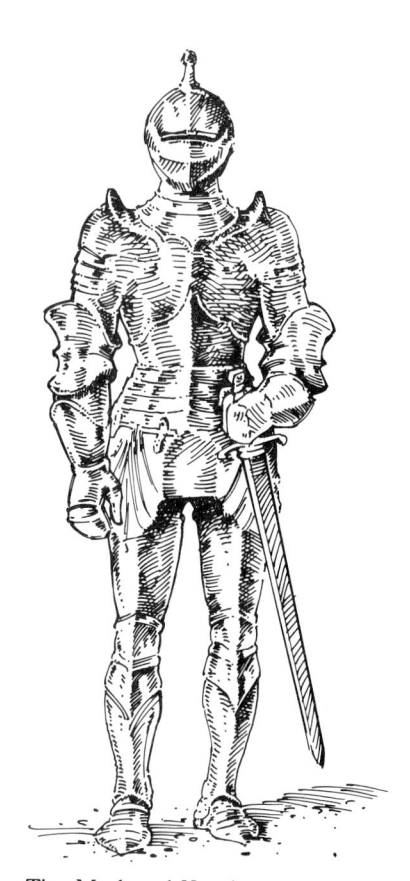

The Medieval Knight in full armor was a gallant figure. The Code of Conduct for Knights was based upon Christian principles.

Chapter 9 Building Christendom: A.D. 800–1500

Pilgrims, equipped with hand-copied guidebooks for the road and handbooks of what to look for upon arrival, were a joyful lot, singing and praying as they traveled. Sometimes there were miraculous cures. Always there were shrines at which to pray and relics to venerate. Chaucer immortalized the medieval pilgrimage in his *Canterbury Tales*.

11. *What religious orders are you familiar with? What needs in the Church do they serve?*

12. *Have you ever made a pilgrimage? What are some pilgrimage places in the United States?*

Schools and Scholars

By the sixteenth century, there were eighty-one universities in Europe. Every university had schools of theology, law, medicine, and art. Latin was the language of the classroom. Students, most of whom were clerics, sat on the floor or, if the classes were too large, in the local church. They listened to lectures, took notes, and then participated in the discussion, debate, and criticism that followed. In this setting, scholasticism, an attempt to take all knowledge—whether known by faith or reason—and arrange it into a systematic form, flourished. Anselm, Abelard, and Bernard of Clairvaux were the forerunners of scholasticism. Albert the Great, Saint Bonaventure, Saint Thomas Aquinas, Roger Bacon, and Duns Scotus represent scholasticism at its peak of development.

Thomas Aquinas, the "dumb ox," as his fellow students labeled him, was to become the most influential mind of the Middle Ages. In his *Summa Theologica* and numerous other works, the "Angelic Doctor" (as Thomas was later called) showed that, since truth is one, true faith and true science cannot contradict each other. In a vision, Christ reportedly told Thomas, "You have written well of me, Thomas, what would you have as your reward?" "Only yourself, Lord," was the reply. The most brilliant man in Christendom refused to write further. "After what I have seen," he said, "all that I have written seems like straw."

The Church: A Spirit-Filled People

The medieval universities that grew out of the cathedral schools seem to have had discipline problems, much as schools do today. Feast days were always occasions for rowdy conduct and pranks. Students suffered from too little money, unexcused absences, and the lure of the local taverns.

---

13. What conflict do you see between faith and reason? Does faith need to make sense?

14. What does Thomas Aquinas' nickname (dumb ox) tell you about the relationship between the way people appear and their true abilities?

Summary

- The Crusades were expeditions sanctioned by the Church to regain the Holy Land from the Muslims.

- Religious friars and sisters renounced all possessions and remained in the world to teach, preach, and help others.

- Great cathedrals were built which served many purposes, and pilgrimages became popular expressions of faith and piety.

- Medieval universities produced scholars like Thomas Aquinas who succeeded in creating a system of Christian knowledge and theology.

SECTION 2
Checkpoint!

■ Review

1. Why were the Crusades organized? Were they successful?

2. What is the difference between the Benedictine monks and the newer orders of friars?

3. What contributions have the various orders made?

4. How were Gothic cathedrals used?

5. Why did faithful Christians embark on pilgrimages?

6. What was the aim of scholasticism?

7. Words to Know: crusade, mendicant, Franciscans, Dominicans, pilgrimage, scholasticism, mystic.

■ In Your World

1. Give a presentation on one of the Gothic cathedrals. Use either slides or pictures. Where and when was it built? What are its distinguishing features (stained glass, relics, arches)? What do we know about its history?

2. Make your own pilgrimage to a local shrine or cathedral. Keep a journal about your journey. How did you get there and how long did it take? What did you see? How did it make you feel? Who else was there? Try to imagine how the medieval pilgrimages compared to your own.

3. Tell the class about one of the women's counterparts of the great medieval orders such as the Poor Clares or Carmelite Nuns. Who founded the order, when was it founded, and what is their special function?

■ Scripture Search

Read the following passages: Psalms 41:1-3; Proverbs 6:6-11, 13:7-21, 14:21, 28:6; Matthew 19:21; 2 Corinthians 8:9; Philippians 2:5-6. What images of poverty are found in these passages? How can you reconcile these different images? How do you think the medieval mendicants used these passages as inspiration and how can you use them?

SECTION 3
Decline

After the thirteenth century, the "greatest of centuries" as it is has sometimes been called, the confusion and scandals during the fourteenth and fifteenth centuries signaled a serious spiritual decline. The Avignon "Captivity" and the Great Western Schism caused papal authority and prestige to decline. Wars and the Black Death created fear and despair. Heresies weakened the faith, and clerical abuses in the Church grew. The Renaissance brought a shift in emphasis—away from God and toward more human endeavors. In all of this, Christ remained with his Church as he promised. It was evident that reform was needed, but the strong personalities needed to bring about reform were not present. In order to understand the Church and its weaknesses and strengths, it's crucial that we understand the errors of this period.

Avignon "Captivity"

In 1305, seeking to escape from the intrigues of Roman politics, Pope Clement V moved the papacy from Rome to the French-speaking town of Avignon, where he and the next six popes lived. This period, from 1305-1378, is sometimes called the Babylonian Captivity, a parallel to the seventy years when the Jews were captives in Babylon.

The cost of the move, of the crusades, and of the extravagant papal court at Avignon resulted in higher Church taxes and widespread resentment. Saint Bridget of Sweden claimed she had a vision in which Christ himself condemned the French popes and accused them of populating hell. Finally, in 1376, Catherine of Siena, a mystic and devoted lover of the Church, convinced Gregory XI to leave Avignon and return to Rome. His death within two years ushered in an even worse disaster—the Great Western Schism.

Chapter 9   Building Christendom: A.D. 800–1500

15. What effects do you think it would have if the Holy Father were to move his residence to another city?

A People at Prayer

Saint Francis wrote many beautiful poems and prayers. In the "Canticle of the Sun," which he wrote in Italian, Francis praised the revelation of God as it is experienced in nature:

"Praise to You, my Lord, for all Your creatures, above all Brother Sun, who brings us the day and lends us his light; lovely is he, radiant with great splendor, and speaks to us of You, O Most High. Praise to You, my Lord, for Sister Moon and the stars which You have set in the heavens, clear, precious, and fair. Praise to You, my Lord, for Brother Wind, for air and cloud, for calm and all weather by which You support life in all Your creatures . . ."

This prayer is a beautiful reminder of the way we see God revealed to us every day through the wonders of nature which we often take for granted.

Who Is the Real Pope?

Within three months, the French cardinals who had elected Gregory's successor, Urban VI, an Italian archbishop, realized their mistake in yielding to the Roman populace, which had demanded an Italian pope. Urban alienated them by making strong remarks against the French cardinals, attempting to reform their lifestyle, and by outbursts of temper that were so violent that even Catherine urged him, "For the love of Jesus crucified, Holy Father, soften a little the sudden movements of your temper." It was too much. The cardinals, declaring their own election invalid, elected a new pope, the Frenchman Clement VII, and returned with him to Avignon. Urban simply created a new set of twenty-eight cardinals, all in one day. It was the beginning of the Western Schism. Strictly speaking, the Great Western Schism was not a schism, since no one had broken away from the Church. Several different people simply claimed to head it.

For the next forty years, the Church was a house divided. The faithful, even the saints, were confused about which pope was Peter's true successor. Nations took sides. Religious orders split over their loyalties. Individual dioceses had two bishops, or none. When the Council of Pisa tried to depose both popes and elect a third, Alexander V, respect for the papacy evaporated. Finally, Gregory XII legalized the beginning of the Council of Constance and then abdicated. The Council of Constance deposed the other two popes and elected Martin V, ending the Western Schism, one of the worst scandals in Christian history.

16. How would you have solved this problem?

17. What do you think happened to the Church as a holy institution during this period?

The Church: A Spirit-Filled People

Wars and the Black Death

Two other situations in Europe upset society and affected the Church: the Hundred Years' War (1337-1453), fought between France and England for control of French territory; and the Black Death. The great heroine and saint of the war was Joan of Arc, a French peasant girl who convinced the dauphin to allow her to lead the French armies against the English. In battle after battle, the "Warrior Maid of Orleans" routed the enemy. Later betrayed and sold to the English, Joan was imprisoned, accused of heresy, and burned at the stake in 1431. Charges of heresy were later revoked and she was canonized in 1920.

Then in 1348, a fatal plague struck Europe. This form of plague was called the Black Death, because the skin of those afflicted turned black. The carriers of this plague were on ships that came to Europe from India and China. Plague victims died in a matter of days. Often, contact with an afflicted person, living or dead, meant contamination.

Joan of Arc, the Maid of Orleans, was canonized in 1920, 500 years after being burned as a heretic.

Abdicate: to give up one's claim to an office or position.

Dauphin: a title given to the eldest son of the king of France. It was used from 1349-1830.

Chapter 9 Building Christendom: A.D. 800–1500

As the plague moved from Italy northward, no European country escaped. Within two years, forty million people, one-third to one-half of the population of Europe, were dead. In six weeks Avignon alone counted 11,000 corpses. As a class, the clergy suffered most—a tribute to their willingness to minister to the dying. Religious houses were deserted and standards for priestly education were lowered. Economic activity was paralyzed and life became so uncertain that people everywhere despaired.

Between the 1350s and the 1450s, life in Europe was a series of strange contradictions. Witchcraft and sorcery flourished, but so did mysticism. Some people abandoned themselves to lives of pleasure, while others, like the Flagellants, practiced excessive penances. Popular piety overflowed in endless processions and miracle plays, and art was preoccupied with death. Cults of the saints and their relics bordered on superstition, even madness. Society suffered from violence, excesses of sensuality, and an absentee clergy. Everything seemed in disarray.

18. How do you think the plague led to some of the excesses and strange habits of people at this time?

Reactionary Heresies

Heresies of the Middle Ages were primarily attempts to create "the perfect Church." The Waldenses, led by Peter Waldo, a layman from Lyons, France, aimed at reforming the Church. Peter's return to Gospel poverty and preaching contained many of the elements that Francis of Assisi and his friars would later add to the Church. The difference was Peter's disobedience to his archbishop and, finally, his rejection of the clergy and the entire Church.

The Cathari (Pure Ones), or Albigensians, mixed rigorous penance and laxity. The "perfect" or "pure ones" were the movement's saints and martyrs. Voluntary suicide by starvation was looked upon as the ideal of sanctity. Ordinary "believers" were assured salvation by means of a kind of deathbed purification rite.

Michelangelo—Art and Inspiration

Michelangelo Buonarrote (1475-1564) is one of the best known artists of the Renaissance. He was born in the town of Caprese in Italy. He was very interested in sculpture as a youth and was apprenticed to a master in Rome. There, he sculpted the famous *Pieta*. He later went to Florence and began to work on the sculpture of *David* which took three years to complete. During this time, Michelangelo struggled with the conflict he saw between his appreciation of the human form and his sensitivity for asceticism and faith. The *Pieta* is a good example of the way he was able to depict both.

In 1505, he was called back to Rome by Pope Julius II. From 1508-1512, Michelangelo worked at painting the ceiling of the Sistine Chapel. The magnificent paintings of biblical scenes, like the Creation and Last Judgment, are evidence of his talent and dedication.

Michelangelo was also given the task of chief architect of St. Peter's Basilica, and he worked on this project until his death. He was so famous during his lifetime that a biography was written while he was still alive. Of his own writings, we have many sonnets (poems) and a short autobiography.

For those who visit the Sistine Chapel and see the other works of this great genius, Michelangelo's religious devotion is clear. His visual contributions to the Church will be with us for centuries to come.

The Sistine Chapel is an excellent example of the work of Michelangelo.

Flagellants: groups of wandering fanatics who scourged themselves until they drew blood.

Absentee clergy: bishops and priests who held several dioceses or parishes and collected revenues without actually living there.

Albigensians: a name taken from their stronghold in the French city of Albi.

Chapter 9   Building Christendom: A.D. 800–1500

For Example

The astronomer Galileo was an innocent victim of the Inquisition.

Innocent III called for a crusade against these "worse-than-Muslim" heretics. The Dominican friars devoted themselves entirely to the work of converting the Cathari and were entrusted with the court of the Inquisition, a tribunal created to inquire into the existence of heresy. This was a common procedure in an age when heresy was considered a dangerous threat to Church and state alike. Those found guilty were given to the civil government for punishment. The excesses of the Inquisition and the abuses to which it led (especially in Spain where it functioned under royal, not Church, direction) make it one of the darker chapters of Church history.

19. Why do you think excessive asceticism is dangerous for body and spirit?

20. What do you think is the best way for the Church to deal with views and acts it considers unorthodox or threatening?

Patrons of the Arts

Just as recent discoveries of ancient manuscripts and the finding of modern archaeological digs have resulted in renewed interest in biblical studies, so the fourteenth-century rebirth of interest in Greek and Roman art and literature, known as the Renaissance, resulted in new creativity throughout Europe.

Religion continued to inspire the arts, as it did during the Middle Ages. The Church sponsored the work of great artists. On the ceiling of the Sistine Chapel in the Vatican, Michelangelo portrayed the creation of Adam and other scenes of Genesis. On its walls, he displayed the *Last Judgment* with fierce realism. Leonardo da Vinci's *Last Supper* and Raphael's superb *Sistine Madonna* rank among the classic works of art. The Madonna, biblical scenes,

Christ, and the crucifixion became immortalized in sculpture, painting, and bronze, reflecting Renaissance attention to the summitry of the human form. Of all Renaissance literature, the *Imitation of Christ* by Thomas à Kempis was most popular. Chaucer's *Canterbury Tales,* Dante's *Divine Comedy,* and Thomas More's *Utopia* are also considered literary classics. Monumental achievements of Renaissance architecture were the Cathedral of Florence and St. Peter's Basilica in Rome.

The Need for Reform

As the popes became engrossed in patronizing the arts and commissioning great religious works, spiritual reform fell by the wayside. Unfortunately, immorality, worldliness, greed, and arrogance became a way of life for many Christians.

Fifty years before Martin Luther, Girolamo Savonarola, 1452-1498, a Dominican friar from Florence, cried out for Church reform in bold, earthly language. "The coffin will soon be opened, and when that time comes, the stench will be such that the whole of Christendom will hold its nose." Radical zeal made him the despotic ruler of Florence and finally led him into heresy. Deserted by his followers, he was convicted and burned at the stake.

The papacy reached the depths of degradation in Alexander VI (1492-1503), who loved luxury and gave his own children the best honors, offices, and benefices the Church could offer. No wonder one visitor to Rome wrote, "I have spent several months in Rome and I have seen prelates and important personages behaving in such a way that if I were to remain here I would be afraid of losing my faith." One historian observed, however, "The ordinary peasant . . . was usually a staunch supporter of the Church. He might grumble about tithes and wax sarcastic at the expense of well-fed lazy clerics, but he still accepted the teachings and the leadership of the Church."

The popes who followed Alexander VI did little to change the situation. With money gained from the "sale" of indulgences or extracted from pious pilgrims, the Renaissance popes had turned Rome into an art center, a poor substitute for the total reform soon to be forced upon the Church by Luther and Calvin.

21. What do you think was the purpose of the artistic contributions made to the Church?

22. Why do you think that the scandals of Church leadership did not filter down to common people or cause them to lose their faith?

Summary

- During the Avignon Captivity, the papacy moved away from Rome to escape scandal, but ended up causing division within the Church.

- Wars and the Black Death destroyed many people in Europe and left those alive in despair.

- Reaction to these disasters led to attempts at perfection which were often heretical.

- The Inquisition was formed to root out heresies, even though it also became guilty of excesses.

- The Renaissance brought new artistic expression in painting and sculpture which focused on meaningful biblical scenes.

SECTION 3
Checkpoint!

■ Review

1. What was the Avignon Captivity?

2. How did the "Western Schism" finally end?

3. Describe the effects of the Black Death on the population of Europe.

4. Why were the Waldensians and Cathari considered heretics?

5. What was the purpose of the Inquisition?

6. How did the artwork and literature of the Renaissance enrich the Church?

7. Words to Know: Avignon Captivity, Great Western Schism, Black Death, Waldensians.

■ In Your World

1. Write a daily entry from the diary of a priest or nun who lived during the time of the Black Death. How do you try to serve the people? What are your fears? How do the healthy treat you and those who are sick and dying? What do you see, smell, and hear around you?

2. Study two pieces of artwork of one of the great artists of the Renaissance, or read one chapter from one of the books mentioned in this chapter. Report on what you have learned to the class. What imagery is used? What contribution do you think the artist/author made to the history of the Church?

■ Scripture Search

Read the following: Proverbs 9:12; Matthew 9:10-13; Luke 10:8-9, 29-37. What do these passages say to you about treatment of those who are sick? How do you think the medieval mendicants and other religious who lived during the period of the plague used Jesus' words and actions as an example? How can you do the same?

CHAPTER 9 Review

■ Study

1. What did Charlemagne do to improve the life of the Church? What did he do that was harmful?

2. How did lay investiture threaten the authority of the Church?

3. Why were monks from the Abbey of Cluny in such demand?

4. Name at least two differences between observance in the Eastern Churches and the Western Church.

5. What reforms did Gregory VII initiate?

6. What weapons were used on both sides in the battle between emperors and popes?

7. What was the "slap heard 'round the world"?

8. What was the purpose of the Crusades and how was that purpose abused?

9. Who were the mendicants and what was their special contribution to medieval Christianity?

10. Explain the importance of a cathedral for a medieval European town.

11. Why did people go on pilgrimages?

12. Who was Thomas Aquinas and what did he do?

13. Why was the Great Western Schism not really a schism?

14. How did the Black Death lead to a period of uneasiness and despair throughout Europe?

15. What were some of the cultural contributions made during these centuries and how do they contribute to the history of the Church?

■ Action

1. Conduct a workshop on the possibility of reconciliation between the Eastern and Western Churches. How hard do you think it would be to work out? What problems do the two Churches face? Would there have to be compromises? By whom and over what issues?

2. Give a presentation which shows an overview of this period. Include both the good and bad events and people of medieval Europe. Focus on those events which you think best represent the place of the Church in society. Use pictures, music, or draw your own images and slides.

■ Prayer

The Jesus Prayer is a short prayer originating in the East composed by Nicephorus the Solitary who lived on Mount Athos in Greece. The prayer is short, only thirteen words, but it is meant to be repeated over and over. Today, this prayer has become popular in both the West and the East.

Nicephorus wrote that preparation for this prayer included sitting alone, becoming tranquil, and breathing slowly. Follow these instructions by finding a quiet spot and sitting quietly for several minutes before beginning. Try repeating the prayer for five minutes silently: "Lord Jesus, Son of the Living God, have mercy on me, a sinner."

Think about how effective this experience was and try again.

CHAPTER

10

Family Rifts: A.D. 1500–1600

OBJECTIVES

In this Chapter you will

- Examine the factors which led to the Reformation.

- Learn about the life of Martin Luther and his original intention in criticizing the Church.

- Read about the consequences of Luther's actions and their influence on others, such as Calvin.

- Follow the path of reform from Germany to Switzerland to England.

- Discover the rebirth and renewal within the Catholic Church at the Council of Trent.

Christ summons the Church, as she goes her pilgrim way, to that continual reformation of which she always has need, insofar as she is an institution of men here on earth.
—"Decree on Ecumenism," #6

The Church: A Spirit-Filled People

SECTION 1
The Launching of the Reformation

Neil Armstrong could take the first step on the moon in the summer of 1969 only because the time and conditions were right. Science, industry, and technology had reached a proper level of development. When Martin Luther, an Augustinian monk and professor at the University of Wittenberg, Germany, nailed his ninety-five theses (including indulgences) to the university church door in 1517, the time and social conditions were right to support a reformation. This chapter will trace the origin of the three major churches established during the Reformation—the Lutheran, the Calvinist, and the Anglican—and explain how the Roman Catholic Church went about reforming and renewing itself.

Luther's Concerns

No one, least of all Luther himself, suspected that criticizing abuses in the Church—including the sale of spiritual benefits—would spark a fire that would engulf all of Europe, separating half of Europe away from allegiance to Rome. Within fifty years, the Roman Catholic Church was wounded and divided, and its authority, teachings, and structure were called into question. A variety of Protestant churches emerged, each carrying within itself the seeds of further splintering and division.

The Reformation was not a consciously organized movement. Its principal leaders, Martin Luther in Germany, John Calvin in Switzerland, and Henry VIII in England, had very little in common besides an ability to respond to the needs of their times. Even the main religious ideas of the

Reformation were not entirely new. Calls for Church reform had sounded long before Luther challenged the abuses associated with the granting of indulgences. In the fourteenth century, both John Wycliffe and John Hus had supported the ideas of an invisible Church and Scripture as the final authority on matters of faith. Both were to be condemned as heretics for their efforts.

Martin Luther was a brilliant, driven man who was offended by corruption in the Church. Luther wanted to reform the Roman Catholic Church, not start a new religion.

The Special Conditions

What were the special conditions in the first half of the sixteenth century that readied society for a permanent break from the Roman Catholic Church? What made the break, once begun, grow and spread? There are no simple answers. In part, the great cultural precursor of the Reformation—the Renaissance—had awakened an interest in the common people, their achievements and needs. Emphasis was on this world rather than the next. Increased education of people led to questions about the traditional faith and the role of the Church. There was a rapid growth in printing and the availability of books, somewhat like the electronic explosion of today. New translations of the Bible helped emphasize the growing interest in its private interpretation. In addition, the rise of nationalism made states and principalities eager to throw off Church restrictions and privileges.

Scandal Continues

Although the Avignon papacy and the Great Western Schism were now history, Peter's successors continued to scandalize many people by living as Renaissance princes. Added to the excesses of the clergy were the rivalries between religious orders, an overemphasis on religious externals, papal politics, frequent mechanical and superstitious approaches to piety, and the peasant unrest in Germany. The ordinary desires of humanity—jealousy and greed—and even the honest desire to correct the abuses of the day in order to return to the simpler age of the Apostles played a part. It is significant that none of the reformers began with a desire to separate from Rome. They only wished to correct what they thought were errors.

---

1. What changes have occurred in the world and in your society since your birth? What problems have those changes caused?

2. What causes people to leave the Church today?

The printing press and new translation of the Bible contributed to the Reformation's quick spread.

Precursor: that which immediately precedes another thing.

Nationalism: pride in and devotion to one nation.

Principality: a territory ruled by a prince.

Chapter 10 Family Rifts: A.D. 1500–1600

On This Rock

The first half of the sixteenth century may be best known for the unsteadiness of the rock which is the Church. We have seen that abuses were widespread. But there were always voices of hope and reason, pleading for reform and a return to the morals of the early Christians. Girolamo Savonarola, a Dominican friar in Florence, Italy, attacked the abuses he saw. Here are some of his accusations:

"You have built a house of debauchery [sin], you have transformed yourselves from top to toe into a house of infamy . . . anyone who has the money enters and does whatever he pleases. But anyone who desires the good is thrown out."

Even in this time of laxity, there were voices of morality crying to be heard. It would take until the middle of the century before people really started to listen. Savonarola was burned at the stake in 1498 for attacking the foundations of the Papacy as well as public morality.

A Tormented Soul

If one were to judge the importance of someone by the number of books written about him or her, Martin Luther (1483-1546) might rank right after Jesus and Saint Paul. He was a highly gifted, generous young man, and, in many ways, a man of genius. His parents were hard-working German laborers. Their strict discipline probably contributed to Luther's image of God as a taskmaster he could never satisfy.

Before joining the Hermits of Saint Augustine, Luther was a diligent, if sometimes moody, law student. After nearly being killed during a thunderstorm, he vowed to become a monk. Just over a year after making this promise, at the age of twenty-two, Luther made solemn vows. Nine months after profession, he was ordained and continued his theological studies.

By the time he was twenty-nine, Luther was in charge of the Wittenberg School of Divinity. He was also suffering from religious scruples and haunted by the thought of hell. Often he said Mass in terror of erring and found himself

The ninety-five theses Martin Luther hung on the cathedral door led to religious and political upheaval across Europe.

The Church: A Spirit-Filled People

unable even to look at a crucifix because of presumed sin. An overwhelming sense of sin caused violent cycles of hope and depression. "I did penance, but despair did not leave me," he wrote.

Without doubt, the extreme fasting and self-inflicted penances which Luther used in an attempt to atone for his sins invited many physical ailments from which he suffered until his death. Even daily confession offered no peace to the tormented monk. "God is not angry with you," his confessor told him. "You are angry with God. If you expect Christ to forgive you, come in with something to forgive, instead of these peccadillos."

The Challenge

Such was the young monk who challenged the archbishop of Mainz and Magdeburg in 1517 at the age of thirty-three. This archbishop stood to profit by the scandalous sermons of a well-known indulgence preacher, Johann Tetzel, a Dominican friar. When the archbishop did not respond, Luther posted ninety-five theses, or positions, on the church door at Wittenberg. Most of his theses were in line with Catholic teaching and his criticisms were modest. But Tetzel's report to Rome, listing the things Luther was supposed to have said, no doubt reflected the bitter Dominican-Augustinian rivalry of his day. Luther's attitude toward Tetzel was anything but hostile, yet he insisted on a fair hearing of Tetzel's and his different ideas. At one point he agreed to stop commenting on indulgences and apologized for some emotional remarks he had made against the pope. Luther, though, would not withdraw his criticism.

In July of 1519, an eighteen-day debate on religious matters with Johann Eck in the town hall of Leipzig made Luther a national figure. It also divided German opinion. In Luther, the people had a spokesman for their grievances against corruption in the Church. The German bishops who were not in sympathy with papal (Roman) claims to Church supremacy were not inclined to stand in Luther's way. Neither were the princes who ruled the provinces of Germany who saw this division as a way to increase their power.

Scruples: a condition of doubt, uneasiness, or extreme hesitation in deciding right from wrong.

Peccadillos: slight faults or minor sins.

Indulgence: the remission of temporal punishment still due for sin after the guilt has been forgiven in the sacrament of Penance, gained through prayer or good works. A small offering could accompany the effort.

A Changing Europe— The New Map

The map of Europe changed dramatically during the sixteenth century. It was a period of upheaval for society in general. There were changes in political boundaries, economics, language, the arts, science, and religion. Several European countries became the modern states we recognize today. Following their development can help us to understand the impact of the other changes that occured during this time.

England, France, and Spain all became independent kingdoms. There were politically motivated intermarriages between royal families. Poland emerged as the boundary between the Roman Catholic and Orthodox Christian worlds. Much of Eastern Europe—Hungary, Austria and Romania—was threatened by periodic invasions of the Turks (Muslims). During this time the Russian church emerged as an independent body. In Germany, the emperor was practically powerless. Seven princes had control of the country, which was divided into principalities.

All of this political activity had a great impact on reform and counter-reform movements. New political leaders arrived on the scene. Lines of communication were established between countries. It was the beginning of the modern era, and we shall see that the Church played a part in influencing and being influenced by the ongoing change.

All of Europe was Catholic prior to 1517. By 1600, Europe was divided by religion. This map shows the religious division of the British Isles around 1600.

The Church: A Spirit-Filled People

The Papal Bull

Scarcely a year after Leipzig, a papal bull arrived in Germany listing forty-one errors in Luther's views. It ordered his writings destroyed, forbade him to preach or teach, and gave him sixty days in which to retract his views under threat of excommunication. Luther wrote a rebuttal entitled "Against the Bull of Anti-Christ." In December of 1520, he publicly burned the bull together with a copy of canon law, representing the Church's authority. Within a month, Luther was excommunicated. In Leipzig, the university students rioted in protest of Rome's decree.

The new printing presses made it possible for Luther's views and writings to be spread quickly throughout Germany and Europe. Luther pointed to the "Romanists" as sources of the decline of Christianity. They wrongly claimed that civil government had no rights over them, that papal decrees stood above the authority of Scripture, and that the pope was above a council of the world's bishops, Luther said. Within a year, he challenged the sacramental system and the Sacrifice of the Mass, stressing the primacy of Scripture, the priesthood of the laity, and the doctrine of justification by faith alone. Through it all, Luther never felt that in condemning abuses he was separating himself from the Church.

With all of Germany now in an uproar, Emperor Charles V decided that Luther should be given a hearing. Instead of being imprisoned as a condemned heretic, Luther was given safe passage to the formal meeting of the emperor and his princes, which was being held at Worms. Under repeated questioning, Luther held firm to his position. "In so much as you have failed to convince me by scriptural proofs," Luther said, "whatever 'retreat' may mean, I cannot and will not do so. Here I stand. May God help me."

Outlawed now by the emperor, Luther was "kidnapped" by friends disguised as outlaws, and for nearly a year was kept safely hidden away in the castle of Wartburg by his friend, Frederick of Saxony. There, though in ill health, Luther translated into German the New Testament. Later, he translated the Old Testament as well.

Anti-Christ: the opponent of Christ expected before the end of the world.

3. Discuss what Luther hoped to accomplish in his challenge of Rome.

4. What do you think is the relationship between Luther's overwhelming sense of personal sin and his later emphasis on the necessity of faith for salvation?

This woodcut is from the title page of one of Martin Luther's original books.

A Final Departure

Luther saw all people as basically sinful and incapable of justification. His study of Paul—in particular of Romans 1:17, "The one who is righteous by faith will live." and Romans 3:28, "For we consider that a person is justified by faith apart from works of the law."—led him to this conclusion. Luther saw the possession of faith, without need of good works, as a guarantee of salvation. In this belief, Luther found peace.

Because Luther rejected much in the hierarchical Church and relied on Scripture alone, many sacraments were eliminated. Since all Christians became a priestly people in Christ, there was no need for a special priesthood, Luther argued, thus no need for a sacramental distinction between clergy and laity. This did away with the need for monastic vows and monasticism itself. As a result, German monasteries and convents were quickly emptied. Many of their former inhabitants became Lutheran pastors and wives of pastors, including Luther and his wife Catherine. Piece by piece, Luther swept away traditional structures of Roman Catholic Christianity—papacy, hierarchy, priesthood, sacraments, religious life, and many traditional practices of Catholic piety.

Summary

- The Protestant Reformation did not start as an organized revolt against Rome. It was meant to bring change from the inside.

- Martin Luther challenged the hierarchy of the Church over its excesses and abuses.

- Luther's actions divided Germany and resulted in his excommunication.

- Luther rejected much of the hierarchical Church, eliminated most sacraments, relied only on Scripture, and disbanded the priesthood.

SECTION 1
Checkpoint

■ Review

1. What were some of the historical factors which led to the Reform movement of the sixteenth century?

2. How did abuses within the Church contribute to dissatisfaction?

3. What event led Luther to become a monk, and how did his own personality play an important role in shaping his religious character?

4. What specific events resulted in Luther's excommunication?

5. What changes did Luther advocate and what reasons or proofs did he supply?

6. Words to Know: Reformation, Wittenberg, ninety-five theses, indulgence, 1517, papal bull.

■ In Your World

1. Arrange to attend a service at a Lutheran Church. Call the pastor and ask to make an appointment to speak to him or her. Record your impressions of the service, and bring questions with you. What characteristics of the service and the church were familiar to you from your reading, and what did you see that was new?

2. Research and then reenact the debate between Luther and Johann Eck. What are Luther's specific complaints about the practices of the Church? How does Eck respond? Have the audience gauge the success of each participant.

3. Write an article for the "Whittenberg Daily Times" for the day after the posting of the ninety-five theses. Be sure to include details about the contents of the document, the circumstances of its posting, and the reactions of all parties involved.

■ Scripture Search

The young Martin Luther was influenced by his reading of Paul. Read the following passages: Romans 1:17 and Romans 3:28. What do you think these verses mean? Did Luther misinterpret them? How do you feel about the balance between faith and works? Can one be effective without the other? Why or why not?

SECTION 2
A New Era

Many factors worked to turn Germany from Catholicism to Lutheranism, but the two main hinges on which the development and spread of Lutheranism swung were the Peasants' Revolt of 1524-1525 and the Augsburg Confession of 1530. In time, the chain of events started by Luther's actions spread to other parts of Europe and as far as England. It left conflict and division as more reforms emerged.

The Lines Are Drawn

Hordes of peasants, fed on Luther's doctrines encouraging the poor to seek equality and social justice, began roaming the countryside, looting castles and cloisters, with such passion and violence that Luther finally begged the princes to "smite, slay, and stab" the rebels. Thousands were butchered. Luther later publicly denied any responsibility for the massacre. He condemned the use of violence, but the Catholic princes and his own conscience held him responsible. The peasants considered Luther a traitor. Many, along with their Lutheran ministers, joined the ranks of the Anabaptist extremists and were persecuted by Lutherans and Catholics alike.

For better or worse, the Peasants' Revolt bound Luther's religious movement to the secular state and placed it under the control of the local German princes. Ironically, the authority of the pope was replaced by the domination of temporal rulers. Moral decline and decadence followed.

Philipp Melanchthon, Luther's faithful friend and follower, and a prominent leader of the reform, wrote, "All the waters of the Elbe would not suffice to weep for the misfortune that has stricken the Reformation." By 1530, the reform had spread throughout Germany. Luther's followers felt the need for some formal statement of beliefs. Melanchthon drew up the Augsburg Confession for the exiled Luther.

Anabaptist: diverse reformation groups who repeated baptism for adults, and interpreted reform doctrine to an extreme.

Augsburg Confession: the basic formula for Lutheran belief.

Chapter 10   Family Rifts: A.D. 1500–1600

Raphael—God Creating the Firmament
Luther's image of God was of a demanding creator, one who judged harshly and was slow to show mercy to sinners.

Luther continued to write, to be consulted, and to preach, but his control over Lutheranism was finished; the movement was no longer in his hands. His original intention, to reform the Catholic Church from within, had instead resulted in the first of the major Protestant churches.

Half seriously, Luther accepted the title "the Pope of Wittenberg," and called himself "God's notary [stenographer] to the Germans." He met the needs of the common people for a Bible translation they could read and understand, a psalter they could pray, a catechism they could understand, and a hymn book with songs of praise they loved to sing. He had each of these books decorated with a variety of lively woodcuts. However, Luther's other writings were often bitter and unrestrained.

In 1546, at the age of sixty-three, Luther died as he had lived, engaged in spiritual conflict. A book, "Against the Papacy Founded in Rome by the Devil," was still in progress. Nine years later, the Catholic-Lutheran boundaries that cut Germany in half were firmly established, and the principle that the religion of the prince was to be the religion of the people became law. With these changes, the seeds of the Thirty Years' War (1618-48)—which was to engulf nearly all of Europe—were sown.

5. *What were some of the good things Luther accomplished?*

6. *What aspects of Luther's reforms have been introduced into Catholicism in this century?*

Calvin—A Prophet with a Mission

"A burning brand snatched from the flames" is an apt description for John Calvin (1509-1564), second of the great Protestant reformers and the movement's major prophet. French by birth, Calvin spent most of his life in exile. His conversion from Catholicism to Protestantism was gradual, stemming both from his university contacts with Lutheranism and his stay with a wealthy Protestant cloth merchant in Paris, whose home harbored religious fugitives. Calvin later fled Paris to Switzerland. There he studied theology and in 1536 wrote the first draft of the *Institutes of the Christian Religion,* a statement of his own religious beliefs. It gave many Protestants their creed and catechism and assured Calvin a role of leadership in the Reformation.

John Calvin preached a form of Christianity which was stern and unforgiving.

Protestant: a name first used in 1529 when Lutheran princes "protested" the Emperor's attempt to weaken Luther's movement by force.

Psalter: the book of Psalms.

Chapter 10 Family Rifts: A.D. 1500–1600

Calvin believed he was a prophet with a mission. He was a brilliant scholar, although one with a cold and reserved nature. He was as severe with himself as he was with others. His religious beliefs were founded on the conviction that God was in control of all life and that no real freedom could be possible, except by God's will. From this conviction came Calvin's doctrine of election and predestination— God "determined with himself what he willed to become of each man. For all are not created in equal condition; rather eternal life is decreed for some, eternal damnation for others" (Institutes 3.21.5). Although accepted widely at first, by the nineteenth century most reform Churches had rejected predestination as immoral.

Like Luther, Calvin relied on Scripture alone and justification by faith. He denied the Catholic understanding of the sacraments and condemned the papacy, clerical celibacy, and monastic vows.

The Geneva Community

The testing ground of Calvin's religious beliefs was the city of Geneva, Switzerland. His first attempt to impose his teachings resulted in his banishment. Four years later, in 1541, representatives from Geneva asked him to return.

Calvin was thirty-two when he arrived in Geneva for the second time. For the next twenty-three years, until his death in 1564, he dominated the city, regulating every aspect of its life. In contrast to Luther's reform, which was controlled by local rulers, Calvin's Church ran the state. His ministers ruled, judged, and punished the smallest infractions of the law. Discipline extended even to dress regulations, curfews, and types of entertainment. Dancing, card playing, and theater were outlawed.

Calvin's God was a harsh judge, someone to fear. The elect, or those saved, were shown by the purity of their personal virtues, and all legislation was intended to make the elect prominent. Under Calvin, Geneva's moral dictatorship became a "reign of terror." In this "Holy City" one could be questioned for lack of attention during a sermon, fined for braiding one's hair, and exiled or burned at the stake for criticizing Calvin.

Calvin trained his ministers—an elite corps of zealous preachers, many of them former members of religious communities—at the university in Geneva. His writings, smuggled into French printing houses, soon flooded France. These ministers were persecuted by French Catholics—a persecution no less terrible than those that the Romans inflicted on the early Christians—who stalked all those who accepted or circulated Calvin's works. Invariably, the blood of the Protestant martyrs, some of whom went to the stake singing psalms, won new converts. The scandal is that, instead of loving one another as Christ had commanded, Christians were slaying one another.

The "Reformed Churches"

Calvin brought to Protestantism the discipline, order, and method Luther had lacked. Calvin introduced lay government to the Church, with its pastors, elders, and deacons, which is now common among the nearly fifty million Christians in Reformed, Presbyterian, and Congregationalist churches, all of which follow Calvin. His unfailing sense of duty and passion to win souls for God overshadowed a seeming lack of kindness and forgiveness.

Calvin was the most radical of the reformers. He rejected all the sacraments and whatever Scripture did not mention. His "Reformed Churches" took root in Switzerland, Scotland, Holland, Hungary, France, and England. Of all the religious revolutionists, Calvinists inflicted the greatest losses on and posed the greatest overall threat to the Roman Catholic Church.

---

7. *How would you react if the restrictions imposed by Calvin in Geneva were imposed on you?*

8. *What do you think Calvin's contributions to reform were?*

Chapter 10 Family Rifts: A.D. 1500–1600

Doctor of the Church, Saint, Mystic

Teresa of Avila (1515-1582) is probably the best known saint of the sixteenth century. She was a Spanish Carmelite known even during her lifetime for her holiness, intelligence, and wit. She was a strong and determined woman who had something to say about every situation. She once told a nun who had resolved to be humble by not expressing clever thoughts, "It's bad enough to be stupid by nature without trying to be stupid by grace." She called herself a "daughter of the Church" and was responsible for establishing many religious houses and restoring strictness and austerity to the religious lifestyle of the Carmelite nuns.

She also had a sense of humor. When her carriage overturned one day, she addressed Christ saying, "No wonder you have so few friends! Look how you treat them!"

She may be best known as a mystic—a person who experiences God's love in direct and piercing ways. She always kept a journal with her and advised others to do the same. She recorded her experiences and her reactions to the natural world around her, which often led her to prayer. For Teresa, prayer is friendship with God.

Teresa's autobiography and other writings are still widely read and enjoyed. On the basis of these writings, Teresa was declared a Doctor of the Church in 1970, along with Catherine of Siena. These were the first women to be so honored by the Church. Teresa is a spiritual guide and inspiration to all who seek communion with God.

Saint Teresa of Avila's mystic writings are read frequently today by people seeking to understand the mystery of God.

Henry VIII—England's First Lay Pope

Two news releases of 1982 made headlines in the story of Roman-Anglican relations. In March of that year, England and the Vatican restored the diplomatic ties broken in the sixteenth century. In June, the visit of Pope John Paul II to England resulted in cordial personal relations with Elizabeth II, Head of the Church of England, and Robert Runcie, Archbishop of Canterbury. These new developments offered sparks of hope for all who dream of Christian unity.

The story of England's break with Rome is the saddest and perhaps the most significant story of the Reformation. As England rose to a position of world empire, the survival of the Reformation was assured. Yet, at the beginning of the sixteenth century, England had less reason than any other European kingdom to break with the Church.

Henry's Problem

Henry VIII had been declared a "Defender of the Faith" for his writings against Luther. However, the duel between Henry VIII (1491-1547) and Pope Clement VII, which began in 1527 over the king's request for a marriage annulment, would soon make that a false title.

Henry VIII of England wanted a son to preserve his kingdom from factional wars. Pope Clement VII's refusal to grant Henry's annulment led Henry to reject the Pope and declare himself head of the Church.

Chapter 10 Family Rifts: A.D. 1500–1600

Communion of Saints

Saint Thomas More (1478-1535) spent his early life studying law and then teaching. He was a member of the English Parliament until Henry VIII made him an official diplomat. He felt called to religious life, but eventually married. When he would not agree with the king's plans to divorce Catherine, Thomas resigned and lived without an income from 1532-1535. When he refused to formally acknowledge Henry as the head of the Church, Thomas spent 15 months in the Tower of London. He wrote many essays while imprisoned. On July 6, 1535, dressed in his best clothes, Thomas was beheaded for his loyalty to Rome. His last words were "I die the king's good servant, but God's first." He was canonized in 1935.

Suddenly, after seventeen years of marriage, Henry felt guilty for having taken Catherine of Aragon, his brother's widow, as his wife. Desire for a male heir and love for Anne Boleyn may have been the real reasons for this request. Legal and religious opinion were against Henry's request for an annulment.

After two years of waiting for Rome's reply, the king refused to send tax payments to Rome. Within five years he had moved to the position of "Royal Supremacy" — "Be it enacted by the authority of this present parliament, that . . . the king of this realm shall be taken, accepted, and reputed the only supreme head on earth of the Church of England, called Anglicae Ecclesia (Anglican Church)." With the exception of John Fisher, Bishop of Rochester, all of England's bishops, appointees of Henry approved by Rome, accepted this claim in silence. Fisher was beheaded for "treason." This was England's new term for declaring that someone did not agree with the king.

Henry stood firm on all other points of Catholic belief. He put to death Protestants who denied Catholic dogma as willingly as he beheaded Catholics who denied his supremacy. He beheaded Thomas More, a one-time friend, for not agreeing with him. In need of money, Henry threatened Parliament when it declined to suppress the monasteries. More than six hundred monasteries were closed or sold, and money poured into the royal treasury. Many of the nobility shared in the profits and so they, too, became supporters of the Reformation in England.

The Church of England

By the time of Henry's death, the Church of England was cut off from Rome, but its doctrine remained Catholic. The move toward Protestant ideas came during the reign of the child king, Edward VI. These ideas were pushed forward by Thomas Cranmer, Archbishop of Canterbury, some of whose Lutheran sympathies now could be implemented freely. The Catholic Mass was forbidden and replaced by a simple Communion service called the Lord's Supper. English became the official Church language, and clerical marriage was legalized. A Book of Common Prayer, a catechism, and new rites for the sacraments included elements drawn from Catholicism, Lutheranism, and Calvinism. Those who refused to attend the new services were fined. Priests who celebrated the old form of the Eucharist were sentenced to life imprisonment.

Six years later, when Mary Tudor (1516-1558), daughter of Henry and Catherine, and a staunch Catholic, came to the throne, the tide briefly turned. During her five-year reign, all anti-Roman legislation was repealed and England enjoyed a brief reconciliation with Rome. Though full of zeal and good intentions, Mary was naive and undiplomatic. Her rigorous persecution of Protestants in high places alienated many. Had Mary been gifted with patience, tact, and a long reign, England might have remained united with Rome. Instead, her drive to restore Roman Catholicism resulted in several hundred Anglican martyrs, and paved the way for a return to a modified Protestantism under Elizabeth I and her successors.

9. How could the break between England and Rome have been avoided?

10. Have you ever been to an Episcopalian (what Anglicans are called in the U.S.) service? What was distinctive about it?

Summary

- As a result of the Peasants' Revolt, Lutheranism was tied to the German states and their leaders.

- John Calvin spurred reform in Switzerland with his doctrine of predestination and strict moral code.

- Henry VIII's break with Rome resulted in a state church whose doctrine is still close to that of Catholicism.

Chapter 10 Family Rifts: A.D. 1500–1600

SECTION 2
Checkpoint!

■ Review

1. How did the Peasants' Revolt change the direction of Luther's reforms?

2. What contributions did Luther make to meeting the needs of the common people in worship and prayer?

3. Explain the doctrine of predestination.

4. Why did Calvin impose such strict laws and regulations in Geneva?

5. What contributions did Calvin add to the reforms initiated by Luther?

6. What started the duel between Henry VIII and Rome, and how was it eventually resolved?

7. Words to Know: Peasants' Revolt, Augsburg Confession, predestination, Institutes, Royal Supremacy.

■ In Your World

1. As a class, discuss a package of reforms for your own class. Let everyone volunteer a possible reform. Debate the pros and cons of each, and come to an agreement. Then enforce the reforms. How do other students react? How do those people whose reforms were rejected feel?

2. Find a copy of either the Augsburg Confession or the Institutes in the library. Read several sections of it and write down what you find most important. Did you find it easy to read and understand? Report back to the class.

■ Scripture Search

Read the following passages: 1 Timothy 2:8-15; Ephesians 6:1-9. Do these regulations seem harsh to you? Why do you think they are included in these letters? What are some regulations in effect today?

SECTION 3
Losses and Gains

The last half of the sixteenth century was filled with change. After Mary Tudor, Protestantism regained support in England. In response, the Catholic Church embarked on its most important program of renewal up to that time. Needed reforms were put into place and the Council of Trent brought together representatives to discuss and put into operation new organizations and practices. This period is marked by the emergence of spiritual personalities and strong leaders within the Roman Catholic Church, who were to affect the history of Christianity for the next five hundred years.

Elizabeth I and Anglicanism

During the reign of Elizabeth I (1558-1603), Catholics in England were an almost hidden minority. She reimposed the Oath of Royal Supremacy—people had to swear their loyalty to Elizabeth as head of the Church. For twelve years Catholics were fined, lost their property, and were imprisoned. Pope Pius V finally excommunicated Elizabeth and absolved her subjects from obedience to her. As a result, the English Catholics (Papists) were thought to be disloyal to the crown.

Elizabeth's retaliation was swift. Laws against Catholics multiplied until even attending Mass, or sheltering a Catholic priest, meant death. Many English Catholics found ways to evade the laws, and priests risked their lives to minister to the faithful.

Some English Protestant sects wanted to see even stronger laws enforced. Certain radical groups, like the Puritans, expressed their dissatisfaction by leaving England for Holland and North America. Slowly, laws against Catholics were reduced or removed. The beliefs and rites of the Anglican Church of England today are very close to those of the Roman Catholic Church.

11. *How do you think loyalty to the Holy Father in Rome might be interpreted as disloyalty to a secular government?*

The Agony of Renewal

With prodding by Luther, Calvin, and Henry VIII, it became obvious that the Catholic Church of the sixteenth century needed reform. The Fifth Lateran Council (1512-1517) issued a warning to Pope Leo X: "These diseases and these wounds must be healed by you, Holy Father, otherwise God Himself will not apply a gentle cure, but with fire and sword will cut off these diseased members and destroy them." The reforms requested by this council were never carried out.

Saint Bernard of Clairvaux (1090-1153) spoke of two kinds of heresy—perverse (or false) doctrine and perverse (or false) living. Perverse living was evident everywhere in the Church, even before the Protestant Reformation. Pope Adrian VI (1522-1523) tried to encourage reform. Of the ten thousand applications for favors, privileges, and appointments that he received the day after his election, he granted only one.

Henry VIII demanded that all bishops sign the Royal Supremacy act naming him head of the Church in England.

Adrian also sent a representative to the Diet of Nuremberg to beg the German princes to act against Lutheranism. He wrote: "We frankly admit that God permits this persecution of the Church because of the sins of men, especially of the priests and prelates. We know that for many years, many abominable things have occurred in this Holy See . . . No wonder that the illness has spread from the head to the members. We promise that we will expend every effort to reform first this Curia, whence perhaps all this evil has come . . ." Unfortunately, Adrian died within a year and all attempts at reform were put on hold for another thirty years.

12. What do you think about Pope Adrian's statement that God permitted the persecution of Catholics because of the sins of others? Do you agree? Why or why not?

13. Do you think that the holiness of the Church was stained by the sins of some of its leaders? What effects would this behavior have on lay Catholics?

The Counter-Reformation

Despite what was happening in Rome, a reform movement was emerging at the grass roots level. New religious orders developed. In Rome, the Oratory of Divine Love, a clerical support group of common prayer and simple living, was organized by Saint Philip Neri. Reform-minded bishops came out of this simple group. Plans for a Church council began. Pope Paul III (1534-1549) appointed a commission of cardinals to study the need for Church reform. Their document, *"The Council of Cardinals on Reforming the Church,"* was the most direct and blunt condemnation of abuses ever to come from within the Church. It did not spare papal court, bishops, religious orders, priests, or financial practices. It was the turning point of the reform. The next step was to establish corrections for these problems.

Perverse: corrupt, wicked, or in error.

Diet: a formal meeting of the emperor and his princes.

Chapter 10   Family Rifts: A.D. 1500–1600

The Council of Trent lasted for nineteen years. The teachings of the Council shaped the Catholic Church for the next four hundred years.

Political conditions in Europe forced Pope Paul III to postpone a Council for eleven years. In 1545 the Council opened at Trent, a city in northern Italy accepted by the pope and the Holy Roman Emperor for the Council. The Council of Trent had three major sessions and two periods of interruptions over nineteen years. Trent encouraged both renewal and reform by reaffirming and redefining the basic truths of the faith in reaction to Protestant teachings, tightening Church discipline, and the removal of ordinary abuses.

A Time of Change

The Council of Trent set the stage for over four hundred years of Roman Catholic Christianity and placed emphasis on both the institutional Church and the sacramental system. In reaction to Protestantism, theologians took care to characterize the Mass as sacrifice, and they paid less attention to the role and importance of Scripture—so central to the faith of the Reformers. At Vatican II, (1962-65) this defensive posture would finally find a balance.

Catholic Missionaries— A New Breed

The renewal which resulted from the Council of Trent brought with it an interest in participating in the discovery of new lands which was taking place. New places and new people meant new opportunities to spread the Good News. Exotic places like China, India, the Americas, and Africa beckoned the more adventurous spirits in the Church. Many of the new religious congregations took on a missionary spirit as part of their vocation. Their members learned additional languages, trained as teachers, and undertook long, and often dangerous, journeys by boat and land.

By the end of the sixteenth century, Christianity had reached the Caribbean, Africa, Latin and South America, India, Japan, and the Philippines.

At first, the missionaries insisted that the newly converted give up many aspects of their native cultures. Eventually compromises were reached as the Church realized how important these cultures were and how much both sides could benefit from their meeting. This missionary work, begun almost five hundred years ago, remains a vital part of Catholic life today.

◆

Trent also made provisions for diocesan seminaries, reorganized the Papal Curia and Inquisition—an official inquiry into a person's beliefs—and created the Index of Forbidden Books—books Catholics were forbidden to read—which was used well into the 20th century.

The popes who followed the Council of Trent dedicated themselves to putting its decrees into operation. They were supported and helped by the new religious communities—Jesuits, Theatines, Ursulines, Oratorians, and others—as well as by a renewal of the Franciscans, Carmelites, Dominicans, and Carthusians.

A People at Prayer

Each of the councils of the Church has opened with a message from those attending. The most recent Church council, Vatican II (1962-1965) was distinctive because its opening message was directed to all people, not just members of the Catholic Church. Here is part of that message: "In this assembly, under the guidance of the Holy Spirit, we wish to inquire how we ought to renew ourselves, so that we may be found increasingly faithful to the gospel of Christ. We shall take pains so to present to the men of this age God's truth in its integrity and purity that they may understand it and gladly assent it." This message clearly represents the desire of the council to renew the Church and to make its mission successful.

Jesuit missionaries worked with native American Indians. Many of these missionaries died for their efforts. Included in this number are the North American martyrs, including Isaac Jogues and John De Brebeuf.

The Jesuits

The Jesuits, in particular, provided a source of strength throughout this period of the Catholic Counter-Reformation. They were founded by Ignatius of Loyola, a Spanish soldier-knight, who organized an elite corps of disciplined scholars and missionaries. They vowed to place themselves at the service of the Holy Father. Jesuits were renowned as professors at the great universities and became advisors and confessors to important officials. Many became canonized saints. Ignatius himself composed the "Spiritual Exercises," a series of thirty-day meditations based on the teachings of the Church and the life of Christ.

14. Why do you think the Council of Trent emphasized the organizational structure of the Church?

The Church: A Spirit-Filled People

The End of an Era

During the last half of the sixteenth century, the Catholic Church reemerged strengthened and renewed. Much of this was due to the appearance of many people who proved to be models of holiness and faith. They include Thomas More, Peter Canisius, Ignatius Loyola, Teresa of Avila, John of the Cross, Vincent de Paul, and Robert Bellarmine, to name a few.

Meanwhile, by the end of the century the political and religious divisions in Europe were complete. Most of Germany and Scandinavia were Lutheran. England was Anglican. Ireland, Spain, Italy, and Poland remained Catholic. Other countries were torn and divided over religion.

Saint Thomas More, the patron of lawyers, was beheaded by Henry VIII. Thomas reportedly said, "I die the king's good servant, but God's first."

Many of Luther's reforms—a vernacular liturgy, emphasis on Scripture, the Church as People of God, the priesthood of the laity, and the need for people to follow their conscience—were advocated by Vatican II. Today's Lutherans believe in a need for good works and have come to substantial agreement with Catholics on the doctrine of the Eucharist. The Anglican Church is even closer in doctrinal belief.

Still, one of the great challenges of our generation is to continue working to heal the wounds that still divide Christians. In the basic profession of faith in Christ as the Savior of the world, we are already one.

15. *What different denominations of Protestants are you familiar with? Do you know how they differ from one another?*

Summary

- Under Elizabeth I, Anglicanism was firmly established in England.

- During the sixteenth century, the Church came to recognize the need for reform.

- The Council of Trent formed part of the Counter-Reformation which rid the Church of many abuses.

- Some changes made include emphasis on the institutional Church, reorganization, and the emergence of new and vital religious congregations.

SECTION 3
Checkpoint!

■ Review

1. What tactics did Elizabeth I and Rome each use in the struggle for power in England?

2. What did Bernard mean by "perverse living"?

3. How did Adrian VI try to initiate reform?

4. What was the Oratory of Divine Love?

5. Name the most important changes that came from the Council of Trent.

6. Words to Know: Council of Trent, 1545, Jesuits, Counter-Reformation.

■ In Your World

1. Hold an imaginary session of the Council of Trent. Discuss changes to be made in Church organization and practices. Make sure all sides are represented (including those bishops who were reluctant to see change). Pass three pieces of legislation, and remember to include measures that will ensure that the reforms will be carried through.

2. During the sixteenth century, the Catholic Church began some of its most important missionary work. Choose one of the people involved in missionary work, or one of the congregations, and give a presentation on where he went and how successful he was. For example, Francis Xavier (India), Francisco Davila (Peru), or Matteo Ricci (China).

■ Scripture Search

Read John 17:20-23. What does this passage say that can be applied to the period of Church covered in this chapter? What do you think it implies about the ways people come to know God?

> **Vernacular:** the native language of a people.

CHAPTER 10 Review

■ Study

1. What was Luther's original intention in criticizing abuses in the Church?
2. What are indulgences and how were they used?
3. How did the climate of the Renaissance contribute to the Reform movement?
4. Who was Johann Tetzel, and how was he involved in the conflict with Luther?
5. What specific criticisms did Luther have of the organization of the Church in Rome?
6. Explain how the political situation in Germany became part of the era of Reformation.
7. What kind of person was John Calvin, and how did his vision of God affect his version of reform?
8. What was the initial reason for the break between Henry VIII and Rome?
9. How did Henry VIII's personal quarrel escalate into a complete split with Rome and the formation of a new Church?
10. What were some of the changes made to distinguish the Church of England from the Roman Catholic Church?
11. What was life like for Catholics under Elizabeth I?
12. Describe some of the attempts made at reform by Rome before the Council of Trent.
13. How did the Council of Trent both reform and renew? Give examples.
14. What role did the new religious congregations play in the Counter-Reformation?
15. What changes has the Church made recently which echo Luther's reforms?

■ Action

1. There are many denominations (groups) of Protestants. Choose one of the following groups and give a short presentation to the class outlining the basic history and beliefs of this group. Be sure to give examples of how this denomination differs from other Protestant denominations. Include some of the following information: name of its founder, date and place it was founded, any special organization or practices. Choose from: Anglicans, Lutherans, Presbyterians, Methodists, Episcopalians.

2. Learn about one of the outstanding individuals of the sixteenth century, such as Teresa of Avila, Philip Neri, Catherine of Aragon, Mary Tudor of England, Elizabeth I, or Thomas More. Choose an important incident in that person's life and present it to the class as if you were that person.

■ Prayer

Despite the turmoil of the sixteenth century, the spirituality of devoted and pious Catholics flourished. Ignatius of Loyola, the founder of the order of the Jesuits, devised a plan specifically for prayer. It included daily time for prayer as well as a four week retreat. The *Spiritual Exercises* are still used today as a guide in spiritual direction. Here is a prayer taken from Ignatius' *Exercises:*

"Lord, teach me to be generous. Teach me to serve you as you deserve; to give and not to count the cost; to fight and not to heed the wounds; to toil and not to seek for rest; to labor and not to ask for reward, except to know that I am doing your will . . . The story of your people, the Church, can discourage as well as encourage us. May the mistakes of the past alert us to our own failings; may the achievements of the past inspire us to make our own world more like the ideal proposed in Jesus' teaching. Without you, we can do nothing. We trust that you are ever with us, especially as we pray together in the name of Jesus the Lord. Amen."

Think about the special significance this prayer has after having read this chapter and learned about some of the failings in the Church. How does this prayer help you to understand and accept those mistakes, and to determine your own role in contributing to the strength and positive aspects of the Church?

CHAPTER

11

From Trent to Vatican II: A.D. 1600 to the Present

OBJECTIVES

In this Chapter you will

- Read about revival in the Church after Trent.

- Discover an emerging missionary movement which went to the new worlds.

- Learn about the split between church and state, and the influence of new philosophies for a changing world.

- Follow the development of Catholicism in the United States.

- Watch dramatic changes take place as Vatican II moves the Church into the modern world, and prepares Catholics to face the future.

Nothing genuinely human fails to raise an echo in the hearts of the followers of Christ. United in Christ, they are led by the Holy Spirit in their journey to the kingdom of their Father, and they have welcomed the news of salvation, which is meant for every man. That is why this community realized that it is truly and intimately linked with mankind and its history.
—"Pastoral Constitution on the Church," #1

The Church: A Spirit-Filled People

SECTION 1
An Era of Change

The period between the Council of Trent and Vatican II was a time of religious wars, revolutions, dramatic changes, and reactions. The pre-Vatican II church was the result of the Protestant Reformation, the Council of Trent, and events in rapidly changing world events. This chapter presents an overview of that story, highlights the growth of the Church in the United States, and summarizes the impact of Vatican II.

After Trent

The reforms of the Council of Trent (1545-1563) were hardly agreed upon when a whole century of religious wars engulfed Europe. Struggles between Catholics and Calvinists divided France and the Netherlands. More devastating was the Thirty Years' War, a Catholic-Protestant conflict which began as an argument over the crown of Bohemia. Three-fourths of the peasant population of Germany perished during this war. It quickly involved all of Europe. By the time it ended at the Peace of Westphalia in 1648, most of northern Europe was Protestant, and most of the south was Catholic.

Saint Vincent de Paul was the leading figure in the seventeenth-century religious revival that began in France. This friend to royalty and slaves alike undertook the tasks of reforming the clergy, preaching missions for the laity, and co-founding religious orders such as the Sisters of Charity, who cared for the sick, the poor, and the abandoned instead of remaining confined to their convents as cloistered nuns did. One hundred years later, even Voltaire, a severe critic of the Church, could say: "My favorite saint is Vincent de Paul." Francis de Sales gave impetus to a growing renewal of the spiritual life among the laity. He and Jeanne Frances de Chantal founded the Visitation Nuns.

This spiritual revival was not without problems. The heresy of Jansenism—which taught that obeying the commandments of God is impossible without a special grace and demanded that its followers adhere to a very strict code of behavior—appealed to the elite and the pious. Its strict moral code and controversy over grace and predestination made it resemble Calvinism. Because it stressed the personal unworthiness of all people, many stopped receiving the Eucharist. Devotion to the Sacred Heart emerged as an answer to the Jansenists. This devotion is widely practiced even today. Jansenism was condemned and had all but disappeared by 1800.

1. *War and conflict produced dramatic changes in Europe. What dramatic changes have occured in your life, and what caused them?*

2. *Who are some of the "saints" in the world today? How do they carry out missions?*

New Worlds for Christ

As northern Europe was becoming more Protestant, Spain's and Portugal's voyages of discovery and exploration opened new worlds to the Catholic Church. Only the first few centuries of Church history rival this time of missionary activity. Wherever Spaniards set foot in the Americas, the Church came with them, supported and dominated by the crown. An army of Jesuits, Franciscans, Dominicans, and secular clergy established Catholicism from California to Argentina. French efforts to evangelize the native Americans of Canada produced a band of heroic martyrs, but little permanent gain for the Church. Still, native Indian populations often suffered from the conquistadors'—Spanish soldiers—greed for wealth. Missionaries tried to protect the natives. Dominican priest Bartholomew de las Casas worked to secure legal protection for the Indians. Peter Claver and Martin de Porres tried to lessen the evils of the slave trade. Until the slave trade ended in the mid-nineteenth century, missionary work in Africa was almost impossible. At its peak, more than twenty-eight thousand slaves per year were taken from Africa.

The missionaries' work was hampered by:
(1) requirements that converts to Christianity accept European culture;
(2) failure to create an effective native clergy;
(3) rivalries between religious orders.

Too often efforts at evangelization were identified with the imperialism and exploitation of the European nations.

In 1622, Gregory XV created the office of the Propagation of the Faith in an attempt to place all missionary activity directly under Roman control. Missionaries were advised in 1659 not to "bring any pressure to bear on the peoples to change manners, customs and uses, unless they are evidently contrary to religion and sound morals." Unfortunately, the directive was not understood and eventually missionary activity practically came to a halt.

---

3. Why do you think it is important not to disrupt a people's culture and customs? Can you think of any practices which might have to be changed as a result of conversion?

From Faith to Skepticism

The Age of Enlightenment was preceded by new philosophies that stressed reason over faith. René Descartes (1596-1650) proposed a philosophy which held that knowledge can be doubted or questioned. As a skeptic, he denied whatever could not be evaluated by using scientific reason, including faith, mystery, and miracles. The French writer Voltaire (1694-1778) wrote of the Church, "I'm tired of being told that twelve men sufficed to establish Christianity, and I'm longing to prove that only one is needed to destroy it."

Chapter 11 From Trent to Vatican II: A.D. 1600 to the Present

Athens and Jerusalem

The war between reason and faith, between philosophy and theology, has been raging for centuries. We read in Chapter 9 about the efforts of Scholasticism to present Christianity as a unified system of understanding. In the early Church, theologians faced competition from philosophers trained in the Greek thought of Plato and Aristotle. Some of those theologians, such as Clement of Alexandria (150-215) and Origen (185-253), were able to integrate some aspects of Greek philosophical thought into emerging Christian thought. Although they were not always successful, they represent a group who welcomed the contributions existing traditions could make.

Another group, whose most outspoken representative may have been Tertullian (155-c. 220), rejected the use of Greek philosophy. Tertullian believed that faith and philosophy have nothing in common. "What indeed has Athens to do with Jerusalem? . . . With our faith we desire no further belief." Athens was the home of several large schools of philosophy at that time, and Jerusalem was still considered the home of the Church.

Tertullian had such a reputation for trying to disrupt the harmony between faith and philosophy that a tradition grew which attributed this saying to him: "I believe because it is absurd." Even though Tertullian never seems to have said this, it illustrates his point of view.

Advocates on both sides of this debate have helped keep the Church balanced throughout the centuries. Education and prayer have ensured this balance.

Those who followed the philosophy deism—a belief in the existence of a God who created the world but has no further involvement in it—accepted only what could be discovered by unaided reason. It makes a clear and unbridgeable separation between Creator and created. Jean-Jacques Rousseau introduced another philosophy which regarded all human nature as completely good and noble. At the same time, discoveries in science and technology laid the basis for the industrial revolution and the emergence of a new money-based economy.

4. How is Rousseau's belief in the goodness of human nature similar to the teaching of the Church?

5. Do you think there is a tension between faith and reason? Why?

Twilight

The papacy of the eighteenth-century was not prepared to handle the revolutions that rocked Western society, especially those in America and France. Political motives dominated papal elections, and no leaders like Peter, Paul, Augustine, or Gregory appeared on the scene. In addition, the Church often seemed opposed to many of the scientific advances of the time. When Galileo Galilei (1564-1642) discovered that the sun, and not the earth, was the center of the universe, he was condemned for teaching what appeared contrary to the Bible. This discovery challenged the credibility of the Church which then held a different belief.

In 1772, Catholic rulers in Europe divided up Poland among themselves and Pope Clement XIV (1769-1774) remained silent. Even worse, he suppressed the Jesuits in 1773 for political reasons. At the time, the Jesuits ran seven hundred colleges and three hundred missions. As a result of Clement's action, the missionary work of the Church was left in shambles. The importance of the Jesuits to the Catholic Church was noted even by Voltaire: "Once we have destroyed the Jesuits, we shall have the game in our hands."

On This Rock

The political, social, and economic upheaval of the nineteenth century marked a crisis for the Church. In 1902, a Catholic scholar named Alfred Loisy published a book called *The Gospel and the Church.* It caused quite a stir at the time. Many of his observations about the Church, taken in light of Vatican II, hardly seem shocking now.

"The message of Jesus consists in the proclamation of the nearness of the kingdom and an exhortation to repentance in order to be able to have a part in the kingdom. As a result of political and intellectual evolution, a great religious crisis has developed everywhere. The best means of remedying it . . . is to appreciate duly the need and usefulness of the immense development which has taken place in the church, to gather its fruits and to continue it, since the adaptation of the Gospel to the changing conditions of humanity is more important today than it has ever been."

Loisy saw the need for the Church to be in the world even as it is not of the world.

Revolution in France

Although national bankruptcy was the immediate cause of the French Revolution in 1789, the revolt was also caused by many factors of French life—unjust taxes, extremes of wealth and poverty, class distinctions, and special privileges. In addition, the Enlightenment had called into question Catholic faith in the minds of educated French people. Hatred of Church privilege and jealousy of its wealth quickly turned into contempt for Christianity itself. At first the lower clergy sided with the Revolution's ideals of freedom and equality. When the National Assembly passed the Civil Constitution of the Clergy in 1790, it created a schismatic French Church which was no longer dependent on Rome. Bishops and priests who refused to accept it were imprisoned, exiled, or guillotined. There was confiscation and destruction of Church property, dissolution of monasteries and religious orders, and abolition of clerical dress and celibacy.

Crown and Altar Tumble

As Napoleon rose to power in France, he saw the Church in anarchy. He understood that law and order in France depended on the restoration of religion, and he pushed for a concordat with the Holy See (Rome). "Go to Rome," he told his ambassador, "and tell the Holy Father that the First Consul [Napoleon] would like to make him a present of thirty million French Catholics." Napoleon used the Church for his own purposes, and eventually even imprisoned Pius VI and his successor. Finally, Pius VII excommunicated him. Napoleon died in exile. Pius VII emerged as the conqueror of tyranny.

---

6. Why do you think the Church was so reluctant to accept Galileo's scientific discovery?

7. How do you think the Church may have suffered during the French Revolution because of the abuses of its past?

The Church: A Spirit-Filled People

Engraved by Peter Aitken from the painting by Jean Paul Laurens
The French Revolution divided the Church. Only with the imposition of order by Napolean did the Church in France come once again under Vatican control. Napolean, however, was no friend of the Church, once even taking Pope Pius VI captive.

Summary

- The period following Trent produced war as well as religious revival.

- Europe's voyages of discovery led to new worlds for Christ and the expansion of missionary work.

- New philosophies stressed reason over faith and initiated a century of political change.

- The French Revolution resulted in a split between religion and government.

Concordat: a formal agreement between a pope and a government concerning the regulation of Church affairs.

Chapter 11   From Trent to Vatican II: A.D. 1600 to the Present

SECTION 1
Checkpoint!

■ Review

1. What was the Peace of Westphalia, and how was Europe changed by its signing?

2. Name two developments in France that illustrate the religious revival there.

3. Why was the office of the Propagation of the Faith created?

4. Define deism and explain how it is an example of the mood of the Age of Enlightenment.

5. Why did the Church have great difficulties during the French Revolution?

6. Words to Know: Vincent de Paul, Propagation of the Faith, Descartes, Enlightenment, Galileo, French Revolution.

■ In Your World

1. Invite a missionary who has served outside the United States to speak to your class about this important part of the Church's work. Where did the person serve and under what conditions? What services did the missionary bring the people? How do you think this experience differed from that of the earliest missionaries?

2. The nineteenth century was a time of rapid change in all aspects of society. Compare the year 1800 with the year 1900. Note a few developments in several areas including science, technology (electricity, for example), transportation, and the status of Catholicism in the world.

3. Draw a map charting some of the missionary journeys undertaken by the Church. Be sure to include as many parts of the world as possible. Use different colors to indicate the different orders who went on these missions.

■ Scripture Search

Read 1 Samuel 8:1-22. It records an event of great political and religious significance for the ancient Israelites. What change do the people demand, and how do both Samuel and God react? Why do you think the people acted as they did?

306

The Church: A Spirit-Filled People

SECTION 2
The Wonderful Century

Some called the 1800s "The Wonderful Century." There was a "flood" of inventions and discoveries. New lands were explored and colonized. Europe's population doubled, and democratic ideas brought the abolition of the slave trade as well as the unification of both Germany and Italy. Revolutions brought independence to Latin America and rocked European tyranny in 1830 and 1848. From England came a new system of thought called socialism or communism devised by Karl Marx and Friedrich Engels. It offered an answer to the evils of capitalism and non-regulation of industry. "Marxism" saw religion as the "opiate of the people." Others have called the 1800s the "Century of Isms." There were atheism, capitalism, conservatism, humanitarianism, imperialism, industrialism, liberalism, materialism, nationalism, secularism, and socialism, to name a few.

Catholicism on the Defensive

If you have ever been put on the defensive, you know how hard it is to see things objectively. In 1815, the Congress of Vienna met to pick up the pieces of Napoleon's empire. The Church's participation in the Congress identified it with the conservative and outdated political systems of Europe. Fear of change strengthened the desire to keep throne and altar united.

Rome's suspicion of liberalism throughout the century alienated the middle class. Society and thought gradually became de-Christianized. Ideas such as Charles Darwin's theory of evolution, Sigmund Freud's psychoanalysis, the separation of church and state, freedom of the press, and a

> **Liberalism:** in the nineteenth century, this meant believing that individual reason and freedom were supreme and were not responsible to any authority.

Chapter 11   From Trent to Vatican II: A.D. 1600 to the Present

church without temporal power put the Church even more on the defensive. The gap between the Church and the everyday world of most people widened.

There were some bright spots during this time. The Society of Jesus was restored in 1814. England dropped its laws against Catholics in 1830. The Oxford Movement in England brought John Henry Newman and others into the Roman Church. These people based their entry into the Church on the intellectual conviction that only Rome had the fullness of Christianity. New horizons opened in the mission fields as new orders and congregations which were devoted exclusively to mission work sent both men and women to the foreign missions. Catholic societies and organizations of all kinds flourished.

Simple People and Popes

Throughout the nineteenth century the Church honored simple people, often the poor: Thérèse of Lisieux (1873-1897), John Bosco (1815-1888), and Bernadette Soubirous (1844-1879). Our Lady's visits to Catherine Labouré and the apparitions at both LaSalette and Lourdes paved the way for the Church's definition of the Immaculate Conception in 1854.

The pontificates of Pius IX (1846-1878) and Leo XIII (1878-1903) sum up the dark and bright sides of the nineteenth-century Church. In the Revolution of 1848, Pius was forced to flee from Rome. His policies and ideas were out of touch with the times, placing the Church in a ghetto separated from the rest of the world.

Only three months after Vatican I and the declaration of papal infallibility (1870), Victor Emmanuel unified Italy, annexed the Papal States, and ended the temporal power of the papacy. Pius declared himself "a prisoner of the Vatican."

Pope Leo XIII is fondly remembered for his concern for the working person. Leo wrote the famous social encyclical, "Rerum Novarum."

Bernadette and the Miracle of Lourdes

In 1858, a fourteen-year-old girl named Bernadette Soubirous was blessed with a miracle. Near the town of Lourdes in southeastern France this peasant girl from a poor family was visited by Mary on several occasions. During these visitations, the two prayed together. Bernadette uncovered a spring in the grotto and followed Mary's instructions to drink from it and to pray for sinners. Although many believed Bernadette, there were also many who doubted her story. She was asked again and again to describe her experiences. Those who believed her clamored to meet her and to visit the grotto where healings were reported to have taken place.

Bernadette was a frail young woman who suffered great physical pain throughout much of her life. But she saw a chapel built at the site of the apparitions of Mary. Lourdes received official recognition as a place of pilgrimage in 1862. Bernadette died in 1879, but the shrine of Mary at Lourdes lives on.

The shrine attracts millions of pilgrims each year. Some are seeking healing, and many others want to pray and reflect at this site of holiness. Mary's appearances at Lourdes and other places, such as Guadalupe and Fatima, symbolize the caring, nurturing, and tender way that God loves us.

Papal infallibility: decreed at Vatican Council I, it states that the Pope will always be free from error whenever he explicitly defines a doctrine as part of the body of divine revelation.

Communion of Saints

Francesca Cabrini (1850-1917) was the first American citizen to become a saint. She was born in Italy and longed to become a missionary to China. Instead, Pope Leo XIII encouraged her to help the Italian immigrants in the United States.

Mother Cabrini came to New York in 1889 with six other Missionary Sisters of the Sacred Heart, an order which she founded. They began the work of teaching, caring for orphans, and founding hospitals. She was a good organizer and a capable businesswoman. She faced opposition from clergy, political upheaval, and lawsuits, yet she persevered and was loved, especially by the Italian immigrants.

Mother Cabrini gave of herself to all sectors of society. She visited those in prison, traveled to large cities and farmlands, and founded orphanages and schools wherever she went. In 1909 she became an American citizen. In 1917, Mother Cabrini died of malaria in Chicago. She was canonized in 1946.

A Papal Renaissance

The world of Leo XIII, Pius' successor, had no boundaries. Like Pope John XXIII in our own times, he "opened windows to let in a little fresh air." His social encyclical, *"Rerum Novarum,"* 1891, supported the labor movement, the rights of workers, and spelled out Catholic teachings on the role of state. Vatican archives were opened to scholars, and Catholic universities were established at Fribourg, Washington, D.C., and the Louvain in Belgium. In Leo XIII, Catholic social action had a champion. Leo's social teachings brought Catholics actively into contemporary society.

8. What do you know about the "isms" mentioned above? Are they still around today?

9. What do you think were some of the consequences of the Vatican's loss of temporal power?

10. How did the actions of Leo XIII mirror the activity of the earliest Christians?

Hope, Despair, and Dreams

In the twentieth century, humanity explored the heavens and walked in space, fought two world wars, and witnessed the advent and disintegration of communism in many parts of the world. It also often lost sight of human dignity and the sacredness of life. The popes during this century have continued to proclaim the Church's teaching on the dignity and sacredness of human life.

Pius X (1903-1914) was a pastoral pontiff. He encouraged the frequent reception of Communion and lowered the age for its reception to seven. Benedict XV's (1914-1922) charity for all victims of World War I helped to end anti-clericalism. Pius XI (1922-1939) accepted a political settlement to the question of the Papal States. The Lateran Treaty (1929) established 108 acres within Rome as the Vatican which has full sovereignty. For the first time since the eighth century the Church stood free of political

Gate of Auschwitz Concentration Camp, Poland
Although Pius XII has been criticized for not doing more to stop the Holocaust during World War II, he attempted to defend Jews throughout Europe.

intrigues and military involvements. Through papal condemnations of the totalitarian governments in Russia, Italy, and Germany, the Church tried to prevent war and the spread of communism. Most of these condemnations went unnoticed, and, in some cases, came too late to do any good.

In 1939, Pius XII was elected pope. Christian nations were again at war. Hitler's systematic massacre of more than six million Jews, known as the Holocaust, as well as America's use of the atomic bomb, seriously undermined the credibility of Christianity and shocked the world. Although Pius' silence during the Holocaust has been questioned, he did succeed in protecting some Jews. At the close of World War II, communist governments took over half of Germany, all of eastern Europe and China, and had strong ties with parts of Latin America, Africa, and the Far East. Communism was a determined and organized foe of the Church. Wherever it was established, persecution of all organized religion followed.

At the same time, many of Europe's colonial empires began to crumble, and the emerging independent nations often welcomed the Church. The creation of native clergies and efforts made to adapt to the cultures of the Third World brought many converts into the People of God.

Encyclical: a papal letter addressed to all the Catholics around the world on matters of Church teaching.

Chapter 11   From Trent to Vatican II: A.D. 1600 to the Present

In the field of Biblical studies, Catholic scholars moved forward on the research of their Protestant brothers. Today, almost fifty different New Testament translations have appeared in English, prepared by committees of Protestants and Catholics. In ecumenism, too, Catholics took their first steps where Protestants had pioneered. Jesuit Father Teilhard de Chardin's writings on the spiritual evolution of creation broke down the barriers between science and religion. Christians in Latin America and Africa were being called to social justice and liberation of the oppressed. In the 1960's, charismatic renewal moved into the Catholic Church.

When Pius XII died in 1958, liberal theological development, bottled up during the former century and a half, was more than ready to emerge. The man who uncorked the bottle was Pope John XXIII. Vatican II broadened the Church's perspective and forced it to look at itself in light of the events of the modern world and the Church's twenty-centuries-long tradition. Before studying the impact of that powerful council, it will be helpful to explore the origin and growth of the Catholic Church in America.

11. *How has the fall of Communism in Europe affected the churches in those countries?*

Conceived in Liberty

Spanish missionaries established the Church in Florida and vast areas of the Southwest. French Jesuits explored the Great Lakes-Mississippi regions during the sixteenth century. But it was the English colonists, stretched along the Atlantic seaboard, who controlled the destiny of the United States. Because of their heritage, they brought their dislike and distrust of "papists" with them. Our earliest statesmen, such as Washington and Jefferson, were deists, and the U.S. Constitution is a document born of the Enlightenment. Thus the religious, cultural, and political values, virtues, and morality of white, Anglo-Saxon Protestants came to be identified with the U.S. ideal.

Toleration of Catholics came with the War for Independence. Charles Carroll was one of the signers of the Declaration of Independence, and, almost without exception, Catholics were committed to the Revolution. To win the support of Catholic France, anti-Catholic prejudices were laid aside.

The Infant American Church

The Constitution of the new nation both guaranteed religious freedom and forbade an established state Church. This left the Catholic Church free to develop under the capable leadership of John Carroll. He was a man of intellect, culture, energy, and vision who saw no conflict in loving both his Church and his country. In 1789 the American clergy elected him as the first Bishop of Baltimore. Carroll's diocese was the entire United States. There were approximately twenty-five thousand Catholics and twenty-four priests. For twenty-six years Bishop Carroll directed the destiny of the infant American Church. In 1790 the first Jesuit college opened in Georgetown. The next year the Sulpicians started a seminary. By 1808 Baltimore was made an archdiocese, and Boston, New York, Philadelphia, and Bardstown (Kentucky) became dioceses. Both the Church and the new nation were moving west.

Bishop John Carroll was the first bishop of the United States. His diocese was Baltimore, Maryland.

Charismatic renewal: refers to the gifts of the Holy Spirit, visible especially in prayer and the creation of community, personal response to the Spirit, and growth in charity.

Sulpicians: a French society of priests who specialized in organizing seminaries and teaching in them.

Chapter 11 From Trent to Vatican II: A.D. 1600 to the Present

Unique in the World

Under Carroll, Elizabeth Seton founded the Sisters of Charity. Their work in education marked the beginnings of the American Catholic school system. Although Carroll struggled with lay trusteeism, organized bigotry from the Know-Nothing Party in New York, and friction between the Irish and French clergy, his vision for the American Church was to be a proof to the world that general and equal toleration was "the most effective method to bring all denominations of Christians to a unity of faith." When he died in 1815, the Catholic Church in the United States was small but growing, totally American, loyal to the democratic system, and unique in the world.

---

12. In what ways do you think that separation of church and state in America is good for the Church?

13. Why do you think a guarantee of religious freedom was important to the founders of the United States?

14. What groups today carry on the ugly tradition of the Know-Nothings?

Coping and Growing

In the decades preceding the Civil War, Irish and German immigrants swelled the ranks of Catholics to over three million, making Catholicism the largest religious group in the United States. Irish settlement in the large cities gave the Church the predominantly urban character it still retains. Methodists and Baptists were the two largest Protestant denominations.

Despite continued hostility from the Know-Nothings, the mid-nineteenth century found the Church not only active in the cities and alive on the frontier, but establishing contemplative communities in Latrobe, Pennsylvania, and Gethsemani, Kentucky. Catholics fought on both sides during the Civil War, and hundreds of religious Sisters volunteered as nurses. Unlike the main Protestant groups, the Church in the North and South remained united after the war.

Post-War Evangelization

From the Civil War to the early 1900s, the United States was again flooded with millions of Catholic immigrants, this time from southern Europe. For the most part they were poor and disenfranchised (without the right to vote), lacking education and knowledge of English. Many groups brought their own priests. The Church's main energies were directed towards Americanizing the immigrants while helping them to preserve their faith. Catholic schools and the thousands

Between 1800 and 1960, the Church in the United States focused much of her attention on "Americanizing" Catholic immigrants.

Lay trusteeism: lay members control of parish government.

Know-Nothing Party: a political party opposed to all foreigners and Catholics.

Chapter 11 From Trent to Vatican II: A.D. 1600 to the Present

of dedicated sisters who staffed them played an enormous role. In 1884 the Third Plenary Council of Baltimore required a Catholic school in every parish. By 1885 Catholics ran 272 orphanages and 154 hospitals, as well as many other institutions that cared for the needs of the immigrant Church.

Preoccupation with the immigrants left few resources for the evangelization of the freed slaves, and most of them turned to the Baptist and Methodist churches. This accounts, in part, for the small number of African-American Catholics today. In 1990 there were approximately one and a quarter million African-American Catholics. The racial prejudice of some white Catholics has also been a factor in the small number of African-American Catholics.

Social Change

On social issues, the Church in America moved in many directions. Baltimore's Cardinal Gibbons (1834-1921) publicly identified the Church with the interests of the working class by championing the rights of organized labor. Convert Isaac Hecker founded the Paulist Fathers and forged an apostolate of the Catholic press. Frances Xavier Cabrini did outstanding ministry among the Italian immigrants. Mother Katharine Drexel reached out as a missionary to the American Indians and the freed slaves.

Frances Cabrini is the first American citizen to be proclaimed a saint.

Twentieth century America brought radical shifts in the Church. It moved from a missionary status in 1908 to the world's greatest source of foreign missionaries. Catholic ghettos fell apart after World War II, and by 1960 most European ethnic Catholics had moved into middle-class America. World War II and the Korean and Vietnam conflicts once more drew on Catholic patriotism. John F. Kennedy's election to the presidency in 1960 demonstrated that American Catholicism had matured. Then came Vatican II.

15. *How does your parish reflect an immigrant tradition?*

16. *What was the importance of the Catholic school system to the immigrant populations?*

Summary

- The 1800s were a time of welcome change and potentially dangerous developments for the world and the Church.

- New ideas threatened Rome which became separated from the world, until Leo XIII brought the Church back into the world.

- The Church in the United States developed quickly under John Carroll.

- Many new immigrants to the U.S. found solace in the Church, and it grew strong.

- The political and social changes of the first half of the twentieth century prepared the Church for Vatican II.

SECTION 2
Checkpoint!

■ Review

1. Why was the 1800s praised by some and not by others?

2. How do the pontificates of Pius IX and Leo XIII illustrate the worst and best aspects of the Church at this time?

3. What contributions did John Carroll make to the development of Catholicism in the U.S.?

4. Name two outstanding figures of American Catholicism and their gifts.

5. What was the Lateran Treaty, and what effect did it have on the Church?

6. Describe the atmosphere in the Church before Vatican II. What changes or new developments led up to it?

7. Words to Know: Lateran Treaty, Know-Nothings, Lay trusteeism.

■ In Your World

1. Choose one outstanding figure of American Church history and present a chapter from his or her autobiography. Read about that person's life and give an oral presentation to the class as if you were that person. Choose a period of his or her life (or an event) which you think shows an important part of his or her character or best illustrates his or her contribution to the Church.

2. As a result of the changes in Eastern Europe, the Church is re-emerging as a force for change and spiritual vitality. With the help of magazine and newspaper articles, explore the new life of the Church in one country. What was its status during the first part of the twentieth century, and how has it changed? Where are there signs of new life? How has the Church played a role in the change?

■ Scripture Search

Reread the story of the Council of Jerusalem in Acts 15. How did the controversy which sparked this council parallel some of the quarrels between different ethnic groups of Catholics in the early 1900s? How do various nationalities, languages, and cultures contribute to the diversity of the Church rather than disrupting its unity?

The Church: A Spirit-Filled People

SECTION 3
The Tidal Wave

The day Pope John XXIII told a group of cardinals he intended to call a general council, he wrote in his diary: "I expected that after hearing what I had to say, they would have crowded around me to express approval and good wishes. Instead there was an unbroken and impressive silence." No wonder! The Church was far from ready for the most significant event since Trent. Pope John's words on October 11, 1962, were prophetic. "You have come to open the Council that God's treasures may be available to all . . . This council will bring us to the right path."

The Council

In many ways, Vatican II was unique. It was the first to deal with the Church's role in the world. It was also much better than any of the preceding councils. There were 2,600 bishops in attendance at the Council. Vatican II was the first council to be so open to internal change, and it was worldwide in its representation. Theologians who acted as advisors to the bishops had the advantage of the historical studies of the previous hundred years. The changes that have developed since the Council, such as Communion in the hand and under both species, are a return to original and more authentic practices.

Council Fathers also made full use of modern technology. Vatican II was the first council to have electric lights, typewriters, telephones, microphones, computers, and worldwide media coverage. Thousands of papers were delivered on the council floor for informal discussion and formal debate.

A People at Prayer

Here is a prayer from Pope John Paul II which focuses on the theme of Christian unity: ". . . help us in a great endeavor that we are carrying out to meet on a more and more mature way our brothers in the faith . . . Through all the means of knowledge, mutual respect, of love, shared collaboration in various fields, may we be able to rediscover gradually the divine plan for the unity into which we should enter and bring everybody in . . . Allow us in the future to go out to meet human beings and all the peoples that are seeking God and wishing to serve him on the way of different religions . . . show us always how we are to serve the individual and humanity in every nation, how we are to lead them along the ways of salvation, how we are to protect justice and peace in a world continually threatened on various sides."

The bishops at Vatican II initiated a revival in the life of the Church with a reform of the liturgy, a revision of Church (Canon) law, and the use of the image of the People of God.

17. How do you think the advances of the twentieth century helped the bishops at Vatican II both during and after the council?

What the Council Said

Can faith be meaningful in today's world? What is the Church's relation to the world? The Council Fathers returned to the Scriptures to discover how the original Church understood itself and chose the People of God as the most suitable image for our time. But because the Church is a mystery—the visible sign of God's presence in the world—nowhere did the Second Vatican Council offer a single authoritative definition of the Church to be accepted by all Catholics.

Following its prophetic voices, Vatican II worked hard to make Catholicism a credible voice to the world. The Church saw itself clearly as in and part of the world, exerting an influence on it and working with it to bring about the reign of God.

John XXIII — The Interim Pope

Angelo Roncalli became Pope John XXIII in 1958. He was expected to serve as an "interim" pope, only filling in for a short time. He was already seventy-eight years old when he was elected. In the end, his five brief years in office ushered in a new age for the Church.

John XXIII was born in 1881, one of thirteen children. He was an accomplished scholar, writer, diplomat, administrator, and could speak seven languages. He served during World War I and afterwards was sent to Bulgaria, Turkey, Greece, and France as an envoy of the Vatican.

After being elected pope, he immediately called for the modernization of canon law. Then, in 1959, he called the Vatican Council, he said, in order "to open a window and let in a little fresh air." He called it *aggiornamento*, or "updating."

The goal of the Council was to seek the unity and peace of all Christians and the world. The Council drew worldwide attention. Although John XXIII died in 1963 before the Council ended, he saw great change initiated, and will always be remembered as the Pope who led the Church into the modern era.

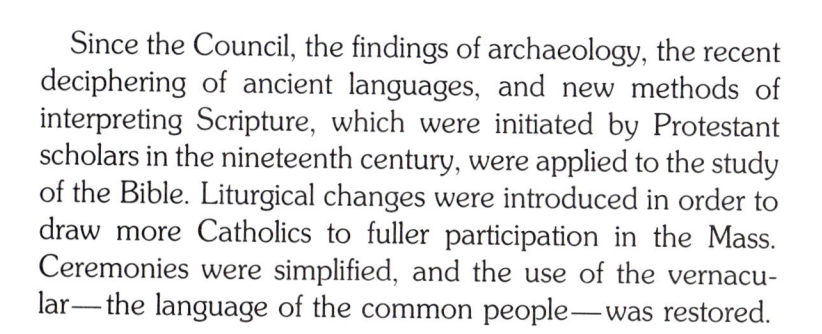

Since the Council, the findings of archaeology, the recent deciphering of ancient languages, and new methods of interpreting Scripture, which were initiated by Protestant scholars in the nineteenth century, were applied to the study of the Bible. Liturgical changes were introduced in order to draw more Catholics to fuller participation in the Mass. Ceremonies were simplified, and the use of the vernacular—the language of the common people—was restored.

The Second Vatican Council strongly supported the need for human freedom, personal dignity, and the democratic process as it called attention to the role of the laity, the need for religious freedom, and the collegial nature of the Church's authority. Christian responsibility for social justice received new emphasis.

18. What additional changes were made at Vatican II?

The Post-Vatican Church

Pope Paul VI inherited a Church with a democratic spirit, but one still caught, at times, in archaic Church structures and ancient problems. Paul continued the effort of John XIII to smooth out these tensions. The World Synod of Bishops that met in 1969 was one such attempt. The first steps toward a reunion with Orthodox Christianity were made in 1964-1965. Mutual excommunications were lifted, and East and West embraced in the persons of Pope Paul VI and Athenagoras I, the Patriarch of Constantinople.

After the death of Paul VI, the largest conclave in history selected John Paul I. During his thirty-four days as pontiff, his joy, holiness, and simple goodness won the world's heart. His untimely death was followed by the election of Cardinal Karol Wojtyla "from a far away nation" (Poland) to be the Bishop of Rome.

John Paul II

John Paul II took office on October 16, 1978. He is the first non-Italian since 1523 to become pope. This pontiff has ruled firmly but also with compassion, a technique he perfected during his years in Poland. While remaining devoted to his native land, where the influence of the Church is strong, he has already traveled the world and embraced its peoples. The attempted assassination of the Pope in 1981 was an indication of the storms facing a pontiff who takes strong social positions. At the same time, the pope has also chosen to help the Church assimilate the many changes initiated by Vatican II.

Pope John Paul II has visited nearly every country in the world during his pontificate.

Predicting the Future

What will the Church of the future be? We know that Vatican II changed not only prayer forms and cultural expressions of piety, but it offered Catholics new ways of viewing the Church, Protestants, non-Christians, worldly progress, law, conscience, and authority. The changes which have followed the Council have not been without problems. Many people are troubled and confused by the vocation crisis, the development of lay ministries, the expanded role for women in the Church, new emphasis on the Bible, and the alienation of Catholic youth. Change has caused many Catholics to leave the Church. Others have welcomed it. Still others have responded with bewildered obedience, saying with Simon Peter, "Lord, to whom shall we go? You have the words of eternal life."

Challenges of the Future

Pessimists look at the Church and see a shrinking U.S. parochial school system, a decline in mass attendance, a drop in clergy numbers and prestige, and a diminishing in the difference between Catholics and other Christians. Optimists look at the Church and note the increased lay involvement in ministry, more shared responsibility from the parish to the national level, a service-oriented authority, and efforts directed toward renewal, evangelization, ecumenism, personal responsibility, and social justice.

Among the challenges facing the Church today is ministry to Hispanic Catholics, who form one-fourth of the Catholic population but who play only a marginal role in U.S. Church life. Other areas of concern include recapturing a sense of Christian community and Gospel simplicity, caring for marginal groups, and working to change unjust social structures. Perhaps the greatest contribution of the U.S. Church to world Catholicism is its two-hundred-year example of unity amid diversity.

In its efforts to recover the original perspective of Jesus and the apostolic community, the post-Vatican II Church sees that there are not two ships afloat on the sea of creation—one, the world, and the other, the Church. There is only one ship, and, as in the Gospel story of the storm at sea, Jesus is on board.

Conclave: the gathering of Cardinals to elect a new pope.

Tracing the Church's story from the Council of Trent to the present reveals dramatic changes as well as resistance to change. Christendom (Catholic Europe) fell apart. Rival nation states used the Church for their own ends. Ignored in the marketplace, the Church closed in on itself and sought security in isolation and uniformity. Two world wars and the emergence of communism threatened and challenged Christianity. Vatican II thrust the Church outward to the modern world, forward toward her separated brothers and sisters, and inward to renewed fidelity to the Gospel and spirit of Jesus.

19. What criticisms have you heard about the changes that have taken place in the Church? Do you agree?

20. Why do you think some people are reluctant to adopt the changes made at Vatican II?

21. What do you think are the biggest challenges facing your Church in the future?

Summary

- Vatican II was unique in many ways, including its size, scope, and use of modern technology.

- Some of the changes which have been made in Catholic practice following the Council include use of the vernacular, Communion in the hand, and fuller participation in the Mass by the laity.

- Change and evolution continue in the Church even after the Council.

- John Paul II has helped the Church assimilate the changes of Vatican II through his extensive traveling.

- The future of the Church depends on its ability to continue integrating changes and meeting the challenges it will face.

SECTION 3
Checkpoint!

Review

1. In what ways was Vatican II different from the councils which preceded it?

2. Why were new developments in Scripture studies so important for the council?

3. How has change continued to be introduced in the Church since Vatican II?

4. What aspects of change have alienated some Catholics?

5. Explain the views of both optimists and pessimists about the future of the Church.

6. Words to Know: John XXIII, Vatican II, John Paul II.

In Your World

1. Have a member of your parish who remembers the Church before the changes of Vatican II come to talk to your class. What specific changes do you see in your own church? How does that person feel about the changes made then and since then?

2. Hold your own council to confront and try to solve one challenge to the Church. Choose an issue which you think is important and discuss ways of dealing with it and implementing change. Your council must confront diversity and difference of opinions. How are you going to reach a final decision? Why did you choose the issue you did?

3. Read part of one of the documents to come out of Vatican II. Choose one which touches on a topic which interests you. Then report back to the class on your reading. What changes did the document make and why? How are they evident in your church?

Scripture Search

Read the following passages: Luke 3:21-22, 12:11-12 and John 16:13. How does the action of the Spirit in Jesus and in the Church affect us today? How is the Spirit active in the Church, in your community, and in the world?

Chapter 11   From Trent to Vatican II: A.D. 1600 to the Present

CHAPTER 11 Review

■ Study

1. How did the Thirty Years' War affect Europe?

2. What made the activities of the Sisters of Charity different from other sisters?

3. How did missionaries spread the message of the Church to the world during these centuries?

4. Explain the philosophies of Descartes and Rousseau and their challenge to the Church.

5. What was the controversy surrounding Galileo?

6. What were the causes of the French Revolution, and how was the Church forced to change because of it?

7. Describe some of the political and economic changes of the 1800s. Why did they put the Church on the defensive?

8. Who were some of the leading figures of the Church during the 1800s?

9. How did Leo XIII move the Church forward to face the twentieth century?

10. How was the Church changed by the events of the two world wars?

11. Discuss the contributions of John Carroll to the political and religious changes of the U.S. and the Church.

12. What did the influx of immigrants do for the Church, and how did the Church provide for its new members?

13. What were some of the reasons for the Second Vatican Council?

14. What was accomplished at Vatican II?

■ Action

1. Add the events in this chapter to a time line. Be sure to cover the whole period from Trent to Vatican II. Choose only events and figures you think are the most important. You might also want to include any discoveries that changed the world.

2. As a class, write a parish bulletin that highlights activities which you think reflect the influence of Vatican II. This might include announcements of meetings, Bible studies, trips, outreach to Hispanics or other groups, or social justice committees.

3. Have a member of one of the religious orders in your parish (or a nearby one) come to class to discuss his or her work. Talk about a religious vocation, and what it means in the twentieth century post-Vatican II Church.

■ Prayer

One of the documents of Vatican II is entitled *"The Constitution on the Sacred Liturgy,"* and it contains a chapter on sacred music. The document notes the ancient tradition of liturgical music and encourages all churches to develop choirs and to use musical accompaniment during prayer.

Choose one of your favorite prayers and find some background music for it. Try some traditional Church music (organ, for example) and play it during your private prayer time. See if you can find other music that enhances your prayer experience. How does the music contribute to your spiritual awareness and concentration? What effect does it have on you during your prayer time, and on the whole congregation during Mass?

CHAPTER

12

Christ Gathering His People Today

OBJECTIVES

In this Chapter you will

- Discover Jesus' mission and how he carried that out.

- Learn about the mission of the Church in the "not yet" of the reign of God.

- Find out about evangelization.

- See the role of catechesis for all members of the People of God, old and new.

- Reflect on the continuing work of missions, ecumenism, and renewal of the Catholic Church.

The faithful who by Baptism are incorporated in Christ, are placed in the People of God, and in their own way share the priestly, prophetic, and kingly office of Christ, and to the best of their ability carry on the mission of the whole Christian people in the Church and in the world.
— "Dogmatic Constitution on the Church," #31

328

The Church: A Spirit-Filled People

SECTION 1
God's Mission for the Church

The Fathers of Vatican II focused on the spiritual meaning and purpose of the Church as the People of God, rather than on the institutional image that had predominated for centuries. The image called for by our times is that of Christ continuing his work in history through his people. The final chapters of this book will explore the insights of the Council into how we, the People of God, work with Jesus to fulfill his threefold mission of teaching, sanctifying, and leading his people to God through loving service.

The Mission of Jesus

"Jesus said to them 'My food is to do the will of the one who sent me and to finish his work'" (John 4:34). That will was revealed through Israel's prophets, priests, and kings, who taught that God wanted to save his people by establishing a kingdom in which they could live free. At first they believed this kingdom meant the possession of their own land. By the fall of Jerusalem it had become obvious to the early Church that the kingdom would be realized in the secret place of each person's heart and grow into a society free of all evil.

The mission of Jesus was to launch that kingdom in order to set right what had been disrupted through humanity's abuse of freedom. Jesus possessed God's Spirit totally and made his Father's will the ruling force of his heart. In him there was no trace of evil. His loving obedience even to death, the ultimate effect of sin, released a divine energy that broke the rule of Satan and set up the new and eternal kingdom of God's love. "All power in heaven and on earth has been given to me," Jesus said (Matthew 28:18). This

Mission: from a Latin word meaning to "send" or "let go."

Chapter 12   Christ Gathering His People Today

authority was precisely his power to crush evil. Jesus not only preached the kingdom—he was the reign of God among us. His mission was to empower us to make the kingdom come in our own lives and in the world.

Jesus carried out his mission of salvation in three ways.

1) He announced that in himself the Father was now offering the gift of salvation.

2) Through this proclamation he gathered together a community of followers, and by his example of service, he led these followers to "kingdom living."

3) Finally, he gave his life in a perfect sacrifice of worship to make us a holy people.

As prophet, shepherd-king, and priest, Jesus fulfilled his threefold mission of teaching, leading, and sanctifying God's people. In this way, he inaugurated the kingdom of his Father.

Already, the activity of the Spirit at Pentecost urged the Apostles to their mission of doing just as Jesus did. They rushed out to announce the Good News of salvation, to receive into their ranks through the life-giving waters of Baptism those who responded to it, and to share with them the remembrance and life of Jesus in the breaking of the bread, the Eucharist. The life of the Spirit led them to cure, help, and serve the people and thus win the respect of still others for the kingdom.

---

1. Discuss what it means to be sent out on a mission.

2. How do you think it is possible to say that the kingdom has arrived in the person of Jesus, and yet is not entirely here?

3. What do you think would be some concrete examples of kingdom living?

The Mission of the Church in Our World

With Jesus, the kingdom successfully broke into our world, and we already possess the Spirit's power for living the life of the kingdom. Even so, the reign of God will not be complete until the end of time. We say it is "already" (accomplished), but "not yet" (fully realized).

Prophet, Priest, and King—Israel's Leaders

In ancient Israel, God used prophets, priests, and kings to prepare the world for salvation. God's plan would culminate in Jesus, who fulfilled all three roles and proclaimed the kingdom.

A prophet in Israel was God's official spokesperson, with the mission to proclaim God's word, to reveal the sacred meaning of events, and to act as the conscience of the people. Among Israel's greatest prophets were Moses, Elijah, and Isaiah.

A priest in Israel was officially set apart as a mediator between God and humanity, especially by offering sacrifices. His action glorified God and sanctified the people. Abraham, Moses, and the other priests offered sacrifices to signify the covenant between God and Israel.

A king was chosen by God to lead the people. David was the model shepherd-king who guided the flock of Israel. He united the people, protected them, and created conditions for a better life.

Jesus fulfilled all three functions of God's saving mission in himself. He is the Word, he sealed the new covenant, and he is the shepherd who gave his life for his flock.

◆

Michelangelo—Moses
Moses is considered one of the greatest of Israel's leaders.

Kingdom living: the lifestyle of those who do God's will as taught by Jesus.

Whenever we pray the Lord's Prayer, we say, ". . . Thy kingdom come." This is a kingdom of peace and justice where all people form a community of love. In this kingdom people from every tribe and nation, speaking every language, will unite in friendship, and rejoice together with God and share the fullness of life. We look forward to this final kingdom—the fullness of life-with hope, but it is already being gradually realized in history. Jesus calls us to form a community of faith, hope, and love, and to serve one another.

Chapter 12   Christ Gathering His People Today

On This Rock

As we have seen, the Good News has spread far and wide in the past three hundred years. Evangelists have been at work all over the world. The RCIA encourages adults to participate fully in the process of initiation.

Before the RCIA was developed, Julius Kambarage Nyerere, President of Tanzania, a country in East Africa, became a member of the Church. He did not start school at St. Mary's until he was twelve. Later he earned a Master's Degree and entered politics.

Through his hard work and perseverance, his country gained independence. He has continued to work to promote justice and equality in Tanzania.

In 1970, Nyerere spoke of the Church at Maryknoll, New York: "Fear of the future, and of the needs of the future, is no part of Christianity. Ours is a living faith: if you like, a revolutionary faith, for faith without action is sterile, and action without faith is meaningless."

As we have seen, the Church always lives in a time of tension. Through these tensions, the Church is shown to be what it is. As "already arrived," it is a sign of the kingdom here on earth. As "not yet" fully realized, it is an instrument of Jesus' own greatest power, the power to shatter the rule of evil and death and to bring forth the kingdom. Jesus commissioned every member of his Church when he commanded, "Go, therefore, and make disciples of all nations" (Matthew 28:19).

To his commission, Jesus added, "And behold, I am with you always, until the end of the age" (Matthew 28:20). With Christ we can make our own future; we can forge his community. While we long for the age to come, we can be God's agents who transform our planet into the global village of peace and justice that is a glimpse of the final kingdom. We not only can, but we must. Joined to Jesus in Baptism, we become his priestly people with the privilege and duty of proclaiming the kingdom. We are capable of co-offering his perfect sacrifice, the Eucharist, and by doing so we become pleasing and holy to the Lord. And by our loving service, we draw others to the service of God.

Vatican II emphasized the role of the laity in the Church as "a participation [through Baptism and Confirmation] in the saving mission of the Church itself" (*"Dogmatic Constitution on the Church,"* #33). "The laity share not in the mission of the clergy, but in Christ's mission" (*"Decree on the Church's Missionary Activity,"* #2). To be a member of the Church is to be responsible for that mission. So strongly did the early Church feel its obligation to be a message-carrying community that every Gospel it wrote ends with a command to be missionary. Not to be so is to betray the Gospel.

---

4. *What signs of global unity have emerged in the past ten years? How have the efforts of the "common people" helped achieve these changes?*

5. *What are some ways people suffer from oppression today, especially in the United States? How is our whole planet suffering?*

6. *How do you think you can be a missionary of the Gospel in your own community?*

The Church: A Spirit-Filled People

A candlelight vigil expresses in a special way that Jesus is the Light of the World.

Gathering the People—Evangelization

The Council Fathers called for an urgent renewal of missionary spirit in the Church. They did not only mean that we should step up our work in the missions "The Church on earth is by its very nature missionary," they wrote (*"On The Church's Missionary Activity,"* #2). There is a difference between the missions, which are efforts to plant the Church in lands where Christ has not been preached, and the mission of the Church, the broader idea of carrying out Christ's total work of salvation. The Council referred to sharing Christ's universal mission as evangelization.

Evangelization comes from the Latin *evangelium,* "the Good News" or "Gospel." Evangelization is bringing the Good News of God's love in Christ to all people by word and witness so that, through the grace of the Holy Spirit, they may accept it, and respond with ever growing commitment to Christ and his Church.

Evangelization is carried out primarily through preaching, catechizing, and missionary work. Yet it involves more than explaining the Paschal Mystery—the death and resurrection of Jesus. It is witnessing to Jesus by our lives.

Evangelization leads to conversion—a turning to Christ. Evangelization is an ongoing process we all need in order to keep our focus on Christ. Responding to the Good News is demanding. It means more than publicly embracing Christ, and even more than accepting Jesus in private prayer. Evangelization is a life commitment to Christ in his Church and a reaching out to evangelize others.

Pope Paul VI summarized the elements of the evangelization process in this order: (1) Christian witness, (2) proclamation of the Gospel, (3) inner acceptance, (4) entrance into the Church community, (5) participation in the signs of grace (sacraments), and (6) initiative in evangelizing others.

An Inquiry Class is one way to reach those people interested in hearing the Good News.

Evangelization is so essential to Christian life that all Church ministries, organizations, structures, and programs exist in order to help the Christian community draw all humankind into one Gospel family, living in love, peace, and justice.

---

7. What obstacles do you think might be placed in your way in your efforts to evangelize?

8. How did Jesus evangelize? Give examples from Scripture.

Summary

- The mission of Jesus, to inaugurate the kingdom of God, was accomplished by his actions and his person.

- The Church has a mission to establish that kingdom through our own actions as the People of God.

- Evangelization brings the Good News to all people.

- It is the responsibility of all Catholics to participate in evangelizing.

Conversion: to turn completely away from present beliefs or behavior.

SECTION 1
Checkpoint!

■ Review

1. How was the will of God revealed before Jesus?
2. What are the three ways Jesus carried out his mission?
3. Explain what is meant by saying that the kingdom of God is "already" but "not yet" present.
4. How is evangelizing carried out?
5. Describe the six elements of evangelization as Paul VI summarized them.
6. Words to Know: mission, kingdom, evangelization, conversion.

■ In Your World

1. Ask some of the members of your parish if they have ever been active in evangelization. Interview someone who has about their experiences. Were they successful? What frustrations did they have? What responses did they get from others?
2. Create a description of "kingdom living." What everyday activities does it include, and what special actions can you add? Be sure to include something about family, work, society, and care of oneself.

■ Scripture Search

Read the following passages: Mark 1:15; John 1:14, 4:34; Luke 4:14-21, 19:9. How do these Scriptures clarify Jesus' relation to the kingdom of God?

SECTION 2
An Evangelizing People

Jesus served as an example in his actions. We seek to imitate him in our own actions. Evangelization and catechesis are at the very heart and soul of the Church's mission. This section examines the when, how, and who of these activities of the mission of the Church.

How to Be a Successful Evangelizer

Evangelizers must be enthusiastic. People seem to respond to the Spirit revealed more in people's action than in their words: caught rather than taught. Convinced Catholics are eager to reveal the great gift of Christ. The aim of evangelization is not to conquer by argument, but to make Christ present to the other. One-to-one encounters are the most successful way to win others for Christ. Eighty-two percent of those who become Catholics do so because someone personally invited them.

Often evangelization is a case of actions speaking louder than words. The way a Catholic reacts to a deep sorrow or forgives an enemy shouts the influence of Christ as nothing else can. A show of sincere interest in others often uncovers in them a longing for peace or forgiveness. Dialogue leads to discussion of Christ and his Church. Evangelizers then share the consolation they find in the Gospel of Jesus and pray for the person in need. The Holy Spirit works in the hearts of the listeners, opening them and stimulating them to respond by breaking with the past and surrendering to God.

Enthusiastic: from *in* and *theos* meaning "in God." It means being inspired by the Spirit.

Communion of Saints

In 1888, at the age of 15, a young girl entered the Carmelite convent at Lisieux in France. By 1897 she had died of tuberculosis, but her short time in the convent was enough to witness to her holiness.

Thérésa of Lisieux was a proud and obstinate child who had already resolved to become a saint. She spent much of her short life fighting her own pride and her doubts. She did so by surrendering to God. She worked hard to do God's will in obedience within the convent.

In the end, Saint Thérésa of Lisieux never surrendered to her doubts, but made them work for her by renewing and strengthening her faith every day. On her deathbed she said, "I will spend my heaven doing good on earth." Her intercession is linked to many miracles. She was canonized in 1925, and today, she and Joan of Arc are the patronesses of France.

Each evangelizer develops a unique style. The Lord uses us as we are. Just as every spiritual value came to you through some other Catholic, other people depend on Catholics like you to learn of Christianity. People hear the Good News of God's forgiveness because you forgive. People see Christian hope because they witness your hope. People are drawn to friendship with God because you risk being their friend. And so the living Lord is experienced in flesh and blood—in the joys and tears of every day living—because you are bold enough to live as if God is a loving Father. The world is converted through your word and witness, and you, in turn, are strengthened in your faith.

9. Why do you think that "fire and brimstone" speeches are not effective in evangelization?

10. How can the media be put to good use as an instrument of evangelization?

Who Needs Evangelization?

God "wants men to be saved and come to know the truth" (1 Timothy 2:4). First among those in need of evangelization is the pilgrim Church, which is imperfect and always in need of reform. Without constant evangelization, the ministries become only jobs and church structures harden. Evangelization helps the Church retain its freshness, vigor, and strength.

Active Catholics

In the United States there are more than fifty-seven million active Catholics. Each of us regularly needs to be awakened to the breadth and depth of our baptismal covenant. We need to increase our understanding of the faith and to be wholeheartedly committed to it. Sharing our faith experience with another is one of the strongest encouragements we can use to further grow in our own faith.

Inactive Catholics

A second focus of evangelization is inactive Catholics. For them evangelization may involve another conversion after a period of being unsure of their beliefs or a complete loss of faith. For this reason, evangelizers must move slowly and sensitively, but with enthusiasm and trust in God, letting Christ go after his lost sheep through them. They must be willing to experience anger or rejection because inactive Catholics are often nursing wounds that need care before they will heal. We can help them with our acceptance and love. Sometimes evangelizers need to apologize on behalf of the Church for wrongs the inactive Catholics may have suffered.

In the story of the Prodigal Son, the Father raced to greet his wayward boy and rejoiced at his son's return.

Those Outside the Church

The third group we are called to evangelize are those outside the Catholic Church. This includes the seventy-three million Protestant Christians in America. Our effort is to proclaim the Lord Jesus to them, as they often proclaim him to us. We encourage them to deepen their faith and gently invite those who might hunger for a more sacramental life to experience Catholicism. In ecumenical dialogue, we try to repair Church disunity. As long as the Body of Christ is broken, our evangelization efforts are hindered.

Chapter 12   Christ Gathering His People Today

A fourth group are religious non-Christians, numbering eleven million in America. This figure includes six million people of the Jewish faith. They are the Chosen People of God. We can, however, continue to share the love of Christ with them. In the fifth group are seventy million people with no religious affiliation. Every Catholic has the mission to reach out to the four to ten people on every parish block who have no church affiliation. Evangelizers need courage to approach these people and to expect to be turned down a dozen times before meeting someone waiting for Christ. Inviting newcomers to their homes, visiting neighbors, and offering service and comfort in times of need are some ways Christians draw others to the faith.

---

11. *How does ongoing evangelization of the active members of your parish illustrate the "not yet" character of the reign of God?*

12. *How can your actions evangelize better than words?*

The RCIA: Evangelization in Action

Every parish includes people just turning to Christ for the first time. They are known as catechumens. David Riggs of Amityville, New York, was baptized according to the Rite of Christian Initiation of Adults (RCIA). This 1974 revision of the baptismal rite restored the catechumenate, which is a period of formation which existed in the early Church.

The RCIA occurs in several stages and each is celebrated by its own rite. David could not say enough about the inspiration, encouragement, and instruction in the faith he received from the parishioners of St. Martin's, who warmly accepted him. The entire community was strengthened in its faith and awakened to renewed commitment as David progressed, but especially his sponsors and godparents.

The RCIA helps people come to understand the Catholic faith.

One of the most exciting developments in sacramental ministry, the RCIA is a powerful agent of ongoing evangelization in the local parish. Since the catechumenate focuses on the Paschal Mystery, and culminates in the celebration of the sacraments of initiation during the Easter Vigil, Lent becomes a period of renewal for the entire parish.

Many people had come to know David during his catechumenate, and so had personal reasons to join the warm applause that welcomed him into the community on that Holy Night of Nights. Although the bishop, pastor, sponsors, and godparents play a role in the candidates' formation, the catechist teaches the Christian vision in formal instructions on the beliefs and traditions of the Church. The parish staff and parishioners provide living witness of the faith, encouraging the candidates to continue on their faith journey. Emphasis is on the *process* of coming to the faith—of experiencing Jesus in the living and loving members of his community—rather than on merely knowing its doctrines, laws, and facts.

As the movement to evangelize gains momentum, God will use more Catholics to reach out to more people. Authorized and guided by the Church, Catholics will be instruments encouraging others to accept the message and love of Christ. It is time to take more seriously the Lord's command, "What you hear whispered, proclaim on the housetops" (Matthew 10:27).

The baptism of a new member is a sign of the vitality of the parish.

Chapter 12　Christ Gathering His People Today

341

13. How does the period of formation in the catechumenate represent a tie to the past?

14. How have you been catechized?

Catechesis

Jane, the daughter of a physician, wanted no part of her school's biology course. Thinking everyone expected her to follow in her father's footsteps, she rebelled at the very thought of biology. After a semester, Jane surprised herself by voluntarily enrolling in physiology.

Genuine conversion is like that. It leads to independent initiative. Anyone who has discovered Jesus wants to know more about him. Catechesis answers the questions that arise after we accept Jesus. Catechesis is not "for children only." Like evangelization, it is a lifelong process. In childhood you passively accept the faith of your parents. Adolescence is the time of coming to a personal ownership of faith. In adulthood you direct your own growth as well as that of others.

The Council's emphasis on evangelization has stimulated a renewal in catechesis, a specific stage in the evangelization and conversion process. Catechesis "aims at developing an understanding of the mystery of Christ" (*"Catechesi Tradendai,"* #20). It is any activity that helps people to hear, understand, interiorize, and respond to God's will in service and celebration. It strengthens personal faith and love, which then are expressed in deeper involvement in Church community.

Content and Methods

The source and content of catechesis is God's Word, which the Church has the duty to interpret. The content of catechesis must be God-centered, Christ-centered, and Trinitarian (through Christ to the Father in the Holy Spirit). It should center around the mystery of God and his great gift

Rebellion and Renewal—Thomas Merton

In 1915, Thomas Merton was born in France. His parents were artists. He was orphaned as a child and spent much of his youth wandering aimlessly without much direction. He felt a deep need for God, even at an early age, but wasn't sure how to satisfy that need. The story of his youth is reminiscent of that of Saint Augustine. He spent a good deal of his time socializing, and even fathered an illegitimate child. Finally, in his early twenties, he began serious study and converted to Catholicism at the Cistercian monastery of Gethsemani, Kentucky. He also became an American citizen.

Merton's biography, *The Seven Storey Mountain*, tells the tale of his journey to God. Merton also wrote many books and articles on prayer and monastic life. He became the Master of Novices and was interested in the use of Eastern methods of prayer, especially contemplation.

In the 1960s, Merton was one of the first voices calling for an end to war, nuclear armament, and environmental abuse. He lived in a hermitage near the monastery and continued to study and pray. At the age of fifty-three, Merton died while attending a meeting of an international group of contemplatives in Bangkok.

Today, Merton is still widely read and talked about. His solitary life has touched many because of his social concerns and his daily attempts to renew himself as he played his part in fulfilling the mission of Christ.

Thomas Merton was a writer, a mystic, a reformer, and a man of peace.

of salvation. Catechesis "must take care to show that the supreme meaning of human life is this: to acknowledge God and to glorify him by doing his will, as Christ taught us by his words and the example of his life, and then to come to eternal life" (*"General Catechetical Directory,"* 39, 41).

Chapter 12   Christ Gathering His People Today   343

Catechesis adapts to the age, development, and readiness of the learners. There is the catechesis of the home, where children almost unconsciously adopt the manner of acting and attitudes of the family members. There are the Catholic schools, which the bishops recognize as a good opportunity to educate Christian children and young people. The bishops call on all members of the Catholic community to do everything in their power to strengthen and maintain Catholic schools. There are parish schools of religion and parish study clubs. In addition, catechesis is carried out in connection with the sacraments: the preparation of children, the RCIA, preparation for marriage, and the preparation of the family for Baptism.

For many years U.S. Catholics derived the support and nourishment they needed for their faith from a Catholic elementary school education followed by lifelong participation in parish liturgies and activities. As more Catholics received higher education, they found their eighth-grade understanding of the faith insufficient to solve the sophisticated problems raised by modern science and technology. Driven by a spiritual hunger for the Lord, many are eager to understand their faith on an adult level, and adult catechesis is enjoying a nationwide resurgence.

New Emphasis in Catechesis

Of all the forms of catechesis, the *"General Catechetical Directory"* (GCD)—guidelines for catechesis for the whole world—states that the chief form is that provided for adults who are able to make a mature decision for Christ. Adults confirmed in faith influence their families, are parish leaders, and can become catechists themselves. In keeping with this trend toward adult catechesis, we are seeing the establishment of catechetical institutes and parish programs, including adult classes, discussions, prayer groups, Bible study groups, and retreat programs.

Viewing the Church as bringing about the kingdom of God in the world, the bishops recommend that catechesis focus on the corporal works of mercy (see Matthew 25:35-40) and social justice. Pope Paul VI called "the cause of human dignity and of human rights . . . the cause of Christ and his Gospel" (*"Call to Action,"* October 1976). Catechists are obliged to speak out on behalf of justice, mercy, and peace. Therefore, catechesis should be concerned with the questions, hopes, anxieties, reflections, and judgments of daily events and should also address contemporary problems. Catechesis interprets the signs of the times in the light of the Gospel message.

15. *What programs does your parish offer for catechesis?*

16. *Why do you think that engaging the body, mind, and spirit are necessary for catechesis?*

17. *What particular issues of human dignity, mercy, and peace, in the U.S. and abroad, should catechists in the Church be addressing today?*

Summary

- The best evangelizers are enthusiastic and sincere.
- All Catholics need continuing evangelization to remain active in faith.
- Other groups needing evangelization include inactive Catholics, the unchurched, Protestant Christians, and religious non-Christians.
- The RCIA offers adults a program of initiation with the catechumenate.
- Catechesis provides us with knowledge and strengthens our faith by focusing on works of mercy and social justice.

SECTION 2
Checkpoint!

■ Review

1. What qualities make a good evangelizer?
2. Identify the five groups in need of evangelization.
3. What is the RCIA, and how has it changed the Church's initiation process for adults?
4. What is catechesis and what forms can it take?
5. Why is catechesis more than just learning dates and doctrine?
6. Words to Know: enthusiastic, RCIA, catechesis.

■ In Your World

1. Learn more about the RCIA. Find out about its three stages and the responsibilities of both initiate and Church during these periods. If people in your parish are involved in the initiation process, talk to them about it. Participate in their baptism and celebrate their entry into the People of God.
2. Devise an evangelization program for your class. Include two objectives: (1) to renew the spirit of your classmates, and (2) to take the Good News outside the classroom in some way. Be sure to discuss how you will accomplish each of these goals.

■ Scripture Search

1. Read the following passages: Romans 1:8-15; 2 Corinthians 4:1-6, 11:24-33; 1 Corinthians 9:16-23. What do they reveal about Paul's evangelizing spirit?
2. Read Luke 15:11-24, the parable of the Prodigal Son. What does it tell you about Jesus' attitude toward anyone who has lapsed in their faith?

SECTION 3
The Many Missions of the Church

Even as the Church in the United States works to revitalize itself and to realize its mission here, it has not forgotten the larger missionary tradition of the Church. Each year, many missionaries travel to places where the Gospel has not yet been preached. These missionaries are often also trained as teachers, doctors, nurses, and administrators. They offer many kinds of help to the people they meet. And they return from their journeys with tales to tell.

Twenty Years in India

Sister Betty Conrad reported to her community about her experiences during twenty years in India as a missionary.

In an effort to accommodate Indian culture, Betty explained that the Western-style furniture in the dining room of the convent was replaced with mats used for sitting on the floor, which is the Indian custom. Traditional musical instruments like the tamboura and tabla now accompanied Indian songs at liturgies. And the administrative offices at the school were now staffed with Indian sisters.

Betty's missionary vocation, like that of all Catholics, came with Baptism. Like the other lay helpers who will return with her, she felt called to exercise her baptismal mission in the foreign missions. Other Christians may be drawn to work in the missions of their own land, to serve the missions by monetary support, or to rear families whose members recognize their missionary responsibilities.

Though much of Betty's work involves providing medical services and teaching "secular" subjects and skills, all of her activities are evangelizing, even when she is not directly

A People at Prayer

Christians through the ages have petitioned God for guidance in establishing the Church in the world. This chapter has examined the place of the Church in today's world and focused on the role of all Catholics in expansion and renewal. The following prayer is taken from the *"Apostolic Constitution,"* a document containing prayers and laws dating from the fourth century. It is a prayer whose meaning has not diminished: "Let us pray for the peace and happy settlement of the world, and of the holy churches; that the God of the whole world may afford us his everlasting peace, and such as may not be taken away from us . . . Let us pray for our enemies, and those that hate us. Let us pray for those that persecute us for the name of the Lord, that the Lord may pacify their anger, and scatter their wrath against us. Save us, and raise us up, O God, by your mercy. Let us rise up, and let us pray earnestly, and dedicate ourselves and one another to the living God, through his Christ."

catechizing or baptizing new members. Just by living Jesus' life in personal service and in sacrifice of home, country, and culture for the kingdom, Sister Betty is a witness to Christ.

New Direction

The Church has always tried to start church communities in non-Christian areas. These efforts were given a new direction by the Vatican II document on the missions. Understanding today that the kingdom is already taking shape in everything good in the world, the Church concentrates on finding Christ present and at work in people wherever they are found. Gradually, as the people are drawn by the witness and faith of the missionaries, the Church puts to the service of Christ all that is valuable in the culture and discourages practices that destroy human dignity or freedom. By teaching the people to help themselves, the Church brings Christ to fuller development.

The growing consciousness that the Church must work in the world to establish peace and justice has repercussions in the interpretation of the mission. Frequently today, the Gospel message is viewed as liberation from all forms of slavery. Working from the beliefs that religion and life are united and that God is concerned about the salvation of the whole person, more and more missionaries see their role including social reform. Like modern Moseses, missionaries try to break down barriers among people, and between God and people, so that humankind will be united as a family and all will be assured of their human rights and dignity.

Evangelization and Progress

Imitating Christ, who cared for the poor and oppressed, missionaries try to reduce poverty, sickness, disease, discrimination, hatred, and social injustice. Missionaries work to correct the causes of these problems, such as lack of skills, education, proper nutrition, medical care, and tools. As the Church helps the people to reduce or eliminate disease, unjust wages, and unhealthy working conditions, it lives out Christian social principles. These include self-appreciation, the dignity of the person, concern for human rights and freedom, and respect for everyone's right to life.

Missions and a Nobel Peace Prize

In this century, the work of tending missions and evangelizing has spread throughout the world. With the help of the media, we are more aware than ever of the people and places touched by the Body of Christ.

Mother Teresa of Calcutta founded the Order of the Missionaries of Charity, and was awarded the Nobel Peace Prize in 1979. She was born in 1910 in Albania. After joining the Institute of the Blessed Virgin Mary, she was sent to India as a teacher. In India, Teresa studied nursing and requested that she be placed in poor communities.

The order she founded flourished with help from many people. She and the other nuns adopted the traditional Indian sari as their habit. Centers for the care of the blind, aged, handicapped, and dying were opened.

Mother Teresa is known worldwide for her acts of mercy. She has saved thousands from death and brought hope to millions more.

Mother Teresa is a sign of hope for the world.

The Sleeping Giant of Evangelization

The land of the Stars and the Stripes is the sleeping giant of evangelization. If every Catholic shared Christ and his message of love, America would be transformed. Only three percent of the Church's time, effort, and money is spent on work with those outside the Church. Yet, if only ten percent of U.S. Catholics would bring one person into the Church, membership would grow by five million.

One of our greatest problems is the size of our parishes. The average Protestant parish has 200 members, but the average Catholic parish has 2,500. Often this large number of parishioners results in many people being treated impersonally. Certainly more priests and parishes are needed. But this also demonstrates the great need for the other ninety-seven percent of American Catholics—the laity—to recognize their responsibility to be ministers.

Like all religions, the Catholic Church in America has lost members in the past two decades. Forty to forty-five percent of young adults between the ages of 18 and 22 leave the Church for a period of time. Marriage to a person of a different faith accounts for some of these people leaving, but stages of maturity, mobility, secularism, and dissatisfaction with Church teachings are other factors. It is heartening that seventy-five percent of those who leave return to the Church after a few years.

We can either respond to evangelizing opportunities for this moment in history, or we can allow the struggles of our ancestors to be wasted; for unless faith is shared, it dries up and dies. The challenge of the twenty-first century is the same as that of the Apostles in the first. The Spirit has orchestrated events to wake up the sleeping giant of the Catholic Church in the United States. Its very future lies in your hands.

18. *What do your parish and diocese do to support the missions?*

19. *Why do you think some young people drop out of the Church and then reenter it later?*

Summary

- Missionaries perform varied functions, both religious and secular.
- Today, missionaries work to establish peace and justice wherever they are.
- Evangelization and human progress are linked together.
- Ecumenism promotes cooperation and understanding.
- The challenge to U.S. Catholics today is to respond to evangelizing opportunities here and abroad.

SECTION 3
Checkpoint!

■ Review

1. What are some of the evangelizing activities that a missionary may perform?
2. How can the Church work in the world in order to bring Christ to others?
3. In what ways do missionaries imitate Christ?
4. Whose responsibility is evangelization?
5. Word to Know: secularism.

■ In Your World

1. Participate in an ecumenical activity of some kind. Contact your parish or diocesan office for information on local ecumenical groups. Attend a meeting or prayer service. How does the sharing of faith and ideas act as a bond between people?
2. Find out where there is missionary work going on near you. Try to arrange a visit or summer session helping out. Keep a journal of your experiences and report back to your class.

■ Scripture Search

Read 1 John 1. What elements of this chapter does it illustrate and how?

Secular: applies to ideas and values that are worldly.

Chapter 12   Christ Gathering His People Today

CHAPTER

12 Review

■ Study

1. How did Jesus both preach and live the coming of the reign of God?
2. What is kingdom living, and how did Jesus' mission give us this concept?
3. What is the difference between the kingdom which is among us now, and the final kingdom fulfilled?
4. What is meant by saying that the Church lives in a time of tension?
5. How does our relationship with Jesus help us proclaim the kingdom?
6. Explain why evangelization is not just a one-time action or experience.
7. In what ways can Catholics evangelize every day?
8. Why do active Catholics need evangelization?
9. How does the RCIA stress the process of conversion?
10. What is the purpose of catechesis?
11. Why is there not just one correct way to catechesize?
12. How do missionaries live out the mission of Jesus every day even when they are not directly involved in religious activities?
13. How does the Church bring liberation to people as it lives its mission?
14. How does missionary activity in other lands today differ from that same activity two hundred years ago?
15. What are some of the reasons for the change in Catholic Church membership during the past twenty years?
16. How has the status of U.S. Catholics progressed since the beginning of the century?

Action

1. Establish letter contact with a missionary. Check with your parish or diocese for a missionary in a place which interests you. Find out about what your pen pal does, and how he or she lives. Report back to the class about what you have learned. Find the place on a map.

2. Make a collage illustrating the various ways your parish promotes the kingdom of God and fulfills the mission of the Church. Be sure to capture as many different activities as you can.

Prayer

Our prayer life often tells us a lot about our own culture. The music we hear, language we speak, and clothes we wear all reflect out particular culture. Although Catholics the world over all use the same prayers, what accompanies those prayers may differ greatly.

In order to try to share the experience of Catholics in another country, try a prayer exercise using the music, language, or dancing of another culture. You may be able to find a recording of traditional African, Indian, or Japanese music in your library. Perhaps one of your classmates can recite a prayer in another language. Recite the Lord's Prayer, which is familiar to all, with the music in the background. How does this very familiar prayer change with unfamiliar music?

Our faith in God and understanding of our Catholic sisters and brothers all over the world is enhanced when we begin to accept and appreciate the unique gifts they bring to the Body of Christ.

CHAPTER

13

Christ Calling His People to Holiness

OBJECTIVES

In this Chapter you will

- Think about what it means to be a holy person.

- Discover how Jesus provides a model for holiness and what struggles we must face to attain holiness.

- Learn about the theological and moral virtues.

- Appreciate the value of all forms of prayer and of our community.

- Encounter the holiness of Mary in her role as Mother of God and of the Church.

"All in the Church, whether they belong to the hierarchy or are cared for by it, are called to holiness . . ." for this is the will of God, your sanctification.
— "Dogmatic Constitution on the Church," #39

354

The Church: A Spirit-Filled People

SECTION 1
All Are Called

At a party, a friend wants you to meet someone special, "someone," she says, "who is good looking, rich, smart, a great dancer, holy, considerate, outgoing, and fun." You might feel uncomfortable if someone were to refer to you as "holy." You probably consider yourself ordinary, and certainly not a saint. Yet all Christians are called to holiness. In Baptism we renounce evil and pledge ourselves to follow Christ. Jesus himself appeared quite ordinary. He ate and slept as we do, and got tired and thirsty. He agonized at the thought of his death, and a crown of thorns was on his head on the cross. To teach us that holiness is for everybody, Jesus called very ordinary people to be his followers.

Equal Privilege of Faith

Perhaps one reason why not many people feel called to sanctity is that holiness is often associated with priests and religious—men and women who have taken the vows of poverty, chastity and obedience in a community approved by the Church. In the Middle Ages the clergy were thought of as the representatives of the people who were considered unworthy to stand in God's presence. Later, religious were included in this preferred circle. This false distinction is still alive today. Vatican II reminded us that although "not everyone marches along the same path, yet all . . . have obtained an equal privilege of faith" (*"Dogmatic Constitution on the Church,"* #30). Because all participate in Jesus' priesthood, "all in the Church . . . are called to holiness" (*"Dogmatic Constitution on the Church,"* #39). This teaching is directed both to the clergy and the laity.

Today the Church is witnessing a great resurgence of interest in holiness, especially among lay Catholics. Their response answers a need in our increasingly secular society where Christians are called to live their faith.

What Is Holiness?

We sometimes think of a holy person as being like a "Goody-Two-Shoes." Yet all true ideas of holiness come from God who alone is holy. In the Hebrew Scriptures, "the Holy One" is represented as infinitely separated from, and far above, all created beings. The Bible often speaks of God's sacredness in negatives. God is completely without sin, and of course, not self-centered, unfair, or unkind. In God there is no death or limitation of any kind, and his holiness is unattainable: "Who is like to you among the gods, O Lord? Who is like to you, magnificent in holiness?" (Exodus 15:11). In comparison with God, not even the angels are holy.

The Hebrew Scriptures reveal God as the possessor of all good qualities to an infinite degree. The word *holiness* derives from a root word meaning "whole." God is holy because God is whole, totally complete. God's holiness is best reflected in the covenant relationship set up with Israel, commanding them, "Be holy, for I, the Lord, your God, am holy" (Leviticus 19:2).

Jesus, Our Model

God's holiness might be frightening because it seems to imply that God is so different than us that it is impossible to communicate with, let alone imitate, God. But nowhere is God's holiness so clearly present as in Jesus, the Son and em-BODY-ment of God. From the Incarnation we learn that God's holiness can become human life. Human holiness is wholeness. The holy person is fully what God created her or him to be, a person re-created in the Holy Spirit. To be fully what God intends us to be is to live aware of God's presence within us, to be open to the Transcendent, and to know and love by God's light and power. Holiness is simply the life of God—love—flowing through us.

John Paul II's description of a Christian further clarifies the meaning of holiness. Transformed by the Spirit "into a new creature, the Christian . . . sets himself to follow Christ

Holiness—A Universal Ideal

Each of the major religious traditions of the world focuses on the meaning and quest for holiness. In the monotheistic religions (those that express a faith in one God), which include Judaism, Christianity, and Islam, that quest is expressed through prayer and action.

We know that our own holiness can never match that of God. God is perfection in all things. For Jews, the holiness of God must be recognized and reverence to God is expressed as acknowledgment of it. Observant Jewish men keep their heads covered at all times (and particularly when in a temple) as a sign of respect. Often you might see the name of the Lord spelled G-d. For Jews, the name of God is so holy it is never written out completely in case the paper on which it is written is destroyed. This shows the importance of the "word" for Jews as well as Christians.

For Muslims, prayer is always preceded by a washing of the body, especially the hands and feet. This symbolizes that one must be pure (holy) before one can pray. Even if a Muslim is in the desert, he must "wash" his hands with sand before praying. Even though Muslims recognize that they are never completely clean (pure), they accept the need to purify body and soul before offering prayer to God.

♦

and learns more and more within the Church to think like Him, to judge like Him, to act in conformity with His commandments, and to hope as He invites us to" ("Catechesi Tradendae," #20).

Holiness has its own mysterious attraction. Dorothy Day (1897-1980), a lay woman who spent her life serving the poor and supporting changes in public policy regarding the poor, discovered holiness in the Gospel: "For her, faith was not a question of avoiding mortal sin and saving one's soul; it was a radical fidelity to the Gospel of Jesus Christ; serving the poor, the brokenhearted, the abandoned . . ."

Transcendent: refers to realities beyond our selves.

Chapter 13 Christ Calling His People to Holiness

1. *What characteristics do you think of when you hear the word holy? Why do you think people don't talk about striving for holiness?*

2. *Name three people who you admire. What qualities of theirs would you like to have and why?*

3. *What characteristics do you think of when you think of God? Which describe things God is not, and which reveal what God is?*

4. *How do you think we can discover what God intends each one of us to be?*

On This Rock

The model of Jesus as a liberator of the poor and oppressed has been especially strong in Latin America. This model of true holiness can be seen in the life of Archbishop Oscar Romero of San Salvador. He was an outspoken critic of violations against human rights in Central America. From the pulpit, he preached about liberation and human dignity. As his support with the people grew, opposition to him in the government became stronger. In 1980, Archbishop Romero was murdered while celebrating Mass. His killers have never been caught. Oscar Romero has become a model of holiness for Catholics because of his commitment to serve the poor of the world, and because he refused to compromise his beliefs even when his own life was in danger.

The Challenge of Holiness

As inviting and desirable as holiness appears, it is not easy to acquire. This is not because God makes it hard for us, but because sometimes we make it hard for ourselves. Forces that may seem beyond our control contradict our best intentions. In some sense, we are like clay, ready to be molded into a work of art (Isaiah 49). Unlike clay, however, we can cooperate with the divine Artist to overcome the defects that threaten God's handiwork—the irrational forces within our hearts that keep us hard and unworkable. We know them as pride, greed, lust, anger, gluttony, envy, and laziness.

While the human body and its emotions, instincts, and sex drives are good, we must direct the body and its emotion in order to build ourselves up, not tear ourselves down. Control of our appetites is an ongoing struggle. Transformation of any kind demands choices in favor of long-range goals, like being thin. The sacrifice of instant gratifications, like sweets, may involve pain and suffering. Jesus never offered us a bumpy-free ride. He said, "Whoever wishes to come after me must deny himself, take up his cross, and follow me. For whoever wishes to save his life will lose it, but whoever loses his life for my sake and that of the Gospel will save it" (Mark 8:34-35).

We are tempted to surrender and give up the struggle. Often we experience self-hatred, loneliness, and isolation. Sometimes we may even try to forget our pain by turning to

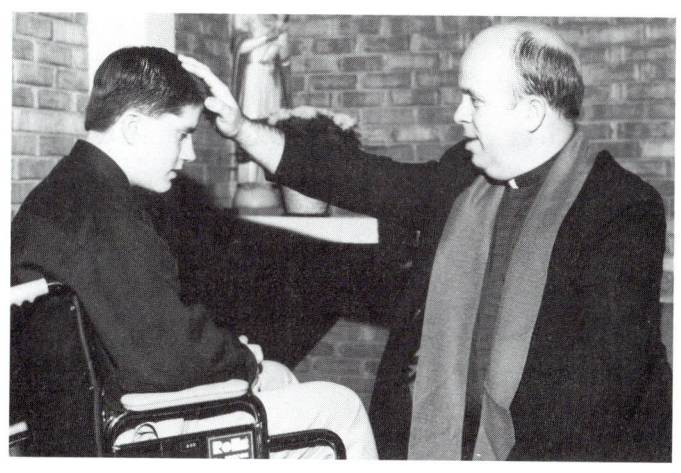

The Sacrament of Penance helps us overcome those things which keep us from holiness.

food, alcohol, drugs, or sex. When that happens, true freedom and fulfillment will be beyond our reach. Only when we give ourselves in faith and love to the Spirit and are fashioned in the likeness of Jesus can we become our true and whole selves. Jesus' healing touch mends our brokenness and gives our hearts the happiness and rest they crave.

5. When was Jesus lonely or tempted? How did he react in each situation?

6. What happens to you when you are feeling alone and in pain? How can turning to God and to your Church community help?

Reflections of God's Holiness

Jesus was the perfect image of divine holiness, and he responded to God in perfect love. He could say, "The Father and I are one" (John 10:30). Sitting at God's right hand, he has led people to holiness in every era.

The saints uniquely reflect God's holiness. Some were witty, others serious. There were literate saints and unschooled peasants; some holy, apparently from youth, and

For Example

For some people, being thin involves a great deal of effort. Not only must the person on a diet give up overeating, he or she must also make a commitment to engage in regular exercise.

others, converted sinners; those with a passionate nature and others who were as cool as a cucumber. Like the widow in the Gospel whom Jesus praises for throwing in her last two coins (Luke 21:1-4), they gave their all to the Lord.

As the saints witness to the Church's holiness, the witness of vowed religious "belongs inseparable to her life and holiness" (*"Dogmatic Constitution on the Church,"* #44). The religious state is not a halfway station between the clergy and laity, but a special gift in the life of the Church. Although considered part of the laity by Canon Law, religious also take the special vows or promises of chastity, poverty, and obedience. Religious dedicate themselves in "an act of supreme love" and are committed to God's honor and service.

The fact remains that the most ordinary person, even the sinner who never gives up trying to respond to God's call to holiness, may become holier—closer to Christ—than a famous cardinal or a consecrated religious. It is helpful to remember that the greatest saint of all was a homemaker and mother.

---

7. *What are some of the temptations that you face in your life?*

8. *Which saints have you used as examples?*

Helps to Holiness in the Church

A loving home environment, caring friends, good experiences, and helping counselors are some human ways of facing and coming to terms with the dark sides of our personality and building our freedom to love. But evil is so strong that we need the special helps to wholeness that are available in the Church: Scripture, liturgy, laws, and other people.

Prayerful reflection on Scripture examines stories of people who have responded to God's call. It helps us to recognize our own story in the history of Israel and in the lives of early Christians. It also provides the healing and strength necessary to follow Christ.

The Church: A Spirit-Filled People

The sacraments and liturgy are indispensable sources of holiness. Baptismal washing symbolizes the process of Christian integration. Drowned in the waters, we die with Christ to destructive elements inside and outside us. At the same time, in the waters of the font, we are raised to the new life in the Spirit we share with our Church community.

Confirmation strengthens our life towards God and mission. In the Eucharist we are healed and sent out by communion with our Savior. The yearly cycle of feasts and the sacraments, especially Reconciliation, keep us on course as we move through the changing conditions of our life.

The Church's rules, moral teachings, and doctrines serve as guides on our journey. Developed from the wisdom of the past, they also keep us heading toward our personal and communal goal: the kingdom.

Finally, the People of God—our faithful relatives, friends, and neighbors, striving for holiness along with us—provide support and example. In turn, our service to them helps us to grow in love.

9. *Which of the ways described above has been the most help to you in bringing you closer to Christ?*

Summary

- All people in the Church are called to holiness.
- Holiness is completeness, being fully what God intended us to be.
- Attaining holiness requires that we learn to control our desires.
- The saints reflect to us God's holiness.
- The sacraments, liturgy, moral teaching, and doctrines are helps to holiness in the Church.

Vow: a solemn promise made to God.

Chastity: purity of character or conduct.

SECTION 1
Checkpoint!

■ Review

1. Is holiness restricted to saints, priests, and religious? Why or why not?
2. What are some of the negative ways God's holiness has been described?
3. In what ways is God holy?
4. Describe the struggle that takes place in our attempts to attain holiness.
5. How do vowed religious live their dedication to God?
6. What are some sources of holiness in the Church, and how do they provide us with help?
7. Words to Know: holy, secular, transcendent, chastity.

■ In Your World

1. Conduct a survey on holiness. Ask ten people to define holiness and to name two people, one living and one dead, who could be called holy. Share your results with the class.
2. Ask a member of a religious order to come talk to your class. This could be someone from your school or from outside. Find out from him or her what the life of a vowed religious is like, and what led him or her to seek that life.
3. Choose music that you think best represents the seven forces within us that work against our efforts at holiness. Explain your choices.

■ Scripture Search

1. Read Romans 1:18-25, 28-32. How does Paul describe sin and what causes it? How does 1 John 2:16 add to this view?
2. Read Deuteronomy 6:4-9, 30:19-20. How do these passages show the place of God and holiness in the lives of the Israelites? What choice are they called on to make?

The Church: A Spirit-Filled People

SECTION 2
Sharing the Power of Jesus

Like other relationships, divine friendship—the life of grace—requires that we share things in common. In order to relate to God who is "other," Christians receive capacities called virtues. These gifts of the Spirit are given in Baptism. They give us a share in the powers of Jesus, and we must exercise them if our divine friendship is to blossom. Just as a child who doesn't use his or her legs will not learn to walk, so we will not learn to order our life to God, others, and ourselves unless we allow these powers to take effect in our lives. "Seek first his kingship over you" (Matthew 6:33), means that our first priority must be our relationship with God. All other things will then be added.

The Virtues

The cross can serve as a symbol to help us remember these gifts. The vertical beam stands for the theological virtues: faith, hope, and charity. They are balanced on the horizontal beam by moral virtues that regulate our relations with one another. In addition to these, God gives us other gifts and charisms.

Faith

The foundation of our relationship with the Holy One is the power to know God, but the process is more complex than merely gathering facts about God. In responding to someone's love, we first interpret the person's offer and then trust ourselves to that person. A Christian responds positively to the offer of God's truth that shines like a light deep within the person. This "yes" is the gift of faith, the first step of love. It is not just an intellectual assent to the plan of God, but a grateful, trustful surrender of one's whole self to God's tender love. It also involves an acceptance of the Church, its traditions, and its beliefs.

Hope

Christians can grow so close to Christ that they put on "his mind" and enter into his very Spirit. They share his absolute trust in the Father's goodness and love in the wonderfully consoling power of hope. By lifting up our hearts and recognizing the promise of God's forgiveness and help to achieve victory over sin and death, hope helps us face meaninglessness, boredom, and other destructive forces in our lives.

Charity

Charity is the power by which Christians are enabled to "dance" in perfect unity with the Father's will, as partners glide together almost as one person. All other virtues spring from and lead to this union, and nothing makes sense without it. People of charity would do anything rather than resist God. Even when they are sick, suffering, or cannot feel as loving as they might want to, they continue to love him above all. Christians love one another for the love of God. The acid test of divine love is this—to love one's enemies.

People who are charitable give of themselves to others, especially in time of need.

The Church: A Spirit-Filled People

Holiness, then, is Christian faith, trust, and love in response to God's offer of himself. It is saying "yes" to the divine command, "Be holy, for I am holy."

---

10. *How are the theological virtues evident in your life and the life of your church?*

11. *What do you think it means to say that holiness is never finished or completed?*

The Cardinal Moral Virtues

Of the four cardinal moral virtues that regulate our relations with ourselves and others, *prudence* is the most crucial. It leads us to choose the best means to serve God in a particular situation. It enables us to distinguish vice from virtue and to choose the good. It is a kind of prayer-filled common sense that guides us to thoughtful, rather than impulsive, patterns of behavior. Prudence makes it easier for us to develop other good qualities—a habit of reflection, power of discernment, and patience.

Justice is the cardinal virtue that inclines and enables us to give all people what is rightfully theirs. It is a social virtue that leads to wholeness in our family, church, and wider society. *Fortitude* provides the strength to handle difficulties in doing good, especially in overcoming fear of ridicule or pain. *Temperance* is the fourth cardinal virtue. It is the power to control or moderate our bodily tendencies in the light of reason and God's plan.

---

12. *Name some other virtues that are extensions of the four cardinal moral virtues.*

Special Gifts

In Confirmation we receive the gifts of the Holy Spirit which supplement our conscience and reason. They make us sensitive and responsive to the Holy Spirit's creative

Cardinal: main or primary.

Discernment: the ability to see clear answers in difficult choices.

Chapter 13   Christ Calling His People to Holiness

Communion of Saints

In this century, many men and women have distinguished themselves in their service to the Church and to humanity. Some of them have already been recognized by the Church as worthy of sainthood. Others we call "saints" because of their lives and actions. One such person was Dorothy Day (1897-1980). She was involved in causes which led her to join public protests, and to be in and out of jail frequently from the age of twenty until her eightieth birthday. At age thirty, Dorothy realized that the cause of human dignity is God's cause. Her work became intimately linked to her Catholic faith. She founded, edited, and wrote for a newspaper called "The Catholic Worker." Those who become involved with it also work in soup kitchens and other facilities aimed at helping the homeless. The Catholic Worker movement attracts many volunteers. Anyone who becomes involved feels the power and commitment of Dorothy Day living on in the day to day work, which reminds us of the dignity and worth of all human beings.

efforts to make us whole. The gifts of the Spirit are like wind to a sail. They gently push us in the direction we need to go to get our lives together. Isaiah lists seven gifts in prophecy of the Messiah, placing wisdom first as the flower of them all, and fear of the Lord last, as its root or beginning (see Isaiah 11:2).

God gives each of us special gifts. How do you share your gifts with the community?

Gifts in Action

When Tammy Dorset turned in to Lost and Found the wallet she found in the lunchroom with its fifteen dollars intact, she exercised her justice. This gift is a disposition to treat others fairly. A sensitive conscience is a sign of this gift.

Jean Donovan left a well-paying desk job to become a lay missionary in El Salvador. She acted by the gift of fortitude that inspires us to undertake difficult tasks with love, patience, courage, and perseverance, and to remain firm when faith is challenged.

People who devote their lives to others in works of mercy demonstrate piety in their lives. Saint Elizabeth Ann Seton (1774-1821), who inaugurated the American Catholic school system, and Mother Teresa of Calcutta, who takes in children from the streets, are examples. Piety makes us look on God as our Father and Mother and so enables us to view creation as God's gift and to fulfill our duties, not in the manner of a slave, but out of grateful love.

Jesus' answer concerning tribute to Caesar demonstrates the gift of council (Luke 20:20-26). This gift helped the

Apostles and saints like Joan of Arc when they were brought before their accusers. Counsel bestows an almost intuitive sense of the right thing to say or do, especially in perplexing situations.

Saint Francis of Assisi, who was very sensitive to God's presence in creation, is an outstanding example of the gift of knowledge, which enables us to correctly grasp the relationship between faith and created things. It also helps us to grow in self-knowledge and to judge the events of our lives in accordance with God's plan.

Understanding and Wisdom

People would wait around the French village of Ars for three days to go to confession to John Vianney, its Curé or pastor. He had an uncanny understanding of the human heart. The gift of understanding penetrates the meaning of the truth of faith and the letter of the law. Under its influence, we grow in comprehension and love of the Eucharist, prayer, Scriptures, and other aspects of the Christian life.

The journal of Pope John XXIII reflects deep wisdom. Almost every sentence shows his concern for becoming the person God meant him to be. People who possess wisdom direct actions in the light of eternal values and try to bring their emotions and passions into the service of the Lord.

Fruits

Christians have evidence of the presence of God's Spirit in the lives of those who heed divine inspiration. As shiny hair, bright eyes, and clear skin mark good health, the fruits of the Spirit indicate vital, wholesome inner life. Jesus said, "You can tell a tree by its fruit" (Matthew 7:20). Saint Paul lists a dozen effects of the Spirit: charity, joy, peace, patience, gentleness, goodness, long-suffering, mildness, faith, modesty, continence, and chastity. Actually, there are as many effects as types of persons because each person is unique.

These dispositions show that "where the Spirit of the Lord is, there is freedom" (2 Corinthians 3:17). God's people are not pressed into God's service. "You are no longer a slave but a son!" (Galatians 4:7).

Continence: moderation.

Outpourings of the Spirit

During the last thirty years, American Catholicism has grown more and more accustomed to the presence and prayer styles of charismatic Christians. In their communal prayer meetings, individuals personally experience spiritual and physical manifestations of the Holy Spirit's power.

Not all charismatic prayer is accompanied by miracles. It is most of all the intense personal experience of the Holy Spirit which can be anything from teaching to singing. Sometimes that gift is extraordinary, like the ability to heal or to receive visions. But a charism is a special gift from the Holy Spirit to an individual and places that person deeply within the Church community. It is a sign of the multi-dimensional nature of the People of God.

Charisms

But the portrait of the Christian is not yet complete. Paul speaks of gifts called charismata. These gifts may be spread as varied talents throughout a group. They may be ordinary like those named by Saint Paul: praying, singing, thanking, advising and consoling, giving service or words of wisdom, administration, and many more such as teaching, preaching, and penetrating hearts (1 Corinthians 14). They may be extraordinary, such as speaking in tongues, healing, visions, and ecstasy.

The problems with charisms is distinguishing which come from the Spirit and which proceed from the destructive elements within us or from worldliness. Saint Paul teaches that genuine charisms are judged, not by their miraculous, brilliant, or extraordinary character, but by whether they serve the community: "To each person the manifestation of the Spirit is given for the common good" (1 Corinthians 12:7). True charismatics—or possessors of the Spirit's gifts—do not separate themselves from legitimate Church authority, but pray to be truly led by the Spirit.

13. *What are the special gifts of the following people: your mother and father, your pastor, your best friend, your worst enemy, yourself?*

Prayer, An Indispensable Means to Holiness

Prayer is at once simple and profoundly mysterious. Saint Paul wrote that we can't so much as acknowledge Jesus as Lord without the help of the Spirit who prays within us (see 1 Corinthians 12:3). Without prayer, holiness is impossible.

Prayer is a personal or community response to our awareness of God's presence. Among the four basic kinds of prayer are:

- adoration, or praise of God and rejoicing in his greatness and availability to us;
- thanksgiving, our response to his generosity to us, which is undeserved;
- contrition, which admits sorrow because our resistance kept us from responding to God's love; and
- petition, which asks for his presence among us and for the coming of his kingdom.

If we want to understand prayer, we should look for examples in how Jesus prayed. He taught us to pray by what he said and did. He prayed often and alone. For long periods of time and frequently in the early hours of the morning or at night, he conversed intimately with his Father. No important decision was made without consultation. In addition to praying, Jesus worshiped in the synagogue and Temple with his fellow Jews.

Participation in Prayer

When we share the life of Jesus, we participate in his prayer. "No one knows . . . who the Father is except the Son and those to whom the Son chooses to reveal him" (Luke 10:22). The prayer of the Church is first and foremost the prayer of Christ. In liturgical prayer (the Mass or Liturgy of the Hours), Jesus as High Priest prays and offers himself through his priestly community, the Church. In the Eucharistic liturgy, he offers perfect worship to the Father and

Many people light votive candles as a sign of their prayer.

Chapter 13   Christ Calling His People to Holiness

invites us to share in that offering and to receive in return our Father's gift of love, especially himself, in the Eucharist. From the earliest days, Christians broke bread together as Jesus had instructed the Apostles to do. In the Eucharist, the sin-offering of Calvary becomes the living bond of unity, joining Christians to God and to one another. In the Eucharist the Christian community finds and celebrates the highest expression of its identity.

Liturgy of the Hours

In another form of liturgical prayer—the Liturgy of the Hours—Jesus is joined by members of the Church to praise God throughout each day, from before the rising of the sun to after its setting. Ideally, the praying community meets seven times during the day and night. Usually this is possible only in contemplative religious orders like the Carmelites, Trappists, and Poor Clares, where this daily prayer is the principal "work" of the community. Traditionally, priests, deacons, and contemplative monks and nuns are committed to pray the Liturgy of the Hours in the name of the universal Church. The seven parts or "hours" of the Liturgy of the Hours each contain a hymn, psalms, readings, and prayers. The books for this worship are prepared and approved by the Church, as are all books used for liturgy.

14. *On what occasions might Christians offer each type of prayer?*

15. *How does the Eucharist bond all Christians to Christ, and to all other Christians throughout the centuries?*

Individual Prayer

Even though the words of the person praying the Hours become his or her personal prayer, liturgical prayer is the communal prayer of Jesus and his Church. In contrast, individual—or private—prayer is "one-to-one" prayer, a personal communion with God as Father or Creator, with Jesus, or with the saints or angels. Like every relationship, individual prayer needs to be cultivated. As it is true that without common worship, private prayer becomes self-centered, so it is true that without private prayer, liturgy grows empty. From Jesus' example, we learn the need for prayerful quiet in solitude. A longing to be with the Father attracted Jesus to set aside times and places to pray. So important is prayer to holiness that since ancient times people have studied and written about prayer. Seldom has interest run so high as now.

Even though you are familiar with the basic distinctions between vocal and mental prayer, you may not be aware that mental prayer can take several forms:

- *meditative—thinking prayerfully or in images about Christ, the saints, or some truth of faith, our insights leading to conversation with them;*
- *affective—praying from the heart without words;*
- *contemplative—prayer of union with God resulting in profound transformation of life.*

You can experiment to find the prayer style that best fits your personality and religious development. Prayer is nourished by virtuous living, asceticism or self-discipline, reading, and writing.

16. *Why do you think silence and solitude are important in prayer?*

Summary

- In baptism we are given the gifts of theological and moral virtues which help us relate to God.
- Faith, hope, and charity are the theological virtues.
- The moral virtues include prudence, justice, fortitude, and temperance.
- All people have special gifts which are developed in response to the work of the Spirit in us, and which may be called fruits or charisms.
- Prayer, individual and communal, is our response to the presence of God.

SECTION 2
Checkpoint!

■ Review

1. What purpose do the theological virtues have?

2. What are the three theological virtues?

3. How do the moral virtues work? Identify two.

4. Give an example of the way the Holy Spirit works in each individual uniquely.

5. How do fruits and charisms give evidence of the presence of the Spirit?

6. What are the benefits of the different types of prayer?

7. Words to Know: virtue (theological and moral), cardinal, prudence, fortitude, temperance, charism, Liturgy of the Hours.

■ In Your World

1. As a class, pray one of the Hours of the Divine Office together every day for a week. How does this activity draw the class closer, and in a different way from your other classroom experiences?

2. Apply one of the four cardinal moral virtues in your life consciously and actively every day for a week. Think about prudence before making decisions, or fortitude in choosing the good despite fear of ridicule. How does conscious practice of this virtue become more and more effortless as the week passes?

3. Practice a form of asceticism, such as fasting. Skip one meal a day for a week. How will you spend the time you usually spent eating? How does your body react? Your spirit?

■ Scripture Search

Read the following passages: 1 Corinthians 14:15; Romans 12:6-8; 1 Corinthians 12:8, 28. What gifts and charisms are mentioned in these verses?

The Church: A Spirit-Filled People

SECTION 3
Many Models of Holiness

Since Vatican II, several Christian communities have formed in an effort to help people find a way to live out their commitment to Christ. You may have friends or relatives who belong to a charismatic prayer group. It is one form of Christian community through which we strive for holiness. Another way to work towards holiness is to focus upon models like the one provided by Mary. She has been a source of solace, help, and holiness for Christians throughout the centuries.

Community, A Help to Holiness

The Catholic charismatic movement was begun in 1966 at Duquesne University by a group of professors who wanted to expand and revitalize their Christian lives. The movement led to a revival of the experience of the Spirit. Many were overwhelmed by the Spirit's peace and joy. They felt reborn to a new life. Encouraged by this outpouring of the Spirit, many charismatic Christians have become vigorously involved in their parishes.

Other types of Christian communities are formed by individuals and families who commit themselves to mutual support in their spiritual lives as well as in other aspects of life. Time, money, facilities, and talents are freely shared. A period of intensive formation is followed by instruction on subjects such as obstacles to Christian living, Christian relationships and service, and Christians and their emotions. This culminates in solemn public commitment to the community.

Chapter 13 Christ Calling His People to Holiness

One of the joys of Christian Community is shared prayer.

A People at Prayer

The Liturgy of the Hours contains the special prayers to be recited at specific times during the day, and at special times during the year. It also contains prayers for the different vocations in the Church and for saints and martyrs. Here is a prayer which is reserved especially for teachers:

"Lord God, you called this person to serve you in the church by teaching his (her) fellow men and women the way of salvation. Inspire us by his (her) example: help us to follow Christ our teacher, and lead us to our brothers and sisters in heaven. We ask this through our Lord Jesus Christ, your Son, who lives and reigns with you and the Holy Spirit, one God, for ever and ever."

17. Have you ever been to a charismatic Mass? If so, what were your impressions?

18. If you could form or join a Christian community, what would its focus be (for example, prayer, social justice, ecumenical work)?

19. What role does your Christian community play in establishing your identity and helping you set your goals as a member of a larger society?

Mary Most Holy

Catholics have always reserved a special place of esteem and love for Mary, who Elizabeth called blessed among women. Though cautioning against viewing her as a goddess, the Council Fathers boldly declared, "Joined to Christ, the faithful must . . . reverence the memory of the glorious ever virgin Mary, Mother of God and of our Lord Jesus Christ" ("*Dogmatic Constitution on the Church*," #52).

Today, when people recognize the need to explore both the masculine and feminine aspects of personality and many question an exclusively male image of God, Mary presents a welcome complement. In her, God's attributes of nurturing, receptivity, long-suffering, and sensitivity are highlighted.

Mary's Call

We learn Mary's high call from Scripture. In the New Testament, Paul is the first to mention the "woman" who bore God's Son. But already in Genesis there is a shadowed reference to "the woman whose offspring would overcome evil" (Genesis 3:15). The Council explains Mary's role in God's plan as that of a second Eve whose "yes" to God ushered in the dawn of our salvation just as the "no" of our first mother, Eve, led us into the dark night of sin and death.

But most of our insights about Mary come from the Gospels. Since they focus on Jesus' ministry, the Synoptics—Matthew, Mark, and Luke—say very little about Mary outside the infancy narratives. John gives Mary a dynamic role only at the beginning and end of the public ministry, and even Matthew's birth story of Jesus is presented from Joseph's point of view.

It is the first two chapters of Luke that present Mary's holiness as a model for us. Gabriel greets her from the start as "the graced one," bidding her rejoice at God's gift. "Hail favored one! The Lord is with you . . . for you have found favor with God," he tells her (Luke 1:28, 30). Mary is a poor young girl from the province of Galilee. She questions such an exalted greeting, not in disbelief, but out of faith and love. For this, her cousin Elizabeth proclaimed her as "she who believed." Mary is above all a woman of faith.

Luke contrasts Mary's response with that of Zachary, the father of John the Baptizer. Although he is a priest who keeps the Law, he doubts Gabriel's announcement that his aged wife will bear him a son. Zachary the priest is struck dumb, but Mary, a woman and lay person, bursts into a song of revelation: it is the poor who are exalted; grace is superior to the Law. Nothing is impossible with God.

God's Presence in Mary

Mary learns that the Holy Spirit wants to grace her with God's presence. The angel waited on the word and faith of a teenage girl. Will Mary voluntarily and freely enter the circle of God's holiness and consent?

"I am the handmaid of the Lord. May it be done to me according to your word" (Luke 1:38). By these words, Mary became the Mother of God.

Complement: something that completes, makes up a whole, or brings to perfection.

Synoptic: taking the same or a common view; used to refer to the Gospels of Matthew, Mark, and Luke which present similar scenarios of Jesus' life and ministry.

Women as Models—Strength, Wisdom, Faith

The Hebrew Scriptures contain many accounts of women who offer us models of virtue and piety. Each, in her own way, acts as an example to us, and reveals how God has acted through both men and women.

Ruth, whose husband had died, remained faithful to her mother-in-law and refused to return to her native country. She chose, instead, to become a Jew, and to go to Bethlehem. For her piety, Ruth became the great-grandmother of David. Joseph was descended from this family.

Hannah, the mother of Samuel, prayed to God to give her a son. When her prayers were answered, she dedicated her son to the Lord and he became one of the great prophets of the Israelites.

Deborah was a great judge of the Israelites. She was known for her wisdom and courage. She settled disputes and even engineered an ambush against an enemy army. And Esther risked her own life as the Queen of Persia—in order to save the lives of every Jew in the kingdom—when the evil Haman had arranged for the mass destruction of the entire Jewish population. As a result of her courage, Haman and his sons were hanged on the very gallows set up for the Jews.

Throughout the history of the Jews, there have been great women who lived their faith in different ways. Each prefigures Mary in some way, and each, in her own way, provides us with an example of holiness and piety.

◆

God prepared Mary as a woman worthy to bear the Son. At her conception she was already freed from original sin and its disorders. Her virginal conception of Jesus was a sign of the holiness of the Son as well as of the mother: she conceived him by faith in her heart before she received him into her womb. Finally, preserved from all personal sin, she was taken both body and soul into glory and exalted by Christ as the Queen of Heaven and Earth. Her Assumption reveals our destiny.

Mary's holiness is seen, not in privileges, but in her faithful service to the Lord. "He has looked upon his handmaid's lowliness," she sang (Luke 1:48). She heard God's word and kept it. Mary's lifelong fidelity led her to the center of the Christian life—the foot of the cross where she lovingly consented to God's plan with the faith that made her Jesus' first and greatest disciple. Mary is known as the Mother of the Church.

20. What are some of the male and female characteristics you associate with God?

21. What is the significance behind God's waiting for Mary's response to the Spirit?

Icon of Our Lady of Tenderness by Fr. John Natusiak, Holy Cross Church, Onamia, MN
The image of the Madonna and Child is a traditional way of proclaiming Mary as the Mother of God.

Mary in Prayer

Probably the best known prayer to Mary is the Hail Mary. It is based on the greeting of the angel Gabriel to Mary in Luke 1:28. Its use can be traced back all the way to the eleventh century. It forms an integral part of the Rosary which reflects on the lives of Christ and his Mother.

When you say this prayer, do you think about Mary as a model of holiness? What does the prayer say about Mary as a holy woman? People for over a thousand years have found great strength through saying this simple prayer from Scripture: "Hail Mary, full of grace, the Lord is with you. Blessed are you among women, and blessed is the fruit of your womb Jesus. Holy Mary, Mother of God, pray for us sinners, now and at the hour of our death. Amen."

Another prayer is Mary's song of redemption, called the "Magnificat," in Luke 1:46-55. In it, Mary recalls the faithfulness of God in protection of the poor and weak against the rich of this earth. What does this song tell you about Mary? Not a weak and helpless woman, but a woman sure of herself, and sure of the Lord.

Mary—Of Us and For Us

Some Christian denominations dismiss Mary's role as intercessor because they claim that Jesus is our only intercessor with God. We remember, however, that Jesus did not hesitate to work his first public miracle at her request (John 2:1-11). While on the cross, he entrusted her as mother to John, the beloved disciple, who represents each of us.

The Scriptures emphasize that Mary is one of us. The American bishops issued a statement clarifying even further what that means. "Mary is not a bridge over the gap that separates us from a remote Christ. Such an approach to her would minimize the deepest meaning of the Incarnation, the fact that He has become a man like us, and that His sacred humanity has made Him the unique mediator between God and us. Mary's greatness is that she brought Him close to us, and her mediation continues to create the spiritual climate for our immediate encounter with Christ" (*"Behold Your Mother,"* #67).

---

22. What role does your mother play in your spiritual development? What qualities does she bring to you?

23. How does Mary speak to each of the following groups differently: mothers, fathers, priests, adolescents, singles, senior citizens?

Summary

- Christian communities and groups provide support and a shared commitment to God.
- Mary is a model of holiness for us.
- Mary's faith and love distinguish her and her role.
- Mary's response to the Holy Spirit makes her worthy to serve God.
- We must remember that Mary brings God closer to us through her human witness.

SECTION 3
Checkpoint!

■ Review

1. Why were charismatic groups first formed?

2. What is the function of a Christian community?

3. How does Mary witness attributes of God?

4. Explain the comparison made between Eve as the first mother, and Mary as the second Eve.

5. In what ways is Mary a model of holiness for us?

6. Explain the "warning" of the American bishops about Mary's role.

7. Words to Know: synoptics, "Magnificat," Immaculate Conception.

■ In Your World

1. Examine the role of Mary in art. Study two or three paintings or sculptures. What events from Scripture are often chosen by artists? How does Mary appear in these works of art? What feelings do you get about her from them?

2. Choose some aspects of Christian life that interest you and dedicate some time discussing them as a class. Think about how that shared time changes you and your classmates.

■ Scripture Search

Look at the crucifixion stories in each of the Gospels: John 19:25-27, Luke 23:44-49, Mark 15:40-41, and Matthew 27:55-56. What does each say about Mary's role? Why do you think there are differences?

CHAPTER 13 Review

■ Study

1. How is God represented in the Bible?
2. In what way is God's holiness made present to us?
3. What are the forces that try to prevent us from seeking holiness?
4. How do the saints act as models for us in their lives on earth and even now in their intercession for us in heaven?
5. Explain the special way that religious seek holiness.
6. How do the sacraments act as a source of holiness?
7. What is the meaning of the cross as a symbol of the gifts given to us that enhance our relation with God and with one another?
8. What is the nature of faith?
9. How do hope and charity bring us closer to God?
10. Define prudence and give an example how it is practiced.
11. What are some of the gifts given by the Spirit?
12. How is the presence of the Spirit evident in a person?
13. Why can the gift of charisms sometimes be difficult to detect?
14. Describe the four basic types of prayer.
15. What is the purpose of the Liturgy of the Hours and how is it prayed?
16. What are the benefits and limitations of private prayer?
17. How does community bring commitment into the public arena?
18. Describe Mary's holiness and how it is described in the Gospels.
19. How does Mary act as a model for us?

▪ Action

1. Give a visual presentation of Mary in her varied roles as they are described in the Gospels. For example, show her particular image as Immaculate Conception, Perpetual Virgin, Mother of God, disciple, and Queen of Heaven and Earth. Choose biblical verses to accompany your drawings or pictures.

2. Focus on a person with whom you are angry or who you consider to be an enemy. Think about the meaning of charity and what Jesus said in Matthew 5:47 about loving one's enemies. What can you do to lessen the anger and hatred between you and that person? How will you react if that person does not respond? How does it make you feel about your own actions and your cooperation with God?

▪ Prayer

The Rosary has been a part of the Church's prayer life for over a thousand years. Developed originally as a peasants' daily prayer, it originally featured the Our Father repeated numerous times. Gradually, the prayer changed to reflect a growing devotion to the Mother of God, and so the Hail Mary replaced most of the Our Fathers.

As a class, pray the Rosary, using each of the 15 Mysteries in Mary's life.

CHAPTER 14

Christ Ministering Through His People

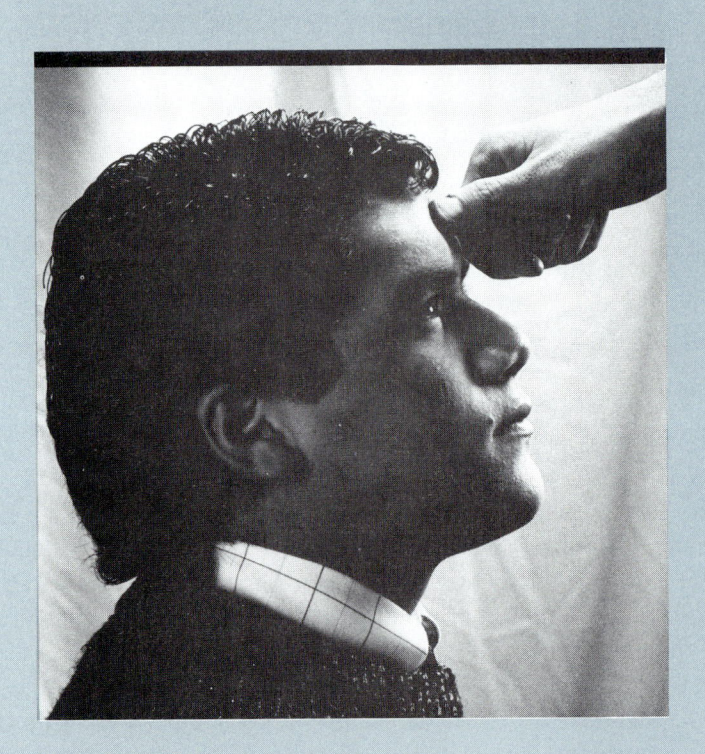

OBJECTIVES

In this Chapter you will

- Learn the meaning of the word "ministry" for the mission of the laity.

- Distinguish different types of ministry in the Church and the world.

- Find out about ordained ministry.

- Discover the role of the pope, bishops, priests, and deacons.

- Understand the place of religious life in the life of the Church.

[Christ] fulfills this prophetic office, not only by the hierarchy who teach in his name and by his power, but also by the laity. He accordingly both establishes them as witnesses and provides them with the appreciation of the faith . . . and the grace of the word . . . so that the power of the Gospel may shine out in daily family and social life.
— "Dogmatic Constitution on the Church," #35

The Church: A Spirit-Filled People

SECTION 1
A Servant Church

If anyone understood the saying "nothing worthwhile comes cheap," it was Jesus. In his ministry, he showed what is today called a "tough love," the kind of love that made him readily available to the people. It was also a love that did not always win him friends. Jesus' love of the people, especially the poor, drove him to preach until he was exhausted. He never turned away from the sick, the lame, or the mobs that continually pressed upon him, and he lovingly gave his life for us all. Jesus inaugurated the kingdom of the Father by a life of dedicated service.

Total Service

Prompted by the Holy Spirit, the Apostles and others in the early Church understood that they too were to serve as witnesses of Jesus' love. They were his chosen instruments to extend his mission throughout the world.

The rapid spread of Christianity could not have come about unless every Christian had used his or her gifts to proclaim the Gospel of Jesus Christ. The early converts turned to "the Twelve" or to their immediate associates, like Paul, for guidance. Better educated than the others, Saint Paul explained that all ministries were the means by which Christ's followers could share in his mission. Using the image of Christ's body, he made it clear that when we use our gifts for the building up of the kingdom, we are Christ to the world and to one another. "For as in one body we have many parts, and all the parts do not have the same function, so we, though many, are one body in Christ and individually parts of one another. Since we have gifts that differ according to the grace given to us, let us exercise them" (Romans 12:4-6a).

All Christ's members are called to share the Spirit's power to sanctify, each in his or her own way. The power of the kingdom rests mysteriously on weakness and humble service like that of Christ. The powerful, strong, or wealthy do not serve better than those who are poor or weak. Saint Paul captured this paradox when he said, "For when I am weak, then I am strong" (2 Corinthians 12:10).

All Called to Ministry

Mission is what the Church does. Ministry is how the Church concretely carries out its mission on a day-to-day basis. Every member's share in Christ's mission is a commission to engage in a particular ministry.

Until Vatican II, the word "ministry" described only the work of the clergy. It was almost as if the only way to participate in the Church's ministry was to become a priest or to join a religious community. The laity—all Catholics, except those who are ordained—should join in Catholic Action—the corporal works of mercy—defined as participation in the mission of the hierarchy.

In the encyclical *"The Mystical Body"* (June 23, 1943), Pope Pius XII broadened the scope of ministry. He reminded the Church that, by baptism, all share in the Mystical Body of Christ and have a proper, active role in the life of the Church. The unique role of the laity, he noted, was in areas where the clergy were ordinarily absent: politics, business, labor, family, the arts, and science. However, because the laity were dependent on the clergy for the sacraments, correct doctrine, and other services, some Catholics still believed that the laity were inferior to the clergy.

The Laity's Essential Mission

Vatican II dramatically expanded the idea of ministry, and emphasized that the laity are essential to the mission of the Church. The clergy cannot substitute for them, nor even be effective without them. Instead, as stated in the *"Dogmatic Constitution on the Church,"* the laity, as do all baptized persons, "in their own way share in the priestly, prophetic and kingly office of Christ and . . . carry on the mission of the whole Christian people in the Church and in the world" (#31).

The Council documents reserved the word "ministry" for the service of ordained pastors, who were to recognize and direct the "charisms," or special gifts, of the laity for the common good. Today, however, respect is steadily growing for the notion that ministry applies to the many ways in which all the People of God fulfill the common mission of Christ.

---

1. How would you define "tough love"? From whom do you receive such love and to whom do you offer it?

2. In what Church ministries do the laity serve in your parish? Do you participate in any?

3. What are some traditional roles in society which have been questioned and are evolving? How does this affect the Church, too?

Types of Ministry

Although the current explosion of ministries keeps the definition of ministry in a state of constant development, some efforts have been made at definition. First, charisms have to be distinguished from apostolic services and ministries. Charisms are those gifts of the Spirit which are rooted in one's very personality or training that are given to Church members to be used in services and ministries. Examples of charisms might be the ability to console mourners, financial expertise, teaching ability, or organizational skills. When such gifts are used only occasionally and spontaneously on behalf of the Church, they are apostolic services. When these services are marked by a certain stability, are used over a long period of time, and are officially recognized by the Church, then they are ministries.

Encyclical: a papal letter addressed to all Catholics around the world.

Ministry within the Church

Today, as the shortage of clergy reaches crisis proportions, individual members of the People of God are experiencing the same sense of responsibility for building up the Church as the first Christians did. Many young people are seeking degrees in pastoral studies, liturgy, the Bible, and theology in order to qualify for such ministries as catechesis, missionary work, liturgical music, Bible teaching, and other roles within the Church.

But members of the laity are involved in hundreds of other ways as well. Sister Margaret Mary Gillard, a parish Director of Religious Education, says that the RCIA program involves the entire parish, which each year averages thirty candidates for initiation. In ministry to the family, there are programs sponsoring family leadership, serving people preparing for marriage, and supporting people who are single, the newlywed and newly married, parents, developing families, distressed families, and families of persons with handicaps. None of these services would be possible without the active participation of parishioners.

For other families, Church attendance is an opportunity for ministry. For the Walkers of North Eaton, Ohio, Sunday Mass is a family affair. Mr. Walker is a minister of the Eucharist. Mrs. Walker is a lector. Their children serve as

Ministry within the Church is done by all members of the community: people with handicaps; young and old; priests, religious, and laity; men and women.

The Church: A Spirit-Filled People

The Church in the Modern World

One of the documents to emerge from Vatican II deals specifically with the place of the Church in today's world.

"The joy and hope, the grief and anguish of the men of our time, especially of those who are poor or afflicted in any way, are the joy and hope, the grief and anguish of the followers of Christ as well. Nothing that is genuinely human fails to find an echo in their hearts.

"The Council exhorts Christians . . . to perform their duties faithfully in the spirit of the gospel. It is a mistake to think focusing on religious duties such as worship exempts one from earthly responsibilities . . . One of the gravest errors of our times is the dichotomy between the faith which many profess and the practice of their daily lives" (*The Pastoral Constitution on the Church in the Modern World,*" #1, #43).

---

acolytes and musicians. Both the Walkers have taught in the Parish School of Religion and helped plan a new building. Their son, Tom, has helped train younger acolytes. The Walkers have made their involvement in the Church a focus of their family life.

Lay Ministries in the World

Jesus did not solve the world's problems in his own time. Christians can't expect to solve the world's problems today either. However, they can respond to people in need. Christians, as they daily venture into the marketplace to work for their living, can make a contribution to society. More and more Christians are coming to understand that their service is unique and valued. They are frequently recognized as conscientious workers.

On This Rock

Many groups have developed within the Catholic Church whose goal it is to address problems of social justice and meet human needs. One of those organizations is Pax Christi (Peace of Christ). Founded in the United States, this organization of religious and lay people is dedicated to fighting hunger, oppression, and injustice the world over. Members of this group get involved in running soup kitchens, protesting at rallies against the arms race, and raising money for needy communities in underdeveloped countries. Pax Christi is especially popular on college and university campuses, and its work attracts many young people with energy and devotion. It is just one way that the Church community extends itself out into the world.

These Christians do not believe that wealth brings happiness or that failure and ridicule are ultimate disasters. They place integrity above success or monetary consideration. People who are weak, poor, elderly, handicapped, and oppressed are given respect, and they carry on their affairs with an eye for promoting causes of justice and charity.

"Action on behalf of social justice . . . is not optional," states the *"National Catechetical Directory,"* "nor is it the work of only a few in the Church. It is something to which all Christians are called according to their vocation, talents, and situations in life" (*"Sharing the Light of Faith,"* #160). So many areas await the Christian influence of dedicated lay workers. Many people will remain without the message of Christ, unless someone brings it to them. But people can hardly be open to Christ's teachings and the sacraments unless their day-to-day needs are met. Jesus healed the sick—whether physically or emotionally—and fed the hungry. His care for those in need attracted many followers.

Christians must regard it among their most important duties to take practical measures to care for people in need, and to do all in their power to work for peace, justice, and freedom for all. Some Catholics understand their mission in such a way that they make employment choices based more on how they contribute to a better world rather than

The caring community identifies the needs of its members and responds to them. Do you know of a parish that provides an interpreter for people who are deaf?

The Church: A Spirit-Filled People

on how well-paying the position is. They will accept their responsibility to put honest candidates who work for Christian values into public office. If they themselves cannot be leaders, they will cooperate in rallies, letter-writing campaigns, boycotts, and other activities for the sake of justice.

---

4. *Name some lay people from your parish who use charisms as apostolic services and as ministries.*

5. *Name the families like the Walkers in your parish. What benefits do you think both the Walkers and the Church derive from their participation?*

6. *Describe some specific actions you could take in the world if you entered one of the following professions: politics, medicine, law, education, journalism, radio and TV.*

7. *Choosing political candidates is a difficult task. Contact your local state representative and ask him or her for his or her position on state spending for one of the following: abortion, the homeless, or drug rehabilitation centers.*

8. *Many people have marched in front of abortion clinics as a protest. Discuss whether this form of protest works for justice or not.*

Summary

- All members of the Church are called to serve the community.

- Since Vatican II, ministry describes ways all the People of God can serve.

- Charisms can be used as apostolic gifts or as ministries in the Church.

- Members of the laity minister in the Church and in the world by living the values of Christ in their professions.

SECTION 1
Checkpoint!

▪ Review

1. How did Jesus show tough love in his ministry?
2. How did the meaning of the word "ministry" change from before Vatican II to after the council?
3. Give an example of a charism.
4. What is the difference between an apostolic service and a ministry?
5. How can lay people become involved within the Church?
6. What does it mean to bring Christ to the world through one's daily life and profession?
7. Words to Know: ministry, tough love, charism, apostolic service, laity.

▪ In Your World

1. As a class, choose a cause that you feel works for peace, justice, or freedom. It could involve writing letters, volunteering time, or participating in a rally. How did you choose your cause, and how do you think it represents a fulfillment of the obligation to act on behalf of social justice?
2. Interview someone in your parish who is active in some form of ministry. Find out what that person does and how he or she first became involved. Be sure to ask what joys and frustrations go along with her or his duties.

▪ Scripture Search

1. Read the following passages: Acts 6:1-6; James 5:13-16; and 1 Corinthians 12:10, 28. Which ministries are described in these verses? How and why did the ministries get started?
2. Read the Sermon on the Mount in Matthew 5:1-12. How could people in some of the following professions apply Jesus' words to their everyday work: store clerk, student, police officer, landlord, mayor, journalist?

SECTION 2
Christian Leadership: Ordained Ministry

All Christians are called to service. If we, as members of the laity, are now to carry out so many ministries formerly associated only with clergy and religious, what is the role of the official, ordained ministers of the Church—the bishops, priests, and deacons?

In response to the Church's new vision of its relation to the world, some members of the hierarchy—pope, cardinals, bishops—now assume a more visible role in the affairs of everyday life. Individual bishops have spoken out on behalf of social issues like world hunger, human rights, and abortion. The Catholic Conference of Bishops has issued statements on nuclear disarmament and peace, the economy, and racism. The main function of ordained ministers, however, is not "political." Their ministry is service to the Christian community.

Roots of Christian Leadership

From among the faithful, some are called by Christ to exercise the ministry of Holy Orders within the community. They include the bishops, priests, and deacons. Their priestly gift—bestowed by the Spirit—is unique, differing in essence and degree from the general priesthood that all the baptized share in Christ. Like the charisms bestowed on other members, their ministry is to be used in the service of the community.

By ordaining men to the priesthood, the Church testifies to and gives sacramental expression to this special call. We hold its ordained leaders in great esteem because, as the

Clergy: ordained ministers. Title taken from the Middle Ages when the ordained were know as "the body of clerks."

Chapter 14   Christ Ministering Through His People

391

Council declared, "Through that sacrament, priests, by the anointing of the Holy Spirit, are signed with a special character and so are configured to Christ the priest in such a way that they are able to act in the person of Christ the head" (*"On the Ministry and Life of Priests," #2*).

The Bishop

Although every Christian is to be a sacrament of Christ to others, the bishop is called to be a special sign of the Church's unity in Christ. Since Jesus sent each Apostle in his own name, the offices of the bishop are the same as those of Christ: the primary teacher, priest, and shepherd in his diocese. The Holy Father, as the chief bishop, signifies the unity of the entire Church.

Every bishop is first a disciple, one called to leave everything and follow the master and to pattern his whole life after him. He is then an apostle, one sent as an official representative of Christ to serve in his name. He is a presbyter or leader, one responsible for the pastoral care of his sisters and brothers in the Church. He exercises leadership, especially by holding fast to the teachings of Christ and by representing the community. The Spirit of leadership is called down upon him through imposition of hands and prayer (Acts 15:6-12). The bishop leads his local pastoral team, the diocesan pastors and their associates, along with the deacons.

In Unity with the Bishop

The ordained fellow workers of the bishop, priests are similarly appointed through laying on of hands and prayer, but they do not receive authority in their own right. As the bishop unifies the local church, the priest is the center of unity in the parish. Under the jurisdiction of the bishop, in whose priesthood he shares, the priest preaches, teaches, and ministers to the faithful, especially in the Eucharist.

The priests of the diocese work together in close unity with the bishop, each making him present in a certain sense in every gathering of the faithful. The priest promotes unity in his parish by facilitating and coordinating all ministries.

Communion of Saints

Basil, Bishop of Caesaria, a large city in what is now Turkey, is remembered for many great contributions to the Church. Born in 330 to a family known for its holiness, he was drawn to the monastic life and spent much time in solitude before returning to the city. He became bishop in 370. Basil fought vigorously against heretics and was known for his sharp mind and knowledge. He visited all parts of his remote diocese regularly, organized a hospital for the poor, and preached often. He worked hard to promote peace and unity not only in the Church but in the city. He died in 379. His legacy lived on through the work of his brother, St. Gregory of Nyssa, and his friend, St. Gregory of Nazianzus.

He is an enabler or catalyst, calling forth and ordering all the gifts of the members of his parish. "[Pastors] must collaborate with their brothers and sisters, including the laity, that all might work together as one for the good of the whole" ("Dogmatic Constitution on the Church," #30).

---

9. Who is the bishop of your diocese? What special services have you seen him provide for your parish?

10. Who is the priest who serves in your parish? How long has he served the parish?

What a Bishop Is and Does

Even though we know our pastors and parish priests better and may be more influenced by them, it is the bishop who is the chief shepherd and teacher of the people of his diocese.

The Greek word from which bishop comes, *episkopos,* means "overseer." Together with the Holy Father and in subordination to him, bishops are the successors of the Apostles for the care of the Church and for the continuation of Christ's mission. As a college, the bishops together with the Pope form the chief governing and teaching body of the Church, where each bishop has the full powers of the priesthood. The bishop is the chief shepherd of the local Church, his diocese. The local bishop has all the authority

Bishops in Latin America place their lives in danger because of their public stand against unjust governments.

Pastoral: refers to shepherding or the gentle guidance that combines direction with service.

College: a group of people who together serve a profession.

Chapter 14   Christ Ministering Through His People

he needs to care for his people. This authority comes from Christ, not from the pope. The bishop is also freed from civil authority to govern the diocese. Priests, who share in the bishop's priesthood, assist him in doing Christ's work in the diocese.

As Teacher

As a teacher, the bishop has many functions. He has the right and duty to preach the Gospel by his words and his own example, and to safeguard Catholic teaching. He establishes seminaries in the diocese which train priests and religious.

The bishop calls for adult education, especially for those parents whose children are preparing to receive the sacraments. He arranges for marriage education courses and other groups or courses which adapt the presentation of Christian doctrine to changing times. Many bishops will regularly write "Pastoral Letters" to their dioceses instructing the faithful on issues of importance. Finally, bishops usually see their preaching opportunities as times to exercise their role as chief teacher of the diocese.

As Priest

As the priest-leader of the diocese, the bishop has the fullness of the sacrament of Holy Orders, so only he can ordain priests and deacons, or consecrate another bishop. The bishop also directs all the celebrations of the Eucharist and is responsible for seeing that the sacraments are worthily administered and received.

The bishop regulates other activities which take place within the diocese, such as Masses in homes, Special Ministers of the Eucharist, granting of faculties to priests to hear confessions, assigning priests to parishes, and other ministries within the diocese. Some of these might include chaplains, prison ministers, and college and high school teachers or administrators.

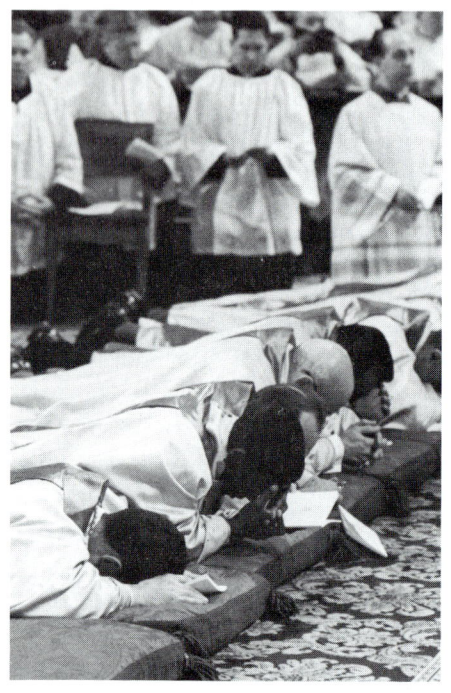

Bishops receive the fullness of ordination.

Infallibility—A Gift of the Spirit

How do we know that the teachings of the Church today are consistent with the revelation of Jesus? How can we be sure that the Church faithfully interprets the Bible? Jesus gave us assistance in the form of a charism called infallibility. Infallibility—a gift of the pope—guarantees to the People of God immunity from error when believing or teaching a truth of faith or morals. It applies to two areas: (1) ordinary Church teaching, such as universally believed truths; and (2) extraordinary teaching set apart by the Church as necessary to Catholicism. These teachings are called dogmas and once they are defined, they can be refined, but never changed.

Infallible teaching is restricted to the college of bishops in Council and the Holy Father when he speaks as the successor of Peter on matters of faith and morals. Official pronouncements like these are rare. None of the documents of Vatican II was declared infallible. The last infallible dogmas declared were the Assumption and the Immaculate Conception.

Catholics are to hold the teachings of popes and bishops, which are authoritative but not non-infallible, in the greatest respect. The understanding of these teachings may change over time as a reflection of growth and changes in the course of history. The private opinions of theologians, bishops, and other on issues in the Church should be respected because of the expertise and wisdom of those who form them, but we are under no obligation to agree or follow them.

The authority of the Church is closely tied to its permanence. Because of Christ's promise to remain with his Church until the end of time, the Church will not deviate in any essential from the Gospel and from its mission.

Pope John Paul II may issue an infallible statement, but has not yet done so.

Faculties: permission granted to a priest by the bishop of a diocese to preach or celebrate the sacrament of Penance in that diocese.

Chapter 14 Christ Ministering Through His People

As Shepherd

The bishop is concerned for the needs of all, not just Catholics, even though Catholics are his first responsibility. He encourages all Catholics to contribute time and talents to their local churches. The bishop also makes provisions for special groups within the diocese, such as migrants and refugees, or helps charitable organizations. The bishop can invite or start religious orders to fulfill needs within his diocese. It is the bishop's responsibility to form new parishes when needed, supplying them with material and spiritual aid.

The bishop acts as a judge in legal cases, and may be assisted by priests who form a tribunal. He gives dispensations to individuals in his diocese from common laws, such as fasting, and can remove an excommunication decree from a person.

Finally, he gives help to churches of his brother bishops, especially to those in need, and collects money, food, or clothing to send to needy people everywhere in the world.

---

11. Has the bishop of your diocese ever written a pastoral letter? Investigate by asking your pastor or calling the chancery office. If there is a pastoral letter, share it with the class.

12. How can you be an active and vital part of these functions which the bishop initiates?

The Petrine Ministry

The Holy Father is the chief bishop of the Church, the successor of Peter, the visible source of the unity of the entire Church, both in faith and communion. He is the Church's supreme teacher, high priest, and shepherd. As bishop of Rome, he, like all other bishops, possesses the fullness of the priesthood, but his is also the highest level of Church authority. Like Peter, who spoke for the Apostles on several occasions, and to whom Jesus gave the power of the keys (Matthew 16:13-20), the bishop of Rome holds primacy, or authority, over the entire Church. If someone were to write a job description of the Holy Father, it would look something like this:

1. To be a visible center of unity in the Church, uniting the College of Bishops and all Catholics in a community of truth, worship, and service.

2. To assemble the bishops in Church Councils, when the need arises, in order to settle questions of major importance and to guarantee the truth.

3. To use his authority and decision-making power for the good of the whole Church.

4. To exercise his gift of infallibility in proclaiming a doctrine of faith and of morals, when the need arises. To clarify issues of faith or morals by writing encyclical letters.

5. To pray ceaselessly for the Church and to attempt, through prayerful study and reflection, to discern God's will for the Church.

6. To show concern for the needs of the whole Church, especially for the poor and oppressed.

13. *What is your impression of the Holy Father? Ask three people not of the Catholic faith what their impressions are.*

Summary

- Ordained members of the Church have a special relationship to Christ.

- The bishop is a disciple, apostle, and presbyter who unifies and leads the community.

- Bishops teach, ordain priests, and guide the community of the faithful.

- The Holy Father is the chief bishop of the Church, and is the supreme teacher, high priest, and shepherd.

- Bishops have jurisdiction over priests and deacons in the daily life of parishes.

SECTION 2
Checkpoint!

■ Review

1. How do ordained clergy differ in their call from the general priesthood shared by all in Christ?

2. What is the bishop's function as disciple, apostle, and presbyter?

3. How would you define the main role of a bishop?

4. Explain the relationship between bishops and priests.

5. Give one example of the duties of a bishop as teacher, high priest, and shepherd.

6. What distinguishes the Holy Father from the rest of the bishops?

7. Words to Know: clergy, bishop, presbyter, pastoral, *episkopos,* faculties, pastoral letters, excommunication, Petrine ministry, infallibility.

■ In Your World

1. Write a short biography of the bishop of your diocese. Include any information you can find about his childhood and education. Find out where he received his seminary training and where he served before coming to your diocese.

2. Prepare an artistic representation of the functions of the bishop. Try to work in as many different aspects of his responsibilities as you can. Think about how you choose the images you will use.

■ Scripture Search

Examine these biblical references to the Petrine Ministry: Matthew 16:18; Luke 22:32; John 21:15-17; Acts 5:1-5, 8-10, 12; 1 and 2 Peter; Matthew 16:13-19. How do these references all contribute to our understanding of this ministry?

SECTION 3
A Life of Service

The lives of priests, deacons, and religious are prepared for the service of the whole Church community. Each group has specific functions and provides special services to the parish. Each requires a special kind of commitment and dedication that comes with the calling to be a part of the People of God.

What a Priest Is and Does

When interviewed about his calling to the priesthood, Father Bob Hartman said, "I wanted to help people on an 'ultimate' level and felt a call to serve Christ in his Church. I consider celebrating the Eucharist and the other sacraments my main responsibility and privilege . . . And, of course, I enjoy preaching and helping others. I work for hours on my homily, and meditate every day to immerse myself in the Scriptures and in the meaning of the Christian life." Father Bob admitted that strengthening his own spirit holds a high place in his life because parishioners expect their priests to be men of prayer, of joy, of example, and of help to those in need.

Father Bob said that he needs and cultivates friends, especially among fellow priests, and he appreciates understanding from his parishioners. He enjoys casual dress but doesn't think a priest should wear the latest fashions, accumulate wealth, or lead a life of leisure.

"It's just as hard for me to keep the humble, serving Christ in my life as it is for anyone else," he admitted. "That's why my parish replaces in my life a wife and children. With all the meetings, activities, and appointments, I could devote all my time to the parish, but I feel the need to be with my brother priests, too. I welcome their support, especially of the older men who are such reservoirs of wisdom." Father Bob also affirmed the need for rest and relaxation to prevent "clergy burnout" and for constantly updating the training he received in the seminary before ordination.

14. *How does your pastor balance parish life with rest and education?*

The pastor of a parish has no more important duty than to know and care for his parishioners.

What a Deacon Is and Does

You have read about the deacons chosen by the Apostles in the New Testament. Deacons today are being prepared to meet contemporary needs of the Church. Reflecting on the Church's growing need for ministries of sacrament, word, and charity, Vatican II restored the diaconate as a permanent ministry open to married and single men. All priests still go through a "transitional diaconate."

The diaconate is an authentic form of ordained ministry distinct from, but also related to, the priesthood. Like the priest, the deacon is an official representative of the Church and assists the bishop. His special ministry is a sign of the

The Church: A Spirit-Filled People

The Church of the Bishop

By the year 200, we can see the emergence of the bishop, priest, and deacon in the Church. By then these roles seem to have been established throughout much of the Christian community. It is clear from writings of this period that the bishop is the person in authority. He is the leader of the community. All other offices, including the priesthood and diaconate, are subordinate to the bishop. Ignatius of Antioch describes the relationship in this way:

"Follow the bishop, all of you, as Jesus Christ follows the Father, and the presbytery as if it were the apostles. And reverence the deacons as the commandment of God. Apart from the bishop let no one do anything pertaining to the Church. Let that be a valid Eucharist which is celebrated by the bishop or by a person appointed by him . . . Apart from the bishop, it is not lawful either to baptize or to celebrate a Eucharist; but whatever he may approve is also pleasing to God, so that whatever you do may be sure and valid."

Most bishops were also accomplished preachers, and they participated regularly in the liturgies. Only in the sixth or seventh century did priests and deacons take over most of the bishop's preaching responsibilities. Many of the great preachers of the early Church, including John Chrysostom and Augustine, were bishops who also had many other responsibilities. Gradually, bishops gave more duties to priests as the size of their dioceses grew and their attention was needed in other areas.

A People at Prayer

Everyone has a vocation in the Church, even if we don't all enter religious life. We need to pray for strength for those who choose to enter into a vowed religious life, and for guidance for all of us in fulfilling our mission in the Church.

Here is a prayer from the Pope's *"Message for the 16th World Day of Prayer for Vocations"* in 1979:

"Lord Jesus, who called those you wanted called, call many of us to work for you, to work with you. You, who enlightened with your words those whom you called, enlighten us with faith in you . . . help us to conquer the difficulties we have as young people today . . . may your love give warmth to this vocation from its very beginning and make it grow and persevere to the end. Amen."

Church's serving the world as he discovers the needs of charity in an area of the diocese and responds to those needs in faith and service. The minimum age for ordination as a deacon is twenty-five, if unmarried, and thirty-five, if married.

Because the deacon usually continues to work in a job outside the Church, he brings a special sensitivity to his ministry. Deacons complement and enrich the work of brother priests and bishops. A deacon's ministry depends on his abilities and on the needs of the diocese and local community in which he serves. He is ordained for the service of the diocese and appointed to a parish and to a particular ministry by the bishop.

By ordination, the deacon is called to special service, which brings about a new relation to the Holy Spirit, and commits his gifts to the good of the entire community. He is united in ministry with the bishop and all ordained priests and deacons and publicly commits himself to the work of God's kingdom.

He may be involved in parish worship functions such as baptisms, marriages, funeral services, and preaching. He may serve in ministries like religious education, ministry to the sick and aged, pastoral counseling, youth and prayer groups, or to special services to a minority community, to prisons, to hospitals, or to people with handicaps.

Deacons may not celebrate the Eucharist, hear confessions, or administer the sacrament of the sick. They continue to support themselves through their own profession, unless they are employed in full-time ministry by the parish or diocese. Their priorities are family, job, and diaconate. Candidates who are not married must vow celibacy, and a permanent deacon may not remarry if his wife dies. The permanent diaconate is growing rapidly with more than nine thousand ordained and about thirty-three hundred candidates in the U.S. in 1990.

---

15. *What special ministry might each of the following deacons do: factory worker, physician, bank president, salesman?*

The Church: A Spirit-Filled People

Religious Life and its Role

Women and men religious are something of a mystery to many people, even to Catholics. When Sister Sandy Manrak publicly consecrated herself to the Church through the Sisters of Saint Joseph, she was following her vocation—her special calling to holiness. Religious life is a gift of God—a charism to an individual, the Church, and the community.

By vowing chastity, poverty, and obedience, religious offer to God their lives and form a special relationship with him not unlike the intimate relationship of Christ and the Church.

Just as a wedding means celebration, Sister Sandy's Final Vow day created a time for rejoicing—her life truly belonged now to the Lord and his people. She had become a unique witness to the power of the Holy Spirit at work in the Church.

Why would a young woman choose not to marry and have children? Still human to the core, Sister Sandy cannot justify her action in human terms. Called by God, in chastity, she gave up having her own family and the love of a husband; in poverty, she relinquished the right to acquire personal possessions; and in obedience to her superiors, she put her life freely into the hands of God. She is a reminder to all that perfect fulfillment can be found only in him.

The vows freed her heart from the obstacles to God's love. She became, in a sense, a sign of the life to come, when each person will be fulfilled in God. She encourages married people to be faithful to one another as Christ is faithful to his Church. To those people pressured by society to amass material possessions and to those who lose their jobs or who can't seem to get ahead, she witnesses that God's kingdom is for the poor in spirit. She reminds people of Jesus' teaching that only in losing life do we find it.

Sister Sandy lives in a community with other people who have taken the same vows. They support one another in prayer and example and together give services to the Church that could not be accomplished by one person. Several hours of prayer each day sustain her dedication and

Religious men and women serve the Church in many ways: as Educators, health care workers, administrators of parishes, as Directors of Religious Education, and as Pastoral Ministers.

Chapter 14 Christ Ministering Through His People

make her a source of spiritual nourishment in her ministry to the aged. Her genuine love for the sisters of her community strengthens the parish families in their efforts to love one another.

To live the Gospel simply and faithfully, responding to the needs of the Church of their time and the special charisms given by God to their founder: this is the daily challenge of Sister Sandy and all religious.

The Spirit at Work

You have seen the Church from many points of view, looking at its nature as explored in the Bible as well as by modern theologians, and calling on your own experiences of it. In studying its origin and history, you saw the many challenging and enriching situations the Church has encountered and survived. Perhaps you marveled that the People of God continued to grow strong as you studied the effects of Vatican II on today's Church.

It is obvious that the Spirit is still at work in his people. No matter how your image of the Church has developed through this study, it is crucial not to allow that image to remain static. Friendship with Christ demands involvement in his Church. Involvement means active participation and constant growth.

Summary

- Priests serve their communities while always continuing to grow in their own spiritual life.
- The diaconate is a form of ordained ministry.
- A deacon continues to work in a job outside the Church, but also serves a parish in a particular ministry.
- People who choose religious life free themselves to serve God.
- Communities of religious give services to the Church and support one another with love and faith.

SECTION 3
Checkpoint!

■ Review

1. How does Father Bob Hartman balance his parish service with his own need for spiritual development?

2. Who may become a deacon?

3. How does a deacon balance work and family responsibilities with service to the Church?

4. In what sacraments may a deacon not officiate?

5. What vows do religious take?

6. What is the purpose of taking vows when entering religious life?

7. Words to Know: deacon, men and women religious.

■ In Your World

1. Invite a deacon from your Church to your class to talk about his vocation and his responsibilities in the Church.

2. Create a symbol or coat of arms for a priest, a deacon, or a religious. It should reflect his or her vocation and responsibilities.

■ Scripture Search

Read Acts 6:1-6. What does it tell you about deacons and their original function in the Church?

Chapter 14 Christ Ministering Through His People

CHAPTER 14 Review

■ Study

1. How did the early Christians all contribute to the spread of Christianity?
2. Explain Saint Paul's use of the image of Christ's body as a model for the Church.
3. What is the unique role of the laity in ministry, according to Pius XII?
4. What are charisms?
5. Give an example of an apostolic service.
6. In what ministries within the Church can all baptized people participate?
7. What is the role of the baptized in bringing the values of Christianity into the world at large?
8. What are some ways people can show that they accept their responsibility as Christians and understand their mission in the world?
9. Who are the ordained ministers of the Church?
10. What are the offices of the bishop?
11. How does a priest function in a parish?
12. What are the three guiding images of bishops?
13. What is the Holy Father's role in the pattern of ordained ministry?
14. What do many priests consider their primary responsibility?
15. Explain the function of a deacon and his place as an ordained minister.
16. How does religious life contribute to the total life of the Church?

■ Action

1. Invite a priest, deacon, and member of a religious order to visit your class. Ask them what drew them to their vocations, how they balance their responsibilities, what they like best (and least) about their vocations, and the greatest satisfactions they receive. How do these interviews give you a better understanding of the many vocations and duties of all members of your Church community?

2. Make a chart of the Church hierarchy as it extends from Rome all the way down to your parish. Put in the names of those people who function in the offices of pope, bishop, priests, pastors, deacons, and religious leaders. How does this chart bring the family of Christians closer together?

■ Prayer

Even though we are used to having our pastor, bishop, and religious lead us in prayer and minister to us, they need our prayers, too. Our ordained leaders pray for guidance just as we do. Very often, we don't think of offering prayers for Church leaders. Maybe we think that they don't really need our prayers, since we presume that they are closer to God than we are. But the truth is that we all need to pray for one another.

Here is a prayer for a pastor. Include this prayer at your daily prayer time. Use it as an opportunity to think about the gifts he brings to your community. "God our Father, in our pastor you gave a light to your faithful people. You made him a pastor of the Church to feed your sheep with his word and to teach them by his example. Help us by his prayers to keep the faith he taught and follow the way of life he showed us. Grant us this through our Lord Jesus Christ, your Son, who lives and reigns with you and the Holy Spirit, one God, for ever and ever."

HANDBOOK

Ecumenism—The Call to Unity

One word sums up the pope's attitude during his trips around the world: respect. Everywhere he goes, the Holy Father shows respect for everyone, including the members of other churches. In his efforts to heal wounds that have festered for over four hundred years, the pope is a one-man ecumenical agent.

The Movement

Ecumenism comes from the greek word *oikos*, which means "house." Ecumenism means "to gather all religions into one house." The ecumenical movement began with Protestants who realized that the factions within Protestantism were too divisive and presented a negative image to non-Christians. In 1948 the Anglicans led the way to the formation of the World Council of Churches. Mergers of smaller Protestant bodies have taken place as a step to fuller unity.

Catholics became active in the ecumenical movement under the leadership of Pope John XXIII, who, with the bishops, made Christian unity one of the goals of Vatican Council II. He set up commissions to begin formal dialogues with members of all Christian churches, Orthodox churches, and with non-Christians, including Jews and even atheists. Vatican II issued *"The Decree on Ecumenism"* and a document *"On Non-Christian Religions."*

Today the Catholic Church no longer refers to Protestants as heretics, but as separated brethren. Through dialogue, the careful study of history, works of charity, constant prayer, and study of Scripture, we hope for reunion in Christ.

We acknowledge that the Catholic Church has been responsible for many misunderstandings, rash judgments, and exaggerations in the past. We must also admit that Christ does work through other churches.

Today, inter-church groups of theologians study ways in which Christians agree on basic issues. On the local level, churches join to worship, pray, and talk together. From time to time, joint declarations of agreement on aspects of the Faith between other communions and Roman Catholics mark milestones on the journey toward better understanding.

Christians can best promote unity by renewing fidelity to Christ, praying together for unity, cooperating in works of charity and social justice, and engaging in serious and scholarly dialogue.

Comparing Faith Affirmations

There are many areas of agreement in beliefs between Protestants and Catholics. These are found in the ancient creeds: the Trinity; Christ's divinity, death, resurrection and Second Coming; the Holy Spirit; the Church; and heaven and hell. However, during the Reformation period, the Catholic Church emphasized other truths and practices not so apparent in Scripture. The following affirmations will find greatest acceptance in the Lutheran, Presbyterian, Anglican, and Methodist churches. Other Protestant bodies modify them to various degrees.

Justification

Reliance on God who saves freely through the death of Jesus is the only act that can forgive sins. No human acts, works, prayers or sacraments will provide salvation. Baptism is essential, but it does not heal human nature (as Catholics believe). Rather, baptism cloaks over sins with the merits of Christ. The Christian must constantly renew faith in Jesus.

> ■ **Catholic Position**—*Faith is essential for an adult, but sacraments, as real acts of Christ, also build our relationship with him. A Christian can grow in grace and holiness by works of love and prayer. The Catholic Church has learned to simplify devotions and to reemphasize the interior spirit of good acts.*

Handbook   Ecumenism—The Call to Unity

Scripture

For Protestants, the Bible is the supreme and final authority on all issues of belief and practice. It seemed to them that people had been depending too heavily on the teaching of churchmen and on external rituals and were ignorant of the Bible. Protestants interpret the Bible by other passages in the Bible and by listening to one another, since the Holy Spirit speaks through every believer.

> ■ **Catholic Position**—*It is true that in the sixteenth century the churchmen did not give Catholics direct instruction on how to read the Bible. This is now corrected. Catholics believe that the College of Bishops and the Holy Father have a special gift from the Holy Spirit to teach a true interpretation of the Bible and avoid error.*

Christ's Priesthood

Protestants believe that worship is the rightful role of the people. Baptism gives all a priestly character. Ministers do not possess any special powers. Each Christian should be priest, counselor, and healer to fellow Christians. Luther and the other reformers eliminated the offering of the gifts at Mass, simplified the consecration, gave communion to all under the forms of bread and wine, further developed hymn singing, and used the language of the people. Reading from the Scripture and preaching were emphasized.

> ■ **Catholic Position**—*Vatican II reasserted the priesthood of the laity, but reaffirmed that within that general ministry there are specialized ministries. One is the special priesthood of ordained ministers whose duties are to see to it that the Gospel is proclaimed, the sacraments celebrated, and spiritual direction given to the community in Christ's name. As leader of the community, the priest presides at the Eucharist, for which he is given a special ministry—to bring Christ's presence in the gifts of bread and wine. He is also empowered to forgive sins in Jesus' name. This ministry is used in service to the community.*

Sacraments

The seven sacraments are not all accepted by Protestants. Only those sacraments clearly described in Scripture are essential. Protestant churches celebrate Baptism and the

Lord's Supper, but the celebrations do not have a meaning agreed to universally within the various Protestant churches. The reformers insisted that Christ's death on Calvary was the one saving sacrifice that can never be repeated and that Jesus is the one and only high priest. So even though Luther retained the name "Mass," he de-emphasized its sacrificial nature and stressed worship and the receiving of the Eucharist. Luther taught that the Real Presence remains with and in the bread and wine, but only during the Mass and not before or after.

> ■ ***Catholic Position**—The Eucharist is not a repetition of Calvary, but a re-presentation of Christ's death to the Father to make it available to each generation. Christ today is still offering his death to God for us, and we unite ourselves with him. The bread and wine are changed into the true body and blood of Jesus, whose presence remains until they no longer have the physical properties of bread and wine.*

Fellowship of Believers

Luther said that the Church is a congregation of saints, visible and invisible, in which the Gospel is rightly taught and the sacraments rightly administered. Protestants emphasize the sharing of faith and fellowship.

> ■ ***Catholic Position**—The same as in the Protestant traditions, with the addition that members are united in common worship and obedience to the teachings of the bishops with the Bishop of Rome.*

Christ as Mediator

Luther and the reformers reacted to the Catholic practice of multiplied prayers and devotions to saints and their relics, and they reacted to what seemed to be extreme devotion to Mary.

The Protestant position is that anyone saved by the blood of Christ is a saint, but since no one's good works can help her or him on earth, neither could a dead Christian help anyone on earth. Only Christ can intercede for people before his Father.

Mary is seen as truly God's mother, a virgin, "the first sinner" to be redeemed by Christ. She moves people to praise God for what he did for her. She was a woman who walked in faith, an example for all.

Handbook   Ecumenism—The Call to Unity

■ ***Catholic Position***—*For the Catholic, Mary is due a special devotion as Mother of God. Mary has a first place among the saints and is active in the lives of God's People. Christ is still our only mediator, but a saint is a friend who can help us, too. Saints intercede for us through Christ.*

Mainline Protestant Churches

The following churches are usually referred to as mainline Protestant: Lutheran, Presbyterian, Episcopalian, and Methodist. This is to designate these churches from other protestant branches which interpret Scripture in a more literal manner. Mainline churches are generally closer in belief to the Catholic Church than are many of the non-mainline churches.

Lutheran

Origin—Founded in the 1500s in Germany by Martin Luther.

Emphases—(1) The need of personal faith in the mercy of Jesus to be saved from one's sins. (2) Bible as the only true source of truth.

Sacraments—(1) Baptism: putting on the merits of Christ as a cloak for one's sins. (2) Lord's Supper: the Real Presence of Christ under and with the bread and wine. (3) Penance: Luther wanted to keep the practice of confession, but did not consider it a Sacrament. The practice of confession died out for many years in the Lutheran Church. Now it is being encouraged, especially the confession of one's sins to a minister. (4) Marriage: a sacrament, but not in the strict sense.

Presbyterian

Origin—Founded in the mid-1500s in Switzerland by John Calvin.

Emphases—Ultimate authority lies in a group of lay people representing a number of churches. The group is called the presbyter (meaning "the elder"). The only true head of the church is Jesus Christ. Predestination: Calvin taught that some people are chosen beforehand for heaven and others for hell. In 1903, the Presbyterians softened this teaching by adding that any person can accept Christ's offering of salvation.

Sacraments—Only Baptism and the Lord's Supper are considered sacraments. The sacraments don't, of themselves, build a relationship with God but are sign of a covenant with Christ. The Lord's Supper only represents or symbolizes Christ.

Episcopalian (American Anglican)

Origin—Initiated in about 1530 in England by King Henry VIII.

Emphases—There are generally three branches of Anglicanism all belonging to the same structural church.
1. High Church: Sacramental worship and ceremonies are very close to everything in Catholic life.
2. Broad Church: This level combines elements of high and low churches at the choice of the local community.
3. Low Church: At this level, there is more emphasis on the Bible, minimization of ritual, a more "Protestant" feel.
Three bonds link the levels together: the Book of Common Prayer, Communion with the Archbishop of Canterbury, and the Bishops as chief pastors.

Sacraments—High Church has all Catholic sacraments. Low Church emphasizes only Baptism and the Lord's Supper.

Methodist

Origin—Began in the 1700s in London by John Wesley, an ordained Anglican minister who wanted to bring religion back to the poor in the cities. He preached a warm, simple faith in Jesus, held prayer meetings in homes, and led the people to Communion at the Anglican Church. His followers became independent of the Anglican Church in America. "Methodism" is taken from Wesley's methodical habits of life.

Emphases—The Methodists espouse simple trust in Jesus as experienced through the action of the Holy Spirit.

Sacraments—They have both Baptism and the Lord's Supper.

Handbook   Ecumenism—The Call to Unity

Index

Age of Enlightenment, 301, 304, 312
Apostles, 96, 99, 103, 173, 184
   definition of, 106
   preparation and mission of, 106–8, 110, 154

Baptism, 8, 39, 62, 63, 72, 95, 115, 118, 128, 164, 178, 179, 206–7, 332, 344, 361, 363, 410, 411, 413
Barbarians, 135, 222–3, 236
Benedictines, 214, 216
Bible, 35, 49, 194–5, 413
Body of Christ, 15, 44–6, 77, 206
   building the, 44–45, 128, 146, 166, 339
   at work, 349

Cardinal virtues, 365
Carolingian Dynasty, 234
Catacombs, Creed of, 207
Catechesis, 72, 78, 115, 122, 342, 344–5
Cathedrals, 95, 249
Catholicism
   characteristics of, 31, 103, 110, 149
   charismatics, 100, 368, 374
   definition of Catholic, 85, 88, 103
   facts about, 85, 165
   government of, 125–127, 136–140, 391–397, 399
   unity of, 25, 96, 103, 145
Christians, first called, 34
Church, the
   Age of, 135
   attitudes toward, 16, 19
   Body of Christ, 15, 44–46, 77, 339, 349
   catechesis in, 342–3
   changing images of, 191
   characteristics of, 85–6, 108, 149, 161
   charismatics in, 100, 368, 374
   Christ's presence in, 60, 98, 161
   as community, 15, 67–8, 79, 355, 368, 373, 378
   community of discipleship, 15, 25, 79, 41, 62
   compared to sheepfold, 36–7
   definition of, 13, 31
   depersonalized image of, 16–7, 22
   direction from Holy Spirit, 148, 154–159, 383, 385, 369
   disunity within, 53
   diversity of gifts in, 47, 366
   doctors in, 14–5, 221
   Eastern, 97, 333–335
   evangelization in, 338–345
   examining ideas of, 13
   Fathers of, 221
   feelings toward, 16–18
   first called, 106
   forgiveness in, 43
   founder of, 377
   guardian of revelation, 167
   as herald of Good News, 71–72
   heresies in, 147, 215
   infallability of, 51–52
   as institution, 62–3, 79, 16
   laity in, 62, 332, 355
   leadership in, 88
   Liturgy of the Hours, 370, 372
   losses to, 226
   magisterium, 168
   marks of, 88–89
   membership in, 22, 44, 13, 99, 106
   in Middle Ages, 251
   ministry of, 62–63
   missions, 291, 330, 347–350
   models of, 59–73
   mystery of, 31, 26, 87, 107
   Mystical Body, 45, 99
   nature of, 22, 59
   the new creation, 37
   the new Israel, 194
   organization of, 88, 96
   origin of, 153, 134
   parish (see *Parish, the*)
   People of God (see *People of God, the*)
   Petrine ministry of, 396
   renewal activities, 43
   a religious mystery, 31
   role of the religious in, 347, 403–404
   roots of, 145–148
   sacramental life of, 14, 69–70, 32
   as servant, 25, 75–6
   source of hope and healing, 75
   structure within, 136–140
   takes root and grows, 54, 39, 147
   turning point in, 173–179
   unity of, 22, 25, 42, 93, 95–96
   universal, 70, 105, 116, 197, 60
   versus the empire, 203–209, 240
   a visible sign, 89, 87
   who belongs to, 108
   youth ministries of, 43, 129
Community
   faith support in, 42–43
   help to holiness, 363–373
   Jesus' call to, 67, 25
   main task of, 67
   as model, 67–68, 63, 164
   in the parish, 68
   in worship, 68
Council of Ephesus, 215
Council of Jerusalem, 106, 182, 183
Council of Nicea, 86, 217, 226
Council of Trent, 13, 139, 287, 290–1, 299, 324
Counter-Reformation, 289–90
Covenant, New, 37
Crusades, the, 245–6

Diakonia, 161–162
Didache, 178
Diet of Nuremburg, 289
Diocesan Curia, 140
Discipleship, 25
   call to, 24–25, 44
   community of, 41
   renewal of call to, 43

Ecumenism, (also see *Handbook*,) 90, 91, 97, 73, 312, 339, 408
Edict of Milan, 203, 211
Eternal life, 38–39, 45, 148
Eucharist, 34, 39, 43, 69, 61, 95, 99, 118–119, 127, 162, 178, 204, 330, 332, 261, 367, 369–70
Evangelization, 72, 149, 332–3, 337–345

Feudalism, 135, 235, 233
Fundamentalists, 72, 149, 151

Good News, 70–72, 25, 99, 149, 159, 161, 166, 179, 195, 120, 154, 218, 330, 333, 338
Good Shepherd, 43, 207
Greek Schism, 238

Heresies, 215
Holiness, 355, 357, 365
   challenge of, 100, 358–9
   charisms, 363, 368
   definition of, 355
   fruits of, 356, 367
   help from community, 360–1, 373
   helps to, 360
   model for, 355–6
   reflections of, 360
Holy Spirit
   in the Bible, 175
   bonding role of, 53, 45, 67, 61
   charismatics, 100, 368
   confirmation, 365
   given to believers, 34, 177, 148
   giving new direction, 59, 63, 337
   guidance in the Church, 53, 59, 63, 107, 147, 197
   in the parish, 107

part of the Trinity, 60–61, 329
  at Pentecost, 156
  planted seeds of salvation, 52
  power of, 54, 158, 188–9
Holy War, the, 245–246
Hundred Years' War, 257

Image
  builders, 59
  Jesus was the perfect, 330, 359
  of sheepfold and shepherds, 36–37, 43, 137
  of vine and branches, 37, 39
Images
  changing, 11
  of Church, 13, 19, 21, 25–26, 41, 62
  complex, 11
  definition of, 8
  influence of, 8–10
  need for, 9
Inquisition, the, 52, 53, 260
Islam, 357
Israel, 49–50, 186, 156, 360
  prophet, priest, and king, 330–1

Jerusalem, destruction of, 187, 191–194, 329
Jesus Christ
  the Body of 36–7, 45, 77, 67, 68, 99, 146, 8, 118
  in the Church, 36–7, 98, 103, 147, 161
  continuing the work of, 41, 194
  faith in, 162
  formed new covenant, 37
  founder of the Church, 101, 148, 150
  gives "new way," 34–35, 37, 181
  Good Shepherd, 37, 207, 330–1
  Head of the Body, 45
  heart of the Mystery, 35
  High priest, 369
  imitating, 44, 68, 75
  Incarnation, 196, 356
  Lamb of God, 36–37
  Last Supper, 162
  mission of, 41, 35, 88, 153, 329, 333
  as model, 41, 103, 356, 360, 369, 371
  the new Adam, 37
  as Redeemer, 37, 50, 153, 195, 76
  sent Holy Spirit, 60, 156
  sharing the power of, 101, 110, 147
  as Truth, 86

Kerygma, 161, 162
Koinonia, 161

Leitourgia, 161, 163

Marks of the Church, 88–91
Martyrs, 99, 164, 193, 203, 205–209
Mercy, mystery of God's, 50
Monasticism, 212–214
Musterion, 33
Mystery (see *Religious Mystery*)

"New way"
  origin of, 34
  living the, 34, 181
Nicene Creed, 82, 88, 226

Parish, the, 116–117
  activities, 78, 127–128
  community in, 116
  lay ministry, 119
  origin of, 135
  as part of diocese, 117, 119–120, 136–138
  pastors and priests, 119–120, 126–7, 136, 139
  purpose of, 67, 115–116, 117
  structures within, 119–120, 125
Peasants' Revolt, 277, 285–6
Pentecost, revelation of, 103–104, 144, 156–159, 330
People of God, 51, 68, 125, 128, 50, 329
  diocese, 136
  in community, 68, 361
  have flourished, 147, 154
  imperfections of, 49–53
  Luther's reform, 267
  uniting in sacraments, 69
  Vatican II, 49
Prayer, 24, 29, 52, 57, 76, 83, 108, 113, 136, 143, 162, 171, 196, 201, 226, 231, 256, 265, 292, 297, 320, 327, 348, 353, 374, 381, 402, 407
  a means to holiness, 9, 29, 88, 95, 369
  private, 29, 265, 370–1

Reformation, protestant, 14, 267–283, 288, 299
Religious Mystery,
  Biblical images of, 35–39
  of the Church, 31–35, 60
  heart of, 34
Renaissance, 255, 268

Second Coming, 165, 197, 153, 156

Thirty Years' War, 278, 299
Trinity, the Holy, 9, 157
  a model in the Church, 60

Unity in the Church, 60–61, 53

Vatican II, 59, 63–64, 69, 90, 107, 117, 94, 49, 86, 108, 118, 215, 241, 290, 292, 294, 297, 304, 317, 319, 324, 329, 332, 348, 373, 408–9

Western Schism, 255, 256, 263

People and Places

Abraham, 49, 331
Adam and Eve, 34, 37
Alexander VI, 261–2
Alexandria, 217, 228
Ananias and Sapphira, 181, 188
Antioch, 52, 103, 178, 181–185, 189, 126, 205, 228
Aquinas, Thomas, 252
Athanasius, Saint, 214, 217, 221
Augustine, 62, 215, 216, 218, 221, 224, 225, 245, 343

Barnabas, 182
Bellarmine, Saint Robert, 13, 14, 293
Benedict of Nursia, 214
Bernard, Saint, 237, 288
Boniface, Saint, 233
Boniface VIII, 243

Cabrini, Mother Frances, 310
Caesaria, 189
Calvin, John, 262, 267, 279–281, 288
Carroll, Bishop John, 313–4
Carthage, 224
Catherine of Siena, 222, 249, 255
Charlemagne (Charles the Great), 233–235
Clare, Saint, 248
Claver, Peter, 300
Clement of Alexandria, 166
Clement of Rome, 221
Clement V, Pope, 255
Clement VII, Pope, 256, 283
Clovis, King of Franks, 223
Constantine, 211
Cornelius, 179, 184, 189, 207
Corinth, 52, 185
Cranmer, Thomas, 284
Cyprus, 178, 182

Damascus, 181
de Chardin, Father Teilhard, 312
Decius, Emperor, 206
de Paul, Vincent, 293, 299
de Porres, Martin, 300
Diocletian, 208
Diognetus, 120
Dominic, 247, 249
Donatus, 218
Donovan, Jean, 366

Drexel, Mother Catherine, 316
Dulles, Father Avery, 15, 62, 67

Eck, Johann, 271
Edward VI, 284
Elizabeth I, 285, 287
Elizabeth II, 283
Ephesus, 197, 206

Francis of Assisi, Saint, 247–8, 258, 367
Frederick II, 241
Frederick Barbarossa, 241

Gamaliel, 176
Geneva, 280
Gregory the Great, Pope Saint, 221, 225
Gregory VII (Hildebrand), 240–1
Gregory XI, 255
Gregory XII, 256
Gregory XV, 301

Henry II, 241
Henry IV, 240
Henry VIII, 267, 283–4, 288
Hippolytus, 139

Ignatius of Antioch, 103, 205, 206
Ignatius of Loyola, 72, 292, 293
Innocent III, 241, 260
Irenaeus, Saint, 221
Israel, 195, 331

James, 24, 137, 164, 185, 187, 250
Jerome, 221
Jerusalem, 187, 191, 228, 245, 302
Joan of Arc, 257, 338, 367
John, Saint, 24, 52, 107, 137, 157, 126, 188, 251, 375
John XXIII, Pope, 59, 310, 312, 319, 321, 367, 408
John Paul I, Pope, 322

John Paul II, Pope, 15, 98, 140, 283, 320, 322, 356–7
Josephus, 191–3
Judas, 156, 175
Justin the Martyr, Saint, 221

Kolbe, Saint Maximilian, 98

Leo the Great, Pope Saint, 223
Leo III, Pope, 233
Leo X, Pope, 288
Luke, Saint, 157, 173, 175, 195
Luther, Martin, 261–2, 267–8, 270, 273–275, 277–278, 288, 294, 412

Mark, Saint, 195
Mary, Mother of God, 9, 24, 88, 154, 159, 107, 98, 219, 309, 360, 373, 412
Matthias, 156, 175
Matthew, Saint, 24, 195, 375
Melanchthon, Philipp, 277
Merton, Thomas (Father Louis), 15, 32, 93, 373
More, Thomas, 261, 284, 293
Moses, 156–7, 331, 348

Napoleon, 304, 307
Neri, Philip, 289
Nero, Emperor, 203–205
Nicodemus, 52

Origen, 221, 302

Paul III, Pope, 289–90
Paul IV, Pope, 162
Paul, Saint, 33, 367, 368, 375
 autobiography of, 183, 196
 conversion, 179, 181
 in early church, 52–53, 106
 image of Church, 44–46, 47
 marks of church, 98
 martyrdom, 191, 204

 missionary journeys, 184–5, 182
 warning to Church, 53
Pepin the Short, 233
Peter, Saint, 50, 137, 179, 195, 261
 in early church, 24, 52
 head of the Church, 106, 211
 leadership of the Church, 154, 156, 164, 175, 188–9
 martyrdom, 164, 191, 204
 the Rock, 154–155
 symbol of Church, 47
Philip, 179
Philip IV, 243
Pius V, Pope, 287
Pius VII, Pope, 304
Pius IX, 308
Pius X, Pope, 233, 310
Pius XI, 310
Pius XII, Pope, 311
Polycarp of Smyrna, 188, 221

Rome, 52, 195, 46
Romero, Archbishop Oscar, 358

Sadducees, 176
Sanhedrin, the, 178, 176
Savonarola, Girolamo, 261, 270
Seton, Saint Elizabeth Ann, 32, 42, 314, 366
Stephen, Saint, 178

Tarsus, 183
Teresa, Mother, 349, 366
Teresa of Avila, 222, 251, 282, 293
Tertullian, 205, 209, 216, 221, 302
Tetzel, Johann, 271
Theodosius, Emperor, 211
Tudor, Mary, 285, 287

Urban VI, 256

Vianney, John, 367
Voltaire, 299, 301, 303